A New Approach to

Understanding and Selecting PERSONNEL

A New Approach to

Understanding and Selecting PERSONNEL

Warren C. Trent

GATEWAY PRESS ● TYLER, TEXAS

A New Approach to
UNDERSTANDING AND
SELECTING PERSONNEL

Copyright © 1985 by WARREN C. TRENT

Gateway Press
P.O. Box 6867
Tyler, Texas 75701

Library of Congress Catalog Number 83-083330

ISBN 0-9613155-0-4

Manufactured in the United States of America

CONTENTS

PREFACE

Many books have been written about personnel selection and the difficulties managers face in performing this crucial management function. Most of these books are useful because they add insight and understanding essential to the selection process. But none offer what managers really need: a systematic approach to identifying those individuals best suited for a particular job. This book presents such an approach. It is based on over 25 years of experience in managing technical professionals in the aerospace industry plus in-depth studies of the basic mental qualities that determine what a person can and will accomplish in life. The book is equally useful in selecting, assigning, and reassigning (current) personnel. And it is, of course, inherently useful to anyone interested in self-evaluation.

The thesis of this book can be summarized in two statements. (1) The procedures commonly followed by managers in selecting and assigning personnel are inadequate because they fail to include many critical variables. (2) Adequate selection procedures which account for all critical variables can be formulated and implemented with the information readily accessible to any prudent manager.

Today, managers generally base personnel selections on information from three sources: psychological tests (IQ and SAT scores, for example), academic records (such as grade-point average and class standing), and years of work experience. IQ and SAT scores indicate ability to absorb knowledge; grade-point average and class standing are gages of the knowledge acquired in a particular course of study; and work experience is indicative of the knowledge gained from a job. In other words, present-day managers tend to emphasize knowledge in their personnel selection process. Too often, little or no attention is given to two other important human qualities: creative problem-solving capability and behavioral characteristics. Each of these qualities significantly influences how well individuals perform in

society, in general, and in the business world in particular. Hence, any procedure that fails to properly consider these qualities has little chance for success.

In view of the recognized inadequacy of current selection procedures, one is not surprised that managers have problems in staffing and operating efficient organizations. The significance and magnitude of these problems are well appreciated by those concerned with personnel management. For example, an often-heard comment by managers is that 20 percent of their personnel are responsible for 80 percent of the accomplishments. Management consultants are even less charitable. Indeed, some have estimated that managers use only 10 percent of their employees' capabilities. Perhaps it is unfair to conclude that these observed deficiencies result from improperly selected personnel. Yet, explaining the poor performance of various organizations is difficult if it is assumed that the selection process has provided personnel properly suited to their assigned jobs.

The problems managers face in effecting suitable personnel selections are numerous. Some stem from the fact that a number of the mental qualities known to affect human performance either have been thought to be unmeasurable or have been ignored. Others arise because managers are unable to properly assess the skills required to do a particular job. And still others arise because managers simply do not understand the true nature of the personnel selection process.

This book addresses these problems with a new approach to understanding and selecting personnel. Its objective is to provide managers with a basic understanding of human mental qualities and to supply the specific procedures and techniques needed for successful personnel selection. The book is both fundamental and practical. It

• presents a conceptual model of the brain that identifies all its major functional processes

• uses the conceptual model to show how the brain interacts with the environment to produce three essentially independent human mental qualities—knowledge, problem-solving capability, and behavioral characteristics

- defines effective mental capability (the quality which determines the level of mental work a person is able and willing to perform)
- presents a systematic procedure for estimating quantitative values for each of the human mental qualities
- establishes a method for quantitatively defining job requirements in terms of human mental qualities
- presents and explains a personnel selection procedure which matches a person's mental qualities with those required for a particular job

The approach is unique with regard to both the variables considered and the procedures used. Unlike other approaches which emphasize knowledge, equal emphasis is placed on knowledge, problem-solving capability, and behavioral characteristics. Since each of these variables is separate and essentially independent, their values are seldom equal in any person. For example, one with a high level of knowledge may or may not have a high level of problem-solving capability or behavioral characteristics.

The levels of all three human mental qualities are important in the selection process, both in combination and individually. It is the combination of qualities that determines the type of job (or profession) for which a person is best suited. Whether one or more mental qualities are relatively high or relatively low makes no difference as long as the combination is at an adequate level. On the other hand, the dominant (highest level) mental quality determines the type of function a person is best suited to fill. More specifically, a person with a high level of knowledge will do best as an analyst; one with a high level of problem-solving capability will do best as a synthesist; another with a high level of behavioral characteristics will perform best as a supervisor; while one with nearly equal levels of all three qualities will serve best as a manager. Conversely, a person with a very high level of knowledge who performs successfully as an analyst is almost certain to fail if he or she is placed in the role of a synthesist, supervisor, or manager.

Since the book is both fundamental and practical, it may be used as either a textbook or a reference book. It is suitable as a textbook because it treats its subject in a basic and teachable form. It is useful as a reference book because it defines a practical and systematic approach to understanding and selecting personnel. And, since it emphasizes basic human understanding, the book is inherently helpful to students and managers in interpreting and applying the most useful behavioral theories and concepts, such as Berne's Transactional Analysis, Blakes and Mouton's Managerial Grid, Herzberg's Motivation-Hygiene Theory, Maslow's Hierarchy of Human Needs, and McGregor's Theory X—Theory Y. The book is particularly well suited for scientists and engineers, since it permits them to treat problems in human understanding in the same systematic and logical manner in which they are obliged to treat equally complex technical problems. It is also well suited for use by the faculties and students of business management schools, practicing managers in various fields, and those persons who are simply seeking a better understanding of themselves and other human beings.

This book does not purport to represent a high level of scientific rigor. Indeed, by intent and necessity, it is both broad and shallow in its treatment. It is broad in that it covers every factor known to have a significant influence on a person's mental qualities. It is necessarily shallow because it treats myriads of factors, and because the influence of some of these factors on human mental qualities can only be assumed or postulated. However, since each necessary assumption and postulate is supported by and is consistent with the most valid data available, I do not believe that anyone of them can be rigorously disproved. More importantly, there is no evidence that these assumptions and postulates are any less valid than many of those accepted and used widely by professional psychologists and behavioral scientists.

The book is divided into four sections: an introduction, followed by three major parts: "The Human Brain," "Human Mental Qualities," and "Personnel Selection."

The introduction presents background information and a synopsis of the book's contents.

Part 1, "The Human Brain," presents a concept which explains how the brain performs its many functions and discusses those elements and characteristics that are germane to the concept. The operating characteristics of the digital computer and those computer elements considered to be helpful in explaining brain functions and processes are discussed. A conceptual model of the brain which accounts for all major brain functions is presented, and the fidelity of the model is demonstrated.

Part 2, "Human Mental Qualities," deals with human knowledge, problem-solving capability, and behavioral characteristics. It introduces the term *effective mental capability,* defined as the ability and willingness of one person to perform in comparison to others. The conceptual model of the brain developed in Part 1 is used in Part 2 to show how the brain and its environment influence a person's mental qualities. How these qualities combine to produce effective mental capability is also shown. Finally, the conceptual model's adequacy in defining a person's effective mental capability is demonstrated.

Part 3, "Personnel Selection," presents the procedures and considerations involved in selecting the personnel best suited for any type of job. The formats and the most efficient techniques for collecting the information needed are defined, and the procedures for estimating a person's knowledge, problem-solving capability, behavioral characteristics, and effective mental capability in quantitative terms are presented and illustrated. A new and fundamental approach to defining job requirements is introduced. Finally, the techniques used in matching human mental qualities and job requirements to make successful personnel selections are identified and illustrated.

After studying and comprehending the principles, concepts, and procedures in this book, the reader will have a much improved understanding of human beings and the personnel selection process. Fortunately, however, effective use of the book does not depend upon complete understanding. For example, a manager can use the selection procedures in Part 3 successfully without fully understanding the concept of human mental qualities developed in Part 2. Considerable insight into and understanding of the human mental qualities covered in Part 2 can also be realized without a complete understanding of Part 1. But Part 1 is of utmost importance for the reader seeking the greatest possible understanding of human beings, since it identifies and explains all the fundamentals and postulates on which the book is based. Indeed, it is this part of the book that gives credence to the concepts and procedures developed and allows them to be used with confidence.

It is not possible to identify all the individuals who have made contributions to this book. Many scientists and researchers, of both the past and present, have identified and described the phenomena of nature upon which the concepts in this book are based. My many friends, colleagues, supervisors, managers, and subordinates in the aerospace industry have—by playing their respective roles—provided the laboratory where the various concepts were evolved, evaluated, and substantiated.

In addition, a number of individuals have made specific and significant contributions to this book. Without implying their endorsement, I gratefully acknowledge the contributions of the following: the late Professor R. C. "Kay" Forman, my teacher in human relations at Texas Christian University, whose unique, practical, and incisive understanding of the human being provided the challenge for the research which culminated in this book; Dr. Eugene Adelmann, a practicing neurologist, who read and provided comments on Chapter 2, "The Anatomy and Physiology of the Brain"; Dr. Raymond M. Kline, Professor of Electrical Engineering, Washington University, who critiqued the electronic digital computer material presented in Chapter 3 and Appendix A; and Dr. J. Richardson Usher, Senior Editor, Sverdrup & Parcel and Associates, Inc., who aided greatly in organizing and editing the final manuscript.

Finally, and by no means last in order of importance, I acknowledge the crucial contributions of my wife Ruth. Her intuitive understanding of human nature was of great value to me in developing the concepts in this book. Moreover, without her encouragement and support, her assistance in preparing the many illustrations, and her willingness to type and retype numerous drafts of the manuscript, this book would not have been possible.

INTRODUCTION

We are making use of only a part of our physical and mental resources . . . the average human being lives far within his limits. He possesses power . . . which he habitually fails to use.

WILLIAM JAMES

It's a fine thing to have ability, but the ability to discover ability in others is the true test.

ELBERT HUBBARD

If you go directly to the heart of a mystery, it ceases to be a mystery.

CHRISTOPHER MORLEY

1

An Overview of Fundamentals, Concepts, and Procedures

Man himself is the crowning wonder of creation; the study of his nature the noblest study the world affords.

GLADSTONE

Personnel selection as managers practice it today is far from an exact science. Indeed, few would even classify it as a mature art. This will undoubtedly remain the case until there is a better understanding of the human being and of the techniques for applying this understanding to the personnel selection process.

The need for a better understanding of the human being has been of consuming interest to leaders and oracles of every major civilization. The ancient Greek philosophers expressed intense interest in the subject when they challenged fellow citizens to "know thyself." And modern philosophers have continued to admonish people to "know yourself and others."

Despite these early and continuing challenges, little has been done to enhance our understanding of the human being. That is not to say progress has not been made, because it has. In fact, significant contributions have been made over the past century by a number of renowned psychologists, neurologists, and behavioral scientists: Sigmund Freud, William James, Abraham Maslow, B. F. Skinner, Wilder Penfield, and Alfred Binet, to name a few. The literature covering the work of these scientists and others working in these fields is extensive, and much of their research data is

precise and elegant. This information in its present form, however, is of little practical value to the manager. But it can be useful. Indeed, when properly interpreted and integrated, it provides a sound basis for a fundamental and systematic approach to understanding and selecting personnel.

Clearly, the information available shows that two important factors affect what a person can and will do in life. One is the person's brain; the other is the environment to which that person is exposed. Thus, to understand human beings and select those best suited for a particular job, the manager must understand

• How the human brain is ordered and how it performs its many functions

• How the brain interacts with the environment to effect human mental qualities (those qualities that control a person's actions and accomplishments)

• How to estimate a person's mental qualities and match these qualities with those required to perform a particular job

THE HUMAN BRAIN

The human brain may be the most researched subject within the entire universe. Even so, little is

2

known about how it performs its many functions. But by making use of the vast quantities of data available from brain research plus related data from other disciplines, a conceptual model of the brain can be defined that accounts for every important brain function.

BRAIN ANATOMY AND PHYSIOLOGY

Brain characteristics and functions are numerous and complex. In a physical sense, the brain is an intricate system of matter that consists primarily of nerve cells. In a functional sense, it is a unique organ of the body that initiates and controls all human activities.

Many characteristics of the brain are well defined. The nerve cell (neuron), the primary constituent of the brain, has been the subject of extensive research and its characteristics have been elegantly defined. The fact that the brain receives, processes, and transmits information coded as electrical impulses is well documented. And specific areas of the brain responsible for a number of its critical functions have been precisely located.

Many other important brain characteristics, although less rigorously defined than those mentioned above, can be postulated with considerable confidence. Of primary interest here are the three brain characteristics known to be associated with human mental qualities. These are the characteristics which provide the brain with the capacity to store information, perform logic-processing operations, and produce human emotions and actions. The character of these brain capacities has not been fully identified. But the fact that such capacities do, indeed, exist is well accepted. It is also generally acknowledged that each of these capacities is seated in a different region of the brain and each is essentially independent of the other. In addition, observations indicate that the characteristics exhibited by each of the three brain capacities vary widely among individuals. This type of variation is in harmony with nature, of course, since the brain is subject to normal genetic variations like other organs of the body.

The brain capacities just described obviously contribute to the mental qualities of every human being. But how they contribute is not at all clear. The brain processes are complex, and definitive information is much too meager for explaining brain operations. Thus, other sources of information and considerable interpretation are needed.

BRAIN-COMPUTER ANALOGY

Because of its recognized similarity with the brain, the electronic digital computer is perhaps the most useful source of supplementary information available. The brain and computer are similar in many ways. They both operate with digital pulse-coded signals. The characteristics of their most basic elements (the brain neuron and the computer logic gate) are amazingly similar. Also, the brain's capacity to store information and perform logic-processing operations are strikingly computerlike. These two brain capacities are, in fact, quite analogous to those provided by the computer memory and central processing units, respectively.

There is, however, an important and fundamental difference between the ways the brain and computer operate. It lies in the method of control. The computer is controlled by operating instructions supplied from the outside by the user, while the brain is controlled by internally generated instructions. How the brain performs this function is much less certain. But two things are evident: there is a control system in the brain, and it is apparently located in those regions responsible for human emotions. This location is in keeping with the obvious relationship known to exist between human emotions and actions. And the large number of nerve fiber connections between this area and other parts of the brain is consistent with the information transfer necessary for control.

Both the brain and the computer can therefore be seen as physical entities that possess capacities to perform specific functions, since each has memory and logic-processing areas that are both separate and independent. Thus, in concept, the brain is essentially a computer in which programmed control (supplied by a user) is replaced by spontaneous control (generated within the brain).

One additional analogy between the brain and computer is useful in understanding the brain. As a prerequisite for operation, each must be supplied information from an outside source. The computer receives the necessary information from the user; the brain receives needed information from its environment.

The environment that supplies information to the brain exists both outside and inside the human body. Exposure to the environment is through a network of nerve fibers that extend to all parts of the body. Through this network, the five senses provide the brain with information from the outside environment. The nerve network similarly supplies the brain with information about body temperature, hunger, thirst, and many other internal physiological characteristics.

BRAIN FUNCTIONS AND PROCESSES

A conceptual model of the brain has been synthesized from information of the type just reviewed. It shows how the brain is postulated to effect information storage and recall (memory), logic-processing (thinking), and control of body actions (logical and emotional). It also illustrates how these three brain characteristics, in combination with information from the environment, determine what a person is mentally able and willing to do.

HUMAN MENTAL QUALITIES

The conceptual model of the brain is very computerlike: the physical brain is analogous to computer hardware, and the information from the environment is analogous to computer software. In this analogy, the hardware parts (or brain elements) responsible for memory, logic processing, and control of body actions are identified as separate entities, each associated with a unique region of the brain. Specifically, memory is associated with the cerebral cortex, in general; logic-processing is associated with the frontal lobe of the cerebral cortex; and control of actions is associated with the brain stem. Appreciation for the nature of these three brain elements is essential to human understanding. Each is independent of the others, and there is essentially no relationship between the characteristics (or capacities) exhibited by each. The capacity of each element is genetically fixed and is thought to change little during adult life; but each varies greatly among individuals, of course.

Like the hardware of a computer, brain elements can function only when supplied with information from the environment. And how well they are able to perform these functions depends upon their inherited capacities plus the quality and quantity of the information received from the environment.

Once a person's brain (hardware) receives information (software) from the environment, it possesses unique mental qualities. These qualities, which depend upon inherited brain characteristics and environmental experiences, are identified here as *knowledge, problem-solving capability,* and *behavioral characteristics*.

Knowledge is determined by the brain's capacity to store and recall information (memory capacity) and the information it is supplied by the environment. Problem-solving capability is determined by the brain's capacity to perform logic-processing operations and the nature of the information it receives from the environment. Behavioral characteristics are determined by the brain's capacity to produce human emotions and actions, in conjunction with related information acquired from the environment.

The combination of these three mental qualities identifies a more comprehensive mental quality, defined herein as *effective mental capability*. This combination of mental qualities, which determines what a person is mentally able and willing to do, has been defined as follows:

$$\text{Effective mental capability} = \sqrt[3]{\text{knowledge} \times \frac{\text{problem-solving}}{\text{capability}} \times \frac{\text{behavioral}}{\text{characteristics}}}$$

(1.1)

where knowledge, problem-solving capability, and behavioral characteristics are defined in consistent units and each is postulated to exert equal influence on a person's effective mental capability.

The significance of Equation 1.1 to managers is readily apparent. It identifies each human mental quality in recognizable form, and it shows how these qualities combine to determine a person's overall capability or effective mental capability. Thus, it provides the basis for greatly improved understanding of the human being, and it affords a definitive framework for selecting personnel best suited for any particular job.

PERSONNEL SELECTION

Using the relationships established by Equation 1.1 in the personnel selection process requires careful consideration of each human mental quality in the equation. The process involves four basic steps: collecting specific information about each candidate, estimating quantitative values for each mental quality, defining job requirements in terms of the different mental qualities, and matching the values of each candidate's mental qualities with those mental qualities required for the job under consideration.

INFORMATION COLLECTION

The information deemed to be most useful in estimating values for the mental qualities in Equation 1.1 can usually be acquired through the use of job application forms, personnel interviewing techniques, and personal reference check procedures. The type of information most useful in estimating a person's knowledge, problem-solving capability, and behavioral characteristics is summarized below:

o Knowledge: early-life social and economic experiences, psychological test scores (IQ, SAT, ACT, etc.) level of schooling completed, quality of schools attended, academic record, specific work experiences, and work accomplishments.

o Problem-solving capability: creative achievements in hobbies, success in writing on complex and multifaceted subjects, creative achievements in college and/or in research, and success as an on-the-job problem-solver.

o Behavioral characteristics: early family-life experiences relative to home stability, social and economic status, religion, discipline, and work; achievements and leadership roles in extracurricular activities; motivation in school studies; commitment to on-the-job responsibilities; success as a supervisor; and courtesy and respect extended to others.

ESTIMATING PROCEDURES

No methods are currently available for quantitatively measuring a person's knowledge, problem-solving capability, behavioral characteristics, and effective mental capability, as defined in Equation 1.1. Yet, by noting their actions and accomplishments, individuals can readily be compared relative to the knowledge they possess, their ability to solve problems, and the desirability of their behavior. In fact, with the type of information identified above, one can make a reasonable comparative estimate of a person's knowledge, problem-solving capability, behavioral characteristics, and, therefore, effective mental capability.

All that is needed is a definitive reference point to provide a basis for establishing quantitative values for each of the human mental qualities. For this purpose, it is convenient to set the reference point for each human mental quality at an average value for the population and establish its numerical value at 100. Since each of these mental qualities depends upon the same variables—brain characteristics and environmental exposures—a similar distribution of their values within the population can reasonably be assumed. If the distribution is further assumed to be normal about the value of 100, a distribution similar to that displayed by the intelligence quotient (IQ) curve results. Accordingly, values of human mental qualities varying from approximately 20 to 180 (plus or minus 5 sigma) can be expected, with very few values occurring beyond these extreme limits.

Estimates of human mental qualities based on the procedures just discussed are, of course, lacking in rigor. But they can provide a new insight and an improved understanding of the human being if they are done with care. And, most importantly, they supply managers with the information necessary for more effective personnel selection.

JOB REQUIREMENTS

The procedures established for estimating human mental qualities make up an essential part of the selection process. Defining the job requirements in terms of the same human mental qualities is another equally important part. Every job in every organization, of course, has unique requirements; and techniques for defining these requirements are essential to the selection procedure. Careful analysis, interpretation, and integration of the information available from many sources show that—in addition to the definition of profession or vocation—two other designations are needed to state job requirements: *effective mental capability* (as defined in Equation 1.1) and the *distribution of human mental qualities*.

The effective mental capability requirements for successful performance in various general job categories have been established, and are summarized as follows:

Job categories	Effective mental capability
Basic study and research	135
Applied research and development	125
Professional service	120
Semiprofessional service	115
Skilled work	110
Semiskilled work	100
Routine work	85

This categorization of job requirements, which has been established from extensive studies, indicates that no specific levels of knowledge, problem-solving capability, or behavioral characteristics are required for any job category. The only requirement is that the combined influence of these three mental qualities provides the specified effective mental capability. However, depending upon the particular job to be performed in a certain job category, specific distributions of knowledge, problem-solving capability, or behavioral characteristics are required. What this requirement is, in each case, depends upon the type of organization involved. Both the organization size and its growth-potential influence the requirement.

For example, under certain conditions the need in a particular job category may be for a person with great quantities of knowledge: an analyst. Under other circumstances a person with high problem-solving capability, a synthesist, may be required. Other conditions may dictate the need for a person with favorable behavioral characteristics: a supervisor. Under still other circumstances, the requirement may be for an individual whose mental qualities are essentially equal: a manager.

Thus, defining a job requirement in terms of human mental qualities involves two steps: defining the job category and then determining whether the need is for an analyst, a synthesist, a supervisor, or a manager.

PERSONNEL SELECTION

Once the job requirements are identified and the human mental qualities of the candidates estimated, the selection process becomes one of selecting the best match between job requirements and the candidates' human mental qualities. In practice there is seldom an exact match. Moreover, the accuracy with which human mental qualities can be estimated and job requirements defined leaves room for error in the selection process. This situation, however, can be dealt with by giving special considerations to the existing distribution of human mental qualities within the organization, the size and growth potential of the organization, and certain practical techniques for dealing with possible selection errors.

PART 1

THE HUMAN BRAIN

The elementary properties of nerve-tissue on which the brain-functions depend are far from being satisfactorily made out.

WILLIAM JAMES, 1890

I am, of course, not claiming some final and complete understanding [of the brain]. That is indefinitely in the future.

J.C. ECCLES, 1977

The brain of a person is in reality that person. Indeed, those mental qualities that determine what a person is capable of accomplishing in life are seated in and controlled by this vital organ.

The human brain is without question the most elegantly constructed and powerful system of matter ever created. It is also extremely complex. Even so, detailed knowledge of the brain is extensive. The basic anatomy of the brain is well established, and the physiological characteristics of many brain elements are well understood. This understanding does not apply, however, to the overall integrated functions of the brain. For example, the integrating functions and processes that permit the brain to effect human consciousness, logical reasoning, memory, emotions, and associated body actions are essentially unknown. Thus, despite our enormous knowledge of the brain, its operation as a functioning system remains vague and mysterious.

Since it is the seat of all human mental qualities, the value of and the need for a better understanding of the brain and its functions are readily apparent. Moreover, because of the large quantities of applicable information available from many sources, a goal for achieving greatly enhanced understanding is a realistic objective. In addition to information about the brain itself, information from other sources provides useful insight into its functions and processes. For exam-ple, much information from controlled experiments and clinical observations is available which relates various brain elements to specific human qualities. The digital computer, which has many characteristics analogous to those of the brain, is also a useful vehicle.

In the following chapters a summary of the available information mentioned above is provided, and a unified concept of brain functions and processes postulated on the basis of this information is presented. Chapter 2 covers the general anatomy and physiology of the brain. It enumerates all the major elements of the brain and identifies their most important features and characteristics. Chapter 3 describes the digital computer and its operating characteristics. Computer components that perform functions similar to those accomplished by the brain are discussed in considerable detail. In Chapter 4, a unified concept of brain functions and processes based on information from Chapters 2 and 3 is discussed. A conceptual model of the brain is defined, its functions are described, and the operating characteristics of the model are discussed and illustrated.

The sources of information used in preparing these chapters are numerous and varied. They include popular publications, advanced technical papers, and very sophisticated textbooks on subjects related to human understanding. A bibliography is provided at the end of Part I.

2

The Anatomy and Physiology of the Brain

The human brain . . . is without any qualification the most highly organized and most completely organized matter in the Universe.

J. C. ECCLES

The brain is the center of all human mental qualities. It is responsible for consciousness, memory, reasoning, emotions, and all associated body actions.

Located atop the spinal cord, the brain is surrounded and well protected by the bone structure of the head. Its shape is somewhat spherical, with local surface convolutions that give its exterior the appearance of an enlarged walnut kernel. The normal brain weighs about 3 pounds, or about 2 percent of the total body weight.

The brain consists of three major subdivisions: cerebrum, brain stem, and cerebellum. The cerebrum, the largest of the three subdivisions, dominates an exterior view of the brain. It is concerned with sensory reception, memory, logic-processing, and voluntary body movements. The brain stem, at the center of the brain mass, is responsible for control of brain operations and life-sustaining processes. The cerebellum, situated below the cerebrum and behind the brain stem, coordinates and effects smooth muscle movements. The external physical features of each subdivision are illustrated in Figure 2.1.

As Figure 2.1 shows, the right and left sides of the brain are essentially symmetrical, with each a mirror image of the other. Figure 2.2, a cross section of the brain at the plane of symmetry, illustrates the internal relationship of the three subdivisions.

The substance constituting the brain mass consists primarily of nerve cells, or neurons. Numbered in the billions, these very sophisticated cells provide the basis for all brain functions and processes. They provide the ability to receive, code, transmit, store, and process information essential to the various brain functions.

The unique characteristics of the neuron which permit it to perform its important functions are discussed in the following section. Later, the anatomical and physiological characteristics of the components which constitute the cerebrum, brain stem, and cerebellum are described.

THE NEURON

The neuron is the primary constituent of the brain. It performs two critical functions: it trans-

9

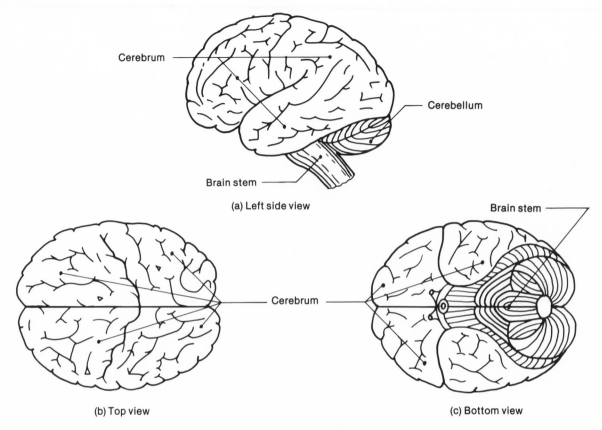

Cerebrum

Cerebellum

Brain stem

(a) Left side view

Cerebrum

Brain stem

Cerebrum

(b) Top view

(c) Bottom view

Figure 2.1 External features of the brain

mits impulses or messages throughout the brain, and it provides the means for processing and storing messages or information.

The size, shape, and other characteristics of neurons vary widely, depending upon location in the brain and the functions performed. Although their anatomy differs greatly, neurons exhibit many fundamental similarities. That is, each consists of three basic parts: dendrites, the cell body, and an axon (see Figure 2.3).

The function of the dendrite is to carry impulses to the cell body. The axon transmits impulses away from the cell body. The neuron may have a few or several thousand dendrites. There is only one axon per neuron; however, the axon often branches into collaterals and in this way transmits impulses to a number of other neurons.

Although there are billions of neurons within the human brain, each is a separate entity; there is no anatomic continuity between them. Thus, impulse transmission along and between neurons involves two different mechanisms.

IMPULSE TRANSMISSION ALONG NERVE FIBERS

The transmission of impulses along a nerve involves a very elegant and sophisticated electrochemical process.

Nerve fibers in all parts of the brain are surrounded by so-called interstitial fluids which contain sodium and potassium ions. The permeability characteristics of the nerve fiber membranes are such that a highly negative electrochemical potential exists across the membrane in a rest (no-transmission) state, as Figure 2.4 illustrates. The fiber membrane is said to be in a polarized (or rest) state when this condition exists, and the resulting electrochemical membrane potential is typically 70 to 90 millivolts negative relative to the outside surface.

Impulse transmission along a nerve fiber involves a process of local depolarization and repolarization. The process—which may be initiated by chemical, mechanical, or electrical stim-

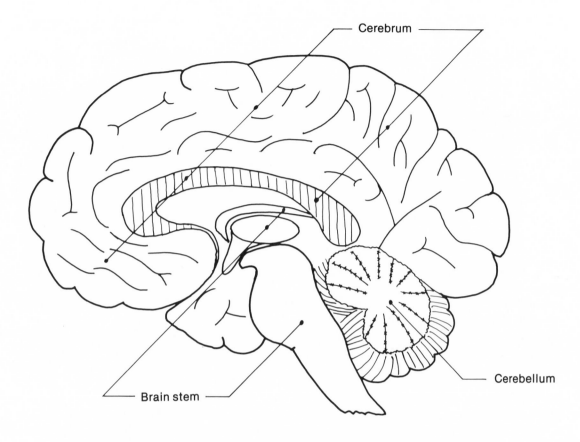

Figure 2.2 Brain cross section through plane of symmetry (median sagittal)

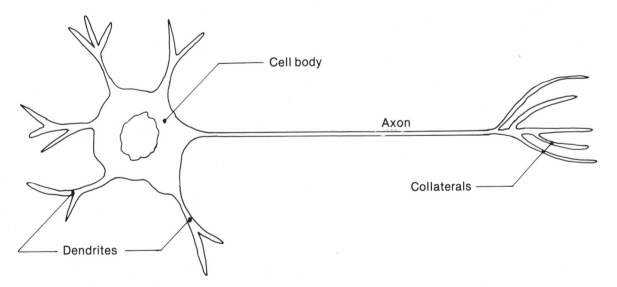

Figure 2.3 Schematic of a simple single neuron

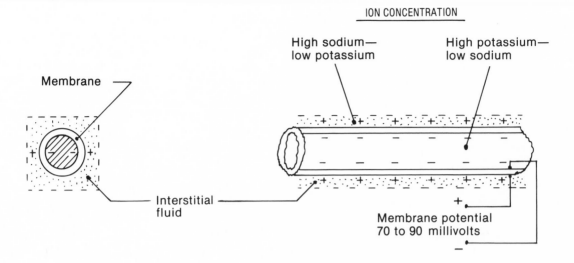

Figure 2.4   Ion concentration and rest-state potential within a nerve fiber

ulation—depends upon a complex transfer of sodium and potassium ions across the neuron membrane, which exhibits varying permeability characteristics. Figure 2.5 illustrates the process that occurs when a nerve fiber is stimulated by an electrical voltage or impulse. Figure 2.5*a* depicts how an impulse signal initiated by a negative voltage moves along a nerve fiber. Figure 2.5*b, c,* and *d* shows how the fiber output is influenced by the input voltage. At very low-input negative voltages there is no fiber output, as shown in Figure 2.5*b*. As the input voltage is changed to a medium-negative value, the fiber produces an output whose frequency is proportional to the input voltage level, and the output frequency increases as the negative input voltage is increased (see

Figure 2.5*b* and *c*). Note that the voltage output of the fiber is independent of the input voltage. Thus, the only effect of changing an input signal to a neuron is a change in the rate at which pulses (essentially on-off signals) are passed along a fiber.

The foregoing discussion serves only to illustrate the similarities and basic characteristics of neuron fibers. On an individual basis, the specific geometrical and functional characteristics of the brain nerve fibers vary markedly.

Anatomically, there are two types of brain nerve fibers. One is coated with an insulating substance; the other is not. The insulator, called *myelin,* is a fatty material which greatly enhances the impulse conduction velocity and frequency

Table 2.1   Certain anatomical and functional characteristics of brain-neuron fibers

CHARACTERISTICS	RANGE OF VALUES	
	Bare Fiber	Myelinated Fiber
Fiber length	1 to 15 centimeters	1 to 15 centimeters
Fiber diameter	0.2 to 1.5 microns	0.5 to 20 microns
Coating thickness	none	0.2 to 5 microns
Maximum frequency response	250 hertz	400 to 1250 hertz
Impulse conduction velocity	0.5 to 2.5 meters/second	3 to 125 meters/second

response characteristics of the nerve fiber. Table 2.1 summarizes some of the anatomical and functional characteristics of the two fiber types.

Myelinated fibers are found in the brain where transmission time and high frequency are crucial. Bare fibers are found where neither of these characteristics is necessary.

IMPULSE TRANSMISSION BETWEEN NEURONS

Impulse transmission from one neuron to another is effected through an interface junction known as a *synapse*. The synapse, in performing this function, is perhaps the most important single

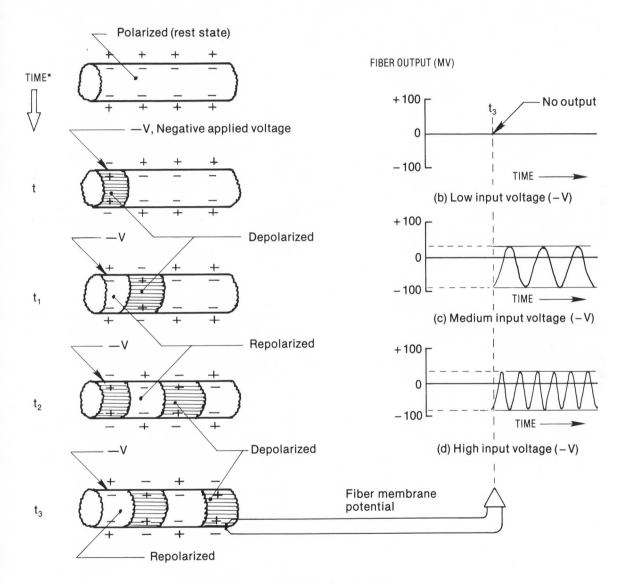

(a) Depolarization/repolarization process

*Time after application of negative voltage

Figure 2.5   Impluse transmission along a nerve fiber

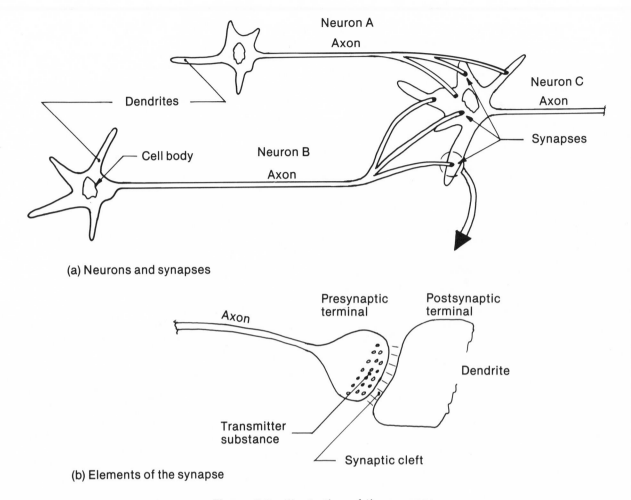

(a) Neurons and synapses

(b) Elements of the synapse

Figure 2.6   Illustration of the synapse

element within the human brain. Synapses exist wherever axon fibers originating from one or more neurons terminate on the surface of a cell body, a dendrite, or (more rarely) the axon of another neuron.

The physical relationship between neurons and synapses is illustrated in Figure 2.6. Figure 2.6a illustrates neurons A and B synapsing with neuron C. Geometrically, the synapse is very small. The distance between the axon fiber terminal and the neuron surface is approximately 0.02 microns at the axon fiber terminal. Figure 2.6b illustrates the primary elements of the synapse.

In controlling impulses, excitatory synapses activate and inhibitory synapses inhibit impulse initiation, depending upon the transmitter substance present in the synaptic terminals. The manner in which the synapse functions to excite the neuron can be explained as follows:

Referring to Figure 2.6b, an impulse reaching the synapse causes a change in the membrane structure and a small quantity of excitatory transmitter substance is discharged into the synaptic cleft. This substance then acts to increase the permeability of the neuron membrane to the sodium ion. Sodium ions present in the surrounding fluid then pass through the neuron membrane and locally increase the positive ions, or charge on the neuron. The quantity of excitatory transmitter substance discharged into the synaptic cleft, and ultimately the charge on the cell body, increases with the frequency of the stimulating input impulse. When the frequency of the input signal at the synapse reaches a certain level, it produces a cell body voltage that is sufficient to cause an impulse to be transmitted along the axon fiber. Thus the synapse acts as an on-off device whose operation depends upon the input frequency.

The inhibitory synapse functions in the same manner as the excitatory synapse, except that the inhibitory transmitter substance acts to decrease neuron membrane permeability to the sodium ion. The result is a decrease in positive ions or charge on the neuron. This increases the existing polarity and, hence, inhibits the initiation of impulse transmission.

As indicated in Figure 2.7, synapses may be widely spread over the neuron. A single brain neuron may have a few or many (up to 200,000) synapses spread over its surface, as indicated in Figure 2.7a. And the synaptic inputs may be either excitatory or inhibitory, as illustrated in Figure 2.7b.

THE NEURON SYSTEM

Within the brain, neurons are grouped into various combinations as appropriate for performing the required functions. Physically, these groups appear in the form of sheaths, hard nuclei, and fiber bundles. They are referred to as *gray matter* and *white matter,* the latter name being associated with the myelin-coated neurons.

It has been estimated that there are at least 10 billion neurons within the human brain. Since the average neuron has approximately 50,000 synapses, the total number of synapses approaches a minimum of 500 trillion. As has already been discussed, each synapse exhibits an on-off characteristic. Accordingly, the brain has the capacity to accommodate some 500 trillion bits of information in binary (on-off) coded form. Thus it is readily apparent why the human brain provides an essentially limitless capacity to store, transmit, and process signals or information.

In performing its functions, the brain receives impulses (or messages) from numerous sources. Information signals from outside the body (sight, hearing, smell, feeling, and taste sensations) are translated by sensors into impulses useful to the brain. Numerous other sensors also communicate information from within the body to various parts of the brain. These include sensors which provide information on a wide range of phenomena. Examples are body balance, muscle position, limb position, hunger, thirst, body temperature, sexual desires, and emotions. In addition, impulses resulting from various brain processes reenter other parts of the brain as information for reprocessing and assessment. In a like manner, messages from the brain to other parts of the body are transmitted by impulses when any body action is necessary.

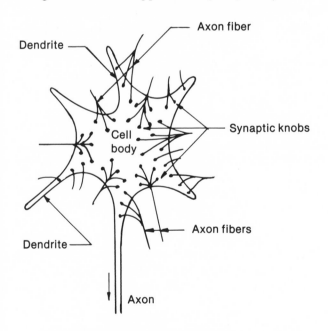

(a) Synaptic knobs on a brain neuron

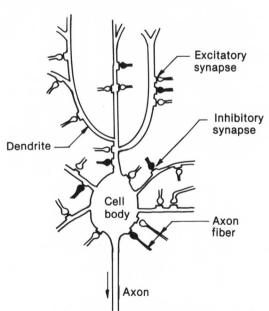

(b) Illustration of brain neuron with excitatory and inhibitory synapses

Figure 2.7 Typical distribution of synapses on a brain neuron

While much is known about the fundamental transmission and operating characteristics of brain neurons, the processes by which impulses are converted into intelligible information is a complete mystery. One thing is clear, however: all information passes to and from the brain in im- pulse form, coded by frequency. Numerous experiments conclusively demonstrate this finding.

Figures 2.8 and 2.9, based on controlled experiments with cats, illustrate the frequency-coding processes associated with brain input and output impulses, respectively. Figure 2.8 shows

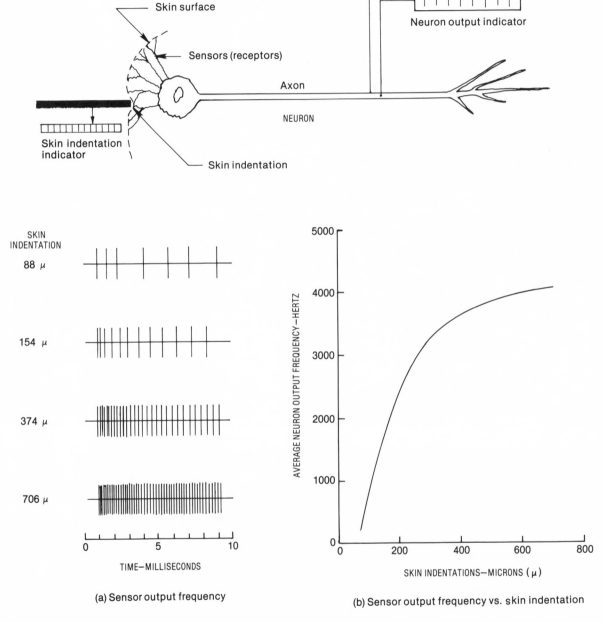

(a) Sensor output frequency

(b) Sensor output frequency vs. skin indentation

Data from John C. Eccles, *The Understanding of the Brain,* New York: McGraw-Hill Book Co., 1977, p. 11. (used with permission)

Figure 2.8 Frequency coding by a cat's touch sensor

how a touch sensor of a cat converts pressure or skin indentation into coded frequency. Both the skin indentation and the discharge frequency of the nerve fiber were measured in this experiment. The correlation between input pressure (skin indentation) and output frequency is clearly shown.

Figure 2.9 demonstrates the effect of impulse frequency output from a brain neuron on the contraction force produced by the leg muscles of a cat. The neuron was pulsed at various frequencies by an inserted electrode in this experiment, and the contraction forces were measured. The con-

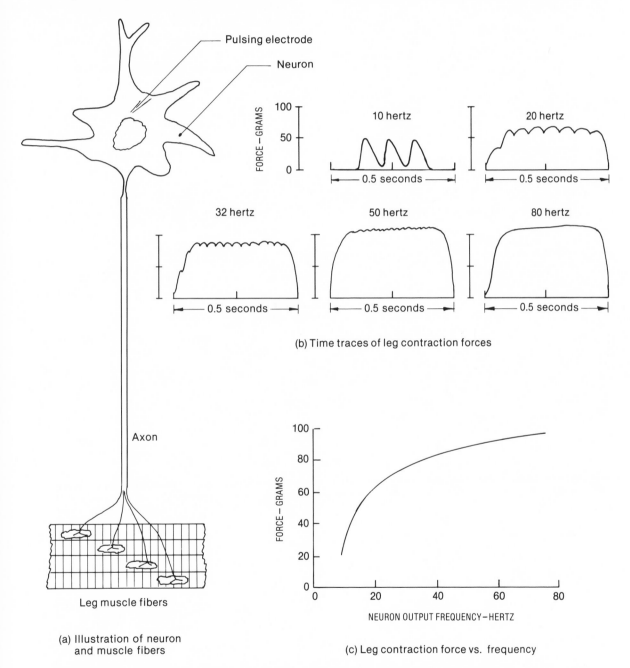

(b) Time traces of leg contraction forces

(a) Illustration of neuron and muscle fibers

(c) Leg contraction force vs. frequency

Data from John C. Eccles, *The Understanding of the Brain,* New York: McGraw-Hill Book Co., 1977, p. 36. (used with permission)

Figure 2.9 Response of a cat's leg muscles to frequency coded input

tractions were typically unstable at very low frequency inputs, but both the time traces (Figure 2.8*b*) and the force-vs.-frequency plot (Figure 2.9*c*) show the contraction force is determined by the output frequency of the neuron.

THE CEREBRUM

More than any other part of the brain, the cerebrum distinguishes the human from the animal. It is by far the largest part of the brain, representing nearly 85 percent of its weight. Located at the top, it completely dominates an external view of the brain (see Figure 2.10). The right and left sides, or hemispheres, are divided into four primary lobes: frontal, temporal, parietal, and occipital (see Figure 2.10*a*). The hemispheres are essentially symmetrical and consist of three major parts: cerebral cortex (gray matter), white matter, and basal ganglia. Figures 2.10*c* and *d* show the relative locations of these parts.

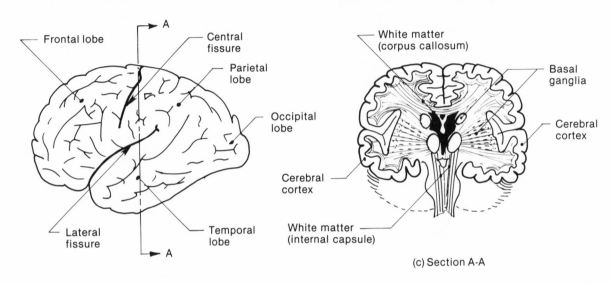

(a) Left side view

(c) Section A-A

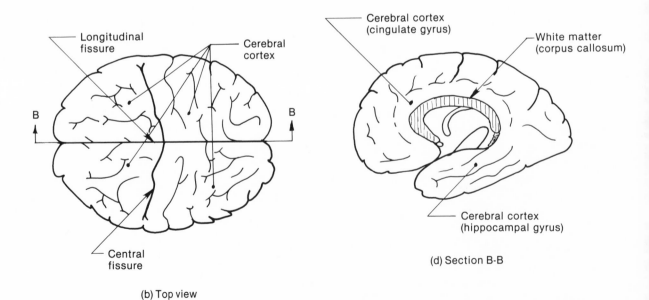

(b) Top view

(d) Section B-B

Figure 2.10   The relationship of certain cerebrum parts

THE CEREBRAL CORTEX

The cerebral cortex is that part of the cerebrum responsible for memory, logic-processing, and voluntary actions. It consists of a six-layer system of gray matter, 2 to 5 millimeters thick, which makes up the outside surface of the cerebrum. The gray appearance results from unmyelinated neurons, the number of which has been estimated to exceed 9 billion. To accommodate this great quantity of neurons, the cerebral cortex surface area is enlarged by numerous folds that create ridges and furrows—referred to as gyri and fissures, respectively. The result is a surface area approximately three times the exposed surface area of the cerebrum (approximately 0.20 square meters).

The cerebral cortex is divided into right and left hemispheres, one being a mirror image of the other. Over 200 million neuron fibers provide for communication between the hemispheres.

THE WHITE MATTER

The so-called white matter of the cerebrum consists primarily of myelinated neurons whose function is to transmit impulses (1) from one hemisphere to the other, (2) from one part of the cerebral cortex to another within the same hemisphere, and (3) from the brain to other parts of the nervous system. The myelinated neurons, which give the white appearance, are important for this function. The myelin coat allows for high-speed impulse transmission between brain parts, thus enhancing processing speed and brain efficiency. Figure 2.10 indicates the main areas of white matter within the cerebrum.

THE BASAL GANGLIA

The basal ganglia are composed of large masses of unmyelinated neurons, or gray matter, located in the central portion of the cerebrum. Figure 2.10c shows the relative position of these components. The functions of these components are not well defined. However, as major interfaces between the cerebrum, brain stem, and cerebellum, they provide primary pathways for information between these subdivisions.

FUNCTIONS OF THE CEREBRAL CORTEX

The cerebral cortex performs the following four basic functions: (1) it receives, codes, and integrates impulse messages from receptors of the sensory sources, (2) it stores and retains information (memory), (3) it performs logic processes on information provided from the memory and sen-

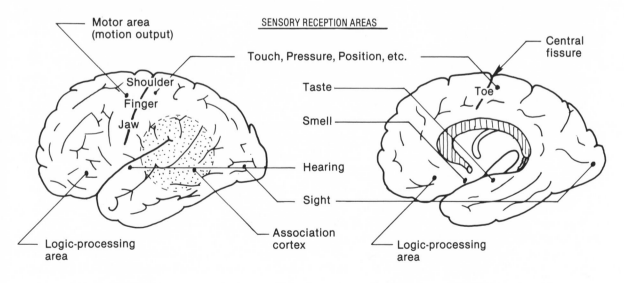

(a) Outside surface

(b) Section through plane of symmetry (median surface)

Figure 2.11 Location of certain functional areas in the cerebral cortex

sory sources, and (4) it initiates voluntary body actions in response to various brain processes. The areas of the cerebral cortex where some of these functions are performed are well defined; others can only be postulated. Some of the areas are identified in Figure 2.11.

Reception, Coding, and Integration

The sensations detected by receptors of the five senses are transmitted to the cerebral cortex by coded impulses. Each sensory receptor projects messages to different areas of the brain, as indicated in Figure 2.11. Through various ingenious techniques and observations these receiving areas of the cortex have been located, some more accurately than others. The sensory reception areas, which receive sensations from touch, pressure, hearing, position, etc., have been precisely mapped. Figure 2.11 shows the general areas associated with sensing impulses from the shoulder, finger, jaw, and toe. The cortex areas which receive hearing and sight are almost as well defined; however, the areas associated with taste and smell are less precisely located.

Messages from all sensory receptors are converted into coded form before transmission to the cerebral cortex, as illustrated in Figure 2.8. Upon reaching the cortex, the impulse messages are further processed and perhaps recoded. These messages then pass into the adjoining cortex (association) area, where they are integrated into meaningful forms. The boundary of the association area is not well established, but is known to overlie the parietal, occipital, and temporal lobes of the cerebral cortex.

The basic functions performed by the right and left hemispheres are essentially the same, with each receiving impulses from the sensory receptors. The hemispheres, however, do not always receive impulses from identical sensory receptors. For example, touch, pressure, and position sensors project impulses from the right side of the body to the left hemisphere and vice versa. In case of the eyes, the right half of each eye projects impulses to the right hemisphere, while the left half of each eye projects impulses to the left hemisphere. The other sensors (hearing, taste, and smell) project impulses equally to both sides of the brain. In any case, however, the myriad interconnecting

neurons provide rapid and almost complete transfer of information between hemispheres.

Information Storage (Memory)

Information storage, or memory, is one of the least understood of the brain functions. Not only is the mechanism of storage unknown; the storage location also remains undetermined. All this mystery notwithstanding, no one doubts the existence of human memory. Only the how and where are in question.

The consensus among specialists is that brain neurons are the devices that make possible information storage and subsequent recall: memory. There is, however, considerable disagreement over how brain neurons perform this function. Some authorities believe that more than one mechanism is involved, because all sensory information inputs are not equally well "remembered." Specifically, certain observations may be remembered, or recalled, for only a short period of time after exposure. Other observations are recallable after extended periods. This situation has led to the concept of so-called short-term and long-term memory.

Short-term memory (or recall) is exemplified by the remembering of a telephone number only long enough to complete the dialing. Some believe the mechanism involves reverberating circuits of neurons. The theory is that information remains encoded as impulses for a short period of time and then disappears. This concept is supported by little experimental evidence.

Long-term memory (or recall) is that which prevails for extended periods, in some instances for a lifetime. This, many believe, involves an anatomical change in the neurons. The hypothesis is that if a system of neurons and associated synapses is repeatedly subjected to the same group of coded impulses (containing a certain message), the neurons will change anatomically as necessary to store the message. Subsequently, when stimulated by an appropriate impulse, the message will be presented to the conscious brain.

The fact that electrical stimulation of certain areas of the cerebral cortex can transfer memory to consciousness has been demonstrated in a number of neurosurgery patients. During the surgical procedure, generally for epilepsy with the patient conscious, electrical stimulations applied to specific areas within the temporal lobe often evoked vivid aural and visual memories. When stimulation ceased, recall disappeared.

Message repetition is apparently the key to long-term memory recall. Repetition may or may not be deliberate on the part of the individual. For example, a passage of literature (message) may be committed to memory, for life, by deliberate repetition. On the other hand, message repetition may be induced by an emotionally charged experience. Such an experience apparently dominates the brain and allows the related impulses, or messages, to circulate repeatedly through the brain until the emotional situation is resolved. Long-term memory recall is thus induced. As examples, few adult Americans living at the times of these events will fail to recall them: the Japanese attack on Pearl Harbor, the assassination of John F. Kennedy, and the lunar landing of Neil Armstrong and Edwin Aldrin. About such emotional happenings, our memories are usually quite vivid in regard to the date, the time of day, our location, our occupation, and our companions at the moment we learned of each of these episodes.

The human memory is generally agreed to be located in the cerebral cortex primarily because that is where most of the brain neurons are. However, it is clear that any particular memory or message is not stored in a single local area of the cortex. Instead, messages appear to be stored in neuron streams (or strings) that traverse many areas of the cortex. Cumulative evidence supports these observations. Experiments with rats show significant retention of memory (maze-running skill) with large percentages of their brains removed. Human beings, likewise, have shown amazing memory retention with large sections of their brains destroyed or severed either by accidents or by certain neurosurgical procedures.

Logic-processing

The mechanism which provides logic-processing within the brain is no better understood than that associated with memory. There are, however, many indications that logic-processing (or human thinking) is accomplished in the prefrontal lobe of the cerebral cortex. It has no other defined function, and the available evidence is very convincing.

Numerous surgical operations known as frontal lobotomies were carried out during the 1940's on patients with severe mental illnesses. This operation consists of removing portions of the prefrontal lobes and severing nerve fibers passing from the prefrontal cortex to the brain-stem area. The operations were generally successful from the standpoint of reducing fear and anxiety, but certain other mental functions were often adversely affected. Common among the ill effects were loss in judgment, foresight, willpower, and problem-solving ability—all apparently associated with the logic process.

Voluntary Body Action

All impulses or messages which result in voluntary body movements are initiated within the so-called motor cortex area at the rear of the frontal lobe, immediately forward of the central fissure (see Figure 2.11). Excitation of local areas of the motor cortex by electrical impulse causes associated parts of the body to move. Hence its functions are well defined and mapped. Generally, the motor cortex located on the left side is associated with movement on the right side and vice versa. However, when movements involve synchronization between sides, as do speaking and swallowing, one side develops more than the other and becomes dominant. It may be either side; but with speech the left side is usually dominant.

As currently understood, the motor area has little or no logic or memory functions but simply responds with the proper motion output impulses when signaled to do so by other parts of the brain.

THE BRAIN STEM

The brain stem is primarily a control and regulation device. Located at the top of the spinal cord, it acts as an interface between the brain subdivisions and the rest of the nervous system. Essentially, all signal impulses (or messages) entering and leaving the brain pass through the brain stem. It is composed of a massive network of neurons which act as sensors, controls, and relays that exert a dominating influence on the health and well-being of every human being.

The functions of the brain stem are obviously enormous. However, those of primary interest here are those performed by the thalamus, hypothalamus, and the reticular formation. The rela-

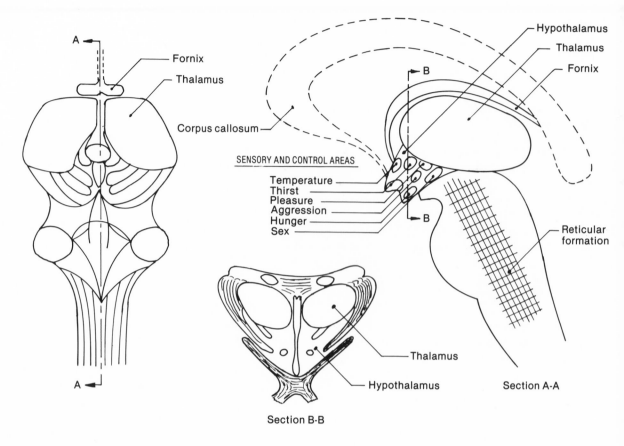

Figure 2.12   The brain stem

tionship of the brain stem to other parts of the brain is illustrated in Figures 2.1 and 2.2. Figure 2.12 shows the relationships of major parts within the brain stem.

THE THALAMUS

The thalamus is located at the top of the brain stem. It interfaces directly with the basal ganglia and projects neuronal fibers to, and receives reciprocal fibers from, essentially every component of the brain. It is often referred to as the relay station of the brain. But its structure and organization indicate its functions are much more extensive than those required of a relay station. In its strategic location, the thalamus is closely associated with the control of most brain processes, including message reception and distribution, memory storage, logic-processing, and body actions. Indeed, the thalamus may well be the center of human consciousness.

THE HYPOTHALAMUS

The hypothalamus occupies a space immediately below the thalamus, as shown in Figure 2.12. Despite its size, its functions are many and varied. Through myriads of neuronal connections, along with other parts of the nervous system, it performs numerous sensory and control functions vital to human survival and enjoyment of life. As a sensory device, it senses (primarily through body-fluid chemistry) such conditions as thirst, hunger, and sexual desires and communicates these to consciousness level. Hypothalamic sensors also detect and communicate to consciousness those bodily conditions which induce emotions varying from pleasure to displeasure and from aggression to indifference.

As a control device, the hypothalamus is directly responsible for regulating body temperature and body water-balance. In addition, it imposes a regulatory influence on the activities of most body glands and organs, including the salivary glands, heart, lungs, intestines, adrenal glands, tear glands, stomach, and gonads.

Many of the various functions performed by the hypothalamus have been demonstrated by experiments or observations in both humans and animals. Furthermore, the general areas of the hypothalamus associated with the different functions have been established, using special electrical and other stimulation techniques. Figure 2.12 indicates the location of some of the most important sensory and control areas.

Some of the experiments which helped to establish and further substantiate certain functions of the hypothalamus are both interesting and convincing. For example, a recently fed animal sought food when stimulated with an electrical impluse in the hunger area of the hypothalamus and continued eating as long as the stimulation was applied. In another experiment, stimulation applied to the sex area caused rats to copulate to exhaustion. Similarly, stimulation applied to the pleasure area of mental patients provided feelings which reportedly ranged from mild to extreme euphoria. In still another experiment, stimulation of the aggression area caused otherwise placid cats to become enraged. In a more dramatic demonstration, an experimenter stood in the middle of a bullring and stopped a charging bull simply by operating a switch in a radio-control device which activated electrodes previously implanted in the animal's brain.

The influence exerted on the various glands and organs by the hypothalamus have been observed clinically, as well as in everyday life. Hunger, for instance, can produce stomach hunger pains; or the sight or smell of food may induce salivation. Adverse conditions (like fear, anxiety, and apprehension) often cause the hypothalamus to provoke increased heart rate, increased breathing rate, intestinal upset, and a number of unfavorable stomach conditions. For example, "stomach butterflies," certain intestinal pains, and even ulcers are known to be caused by fear or apprehension.

RETICULAR FORMATION

The reticular formation consists of a neuron network located deep within the brain stem and below the hypothalamus (see Figure 2.12). It performs a number of vital functions, including the control of breathing and blood pressure. But perhaps its most important function is that of controlling consciousness. This function is accomplished by a matrix of neuron-control circuits collectively known as the *reticular activating system*. It is this system which controls the wake-and-sleep cycle. During sleep it regulates the periods of deep sleep, intermediate sleep, and dream sleep. In the waking period, it determines the level of mental alertness at any one time.

Exactly how the reticular activating system accomplishes its functions is not known. However, it is generally believed to be effected through a system of reverberating neuron circuits which, when excited, oscillate at some relatively high frequency until some of the synapses develop fatigue. As this happens, the output impulse frequency drops, the activating stimulus decreases, and alertness drops. As more synapses in the circuits develop fatigue, brain excitation continues to decrease, and finally sleep is induced. Sleep allows the fatigued synapses to recover, after which a new wake-and-sleep cycle is repeated.

THE CEREBELLUM

The cerebellum is the center of body movement, coordination, and balance control. It is a relatively small ellipsoidal body located behind the brain stem and beneath the cerebrum (see Figures 2.1 and 2.2). It accounts for approximately 10 percent of the brain weight.

While the functions of the cerebellum and cerebrum differ markedly, they share many morphological features. In both, the primary constituents are neurons, with the most advanced functions being restricted to the outer layers, or cortex. The surface of each is folded into ridges and furrows to increase the cortex area. However, unlike the cortex of the cerebrum, which has six layers of neurons, the cerebellum cortex has only three.

In performing its functions, the cerebellum receives impulses from the motor cortex of the cerebrum when it initiates body movement, and from sensors throughout the body which define muscle tension, tendon tension, position of joints, and certain body pressures. Movement impulses initiated in the cerebrum are transmitted simultaneously to the activating muscles and the cerebellum. Almost instantaneously, the body tension and position sensors transmit the new body position to the cerebellum. Thus, both the command impulses and impulses which define the resulting body position are available in the cerebellum for movement coordination and balance control.

Input impulses alone, however, are not adequate to ensure smooth and balanced movements. The cerebellum presumably provides this phenomenon through memory, which is developed through continuous and refined repetition of the desired motions. Physical skills, consequently, depend greatly upon the cerebellum and the extent of accurate repetition.

THE LIMBIC SYSTEM

The limbic system, a group of brain components which form the interface between the cerebrum and brain stem, is of special significance. It is concerned with memory and human emotions and has often been referred to as the emotional brain. Components of the limbic

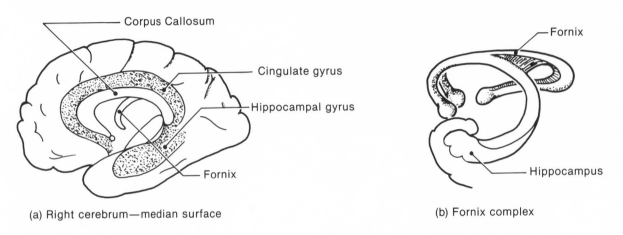

(a) Right cerebrum—median surface

(b) Fornix complex

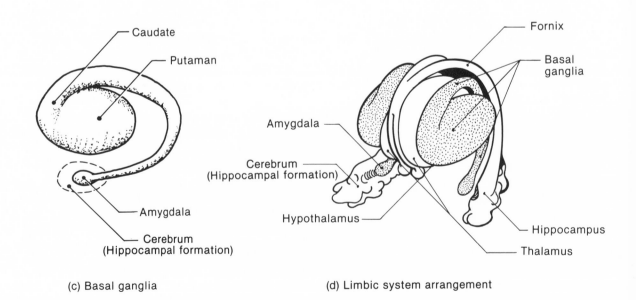

(c) Basal ganglia

(d) Limbic system arrangement

Figure   2.13   The limbic system

system are located in both the cerebrum and the brain stem; they are interconnected through very complex neuronal circuits. Within the brain stem, the most important parts of the limbic system are the hypothalamus and certain parts of the thalamus. The major cerebrum parts are the basal ganglia, hippocampus, and cingulate gyrus. Figure 2.13 shows each of these parts and the general arrangement of the components and their interfaces.

The detailed processes and specific functions performed by the limbic system are essentially unknown. The system does, however, provide an interface for the interchange of emotional impulses between the brain stem (primarily the hypothalamus) and the memory and logic centers of the cerebrum. In addition, certain areas of the limbic system are associated with long-term memory recall. The mechanism is not understood, but available data clearly show that damage to certain portions of the hippocampus results in loss of ability to store and recall new information.

3

The Electronic Digital Computer

Many psychologists, myself included, are indebted to computer technology for a wealth of new ideas which seem to be helpful in understanding man.

ULRIC NEISSER

The electronic digital computer is a modern development of immeasurable significance to society. It helps the human brain with mental tasks in much the same way mechanical machines help the human body with physical tasks. In fact, the computer exhibits many brainlike qualities, perhaps because it was created to relieve the brain of certain laborious mental tasks. For example, it stores information (memory), performs logic-processing operations (thinks), and controls its own operations (actions) as directed by the user. There is even greater similarity at more basic levels.

COMPUTER AND BRAIN SIMILARITIES

Both the electronic digital computer and the brain operate with binary coded information. That is, each stores, processes, and transmits information in terms of on-off (plus-or-minus) signals. These functions are performed in the digital computer by combinations of three types of very simple electronic circuits, identified as AND, OR, and NOT gates (or logic gates). Typical circuits suitable for these functions are illustrated in Appendix A, Figure A.3. These functions are performed in the human brain by various combina-

tions of neurons and their synapses, as described in Chapter 2.

How the computer functions is, of course, well understood by the designer. But no one has yet provided a complete and comprehensive explanation of how the brain performs its many functions. Because of the recognized similarity between the brain and the digital computer, however, the computer provides a basis for greater insight and understanding of the human brain.

Accordingly, the following concept of how the human brain performs its many functions and processes draws heavily on the similarity that is known to exist between the brain and the digital computer. The computer fundamentals and system-operating characteristics considered in establishing this new concept are reviewed below. The fundamental considerations are summarized in Appendix A under the following headings: "The Binary Number System," "Control and Processing Functions," "Memory Functions," and "Input and Output Functions."

THE COMPLETE COMPUTER SYSTEM

In concept, the digital computer system is rel-

26

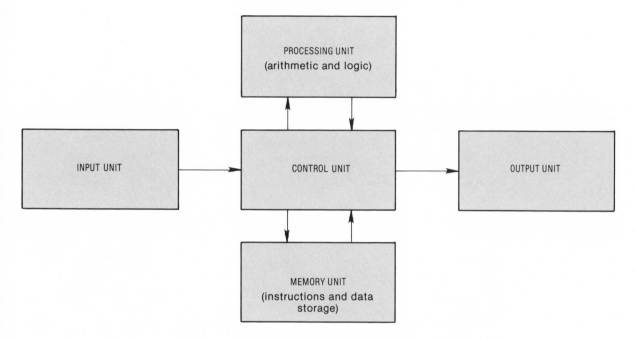

Figure 3.1 Block diagram of an electronic digital computer

atively simple, as the block diagram in Figure 3.1 shows. Basic data and operating instructions enter the computer through the input unit and are stored in the memory unit. All operations are directed by the control unit, which operates from instructions stored in the memory unit.

The fundamental functions of the various computer units are relatively simple and easy to understand. As an integrated system, however, the large high-speed digital computer is extremely complex. Despite the relative simplicity of the components, it is humanly impossible to comprehend all the simultaneous activity occurring in an operating computer system. Thousands of gates and digit storage devices are in operation at any particular time, controlled and synchronized by an accurate and sophisticated timing system, or clock. An adequate discussion of the interactions, interfaces, and operation of the complete system would require many chapters and will not be attempted here. Some of the more important operating characteristics of the complete computer system are summarized below, however.

SYSTEM OPERATION

Figure 3.2 is a schematic diagram of a complete computer system. It illustrates both the flow of information as directed by a user-prepared program (software) and the functions performed by each unit of equipment (hardware).

A computer is useful only when the user has adequately defined the problem to be solved and stated it in terms compatible with the computer. Since the digital computer can store and process information only in binary coded form, all user inputs must be converted to binary (or machine) language. In making this conversion, the user may use special input languages such as the so-called high-level language or symbolic language identified in Appendix A. The necessary procedural instructions and data must then be recorded in a form suitable for input to the particular computer. Typical devices include punched cards, typewriter, and magnetic tapes. Depending upon the language selected by the user, a compiler or an assembler unit is then used to translate the input language to machine language (see Figure A.17, Appendix A).

Information from the input unit enters the control unit which directs all computer operations. The control unit passes all input data directly to the memory unit; it uses instructions received from memory unit to control all processing operations; and it provides the commands for data release to the output unit.

The memory unit stores all computer operating

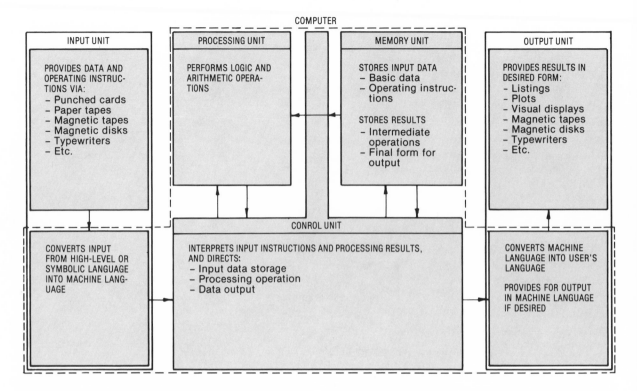

Figure 3.2 Functional diagram of an electronic digital computer

instructions and basic data associated with the problem at hand. It also stores intermediate data developed during a problem solution as well as the final problem results.

The processing unit is the component which permits problem-solving. Large quantities of data could conceivably be stored in the memory unit of a computer without greatly involving the processing unit. Supplied with appropriate instructions, the stored data could be retrieved and arranged in output form with little assistance from the processing unit. The processing unit is indispensable, however, when operations involving logic and arithmetic are required. Taking its directions from the control unit, the processing unit interacts with both the control and memory units in performing its problem-solving function.

The output unit can provide output results in two ways. If so commanded by the control unit, it can provide results in machine language either for storage or for further computer usage. Its most important function, however, is to translate machine language results into an intelligible language for the user. The output may be provided in var-

ious forms including listings, plots, visual displays, and tapes.

COMPUTER CAPACITY

The capacity of a high-speed digital computer is determined by the capacities of its memory and processing units. Memory unit capacity is measured by the number of binary digits (bits) it can store, and processing unit capacity is best defined as the millions of instructions per second (mips) it can accommodate. The size of each unit required depends upon the type of problem to be solved. For example, data handling or sorting problems may require large memory and little processing capacity. A complex iterative mathematical problem, on the other hand, may need large processing and little memory capacity.

In special-purpose applications which use a computer for only one type of problem, it is possible to match memory capacity and processing capacity for optimum operating efficiency. In most applications, however, large high-speed digital computers are used as multipurpose machines that must accommodate numerous types of problems. Consequently, the problem requirements usually do not exactly match the machine's memory and processing capacities. This does not mean that the computer capacity is inadequate. Even so, for a typical problem, the memory capacity or processing capacity of a particular computer will probably be either too large or too small. Thus, for most problems, the required computer capacity can be achieved only through special programming, which inherently results in less than optimum operating efficiency. For example, if the memory unit is too small for a particular problem, the processing unit must be programmed to perform functions that could be more efficiently done by the memory unit.

The effects of this type of programming on computer capacity and efficiency obviously depend upon the relative influences of memory capacity and processing capacity. These influences cannot be precisely defined, but two useful observations are readily apparent: First, high levels of memory capacity and processing capacity result in high computer capacity, and low levels of memory capacity and processing capacity result in low computer capacity. Second, there is a reciprocal

relationship between memory and processing capacity. That is, if a constant level of computer capacity is to be maintained, any decrease in memory capacity must be accompanied by an increase in processing capacity, and any decrease in processing capacity must be accompanied by an increase in memory capacity. In more general terms, these observations can be stated symbolically as follows:

Computer capacity
= f (memory capacity $\times$ processing capacity)
where f is a functional coefficient.

The significance of these relationships in understanding computer capacity is clear from Figure 3.3. Figure 3.3a shows how the different levels of memory and processing capacity influence computer capacity in a family of digital computers. Figure 3.3b illustrates how computer capacity and efficiency are influenced by changes in memory and processing capacity. In this figure, point A represents a computer in which computer capacity, memory capacity, and processing capacity are perfectly matched for a specific problem. Thus, any change in either memory or processing

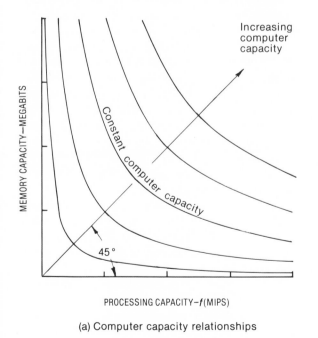

(a) Computer capacity relationships

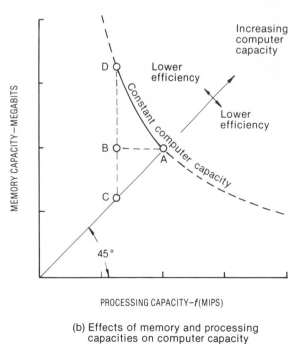

(b) Effects of memory and processing capacities on computer capacity

Figure 3.3 Computer capacity as a function of memory and processing capacities

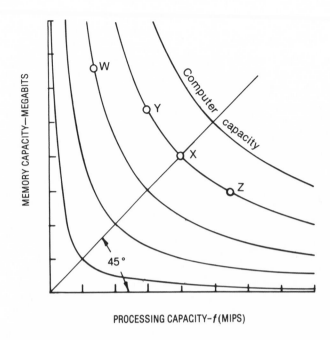

Figure 3.4 Specific computer characteristics

capacity will result in a change in both computer capacity and efficiency. For example, a reduction in processing capacity will move point *A* to point *B*, between points *C* and *D*. From the efficiency standpoint, the best way to regain the computer capacity available at point *A* is to increase processing capacity. However, the same computer capacity at reduced efficiency can be achieved by increasing the memory capacity and reprogramming the computational procedure. Such a computer is identified as point *D*. This computer, as well as any computer identified along line *AD*, will have a capacity equal to the computer represented by point *A*, but at a reduced efficiency.

In computer design, any value of capacity may be selected for either the memory or the processing unit, since each is an independent element. In Figure 3.4, points *W*, *X*, *Y*, and *Z* represent specific computers, each with a fixed capacity. The computers defined at points *X*, *Y*, and *Z* are equal in capacity. For the specific problem under consideration, *X* represents a computer with perfectly matched memory and processing capacities, *Y* represents a computer with larger-than-optimum memory capacity, and *Z* represents a computer with larger-than-optimum processing capacity. Point *W* represents a lower-capacity computer and illustrates a design in which the

memory unit is disproportionately larger than the processing unit relative to the problem to be solved. The computer characteristics are, of course, greatly oversimplified in these examples. Nevertheless, they serve to indicate the importance of properly matched memory and processing units for a particular problem, and they illustrate the unfavorable computer characteristics which result from an improperly matched design.

COMPUTER CAPABILITY

As defined here, *computer capacity* refers to the combined capacities of the computer memory and processing units. These are fixed quantities in any particular computer and are a function of the hardware involved. Every computer, therefore, has a finite and definable capacity. As the term implies, however, computer capacity represents only a potential, not a capability. Utilizing the available capacity and converting it to capability requires perfect computer programming. The memory unit must be filled with the proper data, and the processing steps must be perfectly defined.

Figure 3.5 shows the difference between computer capacity and computer capability. The upper curve in Figure 3.5*a* represents a family of computers with equal computer capacities. Points *A, B,* and *C* in this figure symbolize three separate computers which have different memory and processing capacities, as indicated in Figure 3.5*b*. If each computer were perfectly programmed,

computer capability would equal computer capacity and the points *A, B,* and *C* would represent computer capability. Since this can never happen, computer capability is always less than computer capacity, as indicated by points *A', B',* and *C'*.

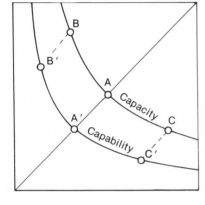

PROCESSING CAPACITY - f(MIPS)

(a) Computer capacity and capability

| | | COMPUTERS OF EQUAL CAPACITIES | |
		A	B	C
Memory capacity for ➡		Short table of data	Complete table of data	No table of data
Processing capacity for ➡		Data interpolation	Little data interpolation	Equations of relationships

(b) Computers of equal capacities

Computer capacity = f (memory capacity × processing capacity)

= f (MEGABITS × MIPS)

Computer capability = f (MEGABITS × MIPS) E_k*

*E_k represents the efficiency with which the computer is programmed

Figure 3.5   Computer capacity and capability characteristics

4

A Unified Concept of Brain Functions and Processes

The aim of a model is, of course, precisely not to reproduce reality in all its complexity. It is rather to capture in a vivid, often formal, way what is essential to understanding some aspects of its structure or behavior.

J. WEIZENBAUM

The brain is unquestionably the most important organ within the human body. It is also the least understood. Even so, the basic anatomy of the brain is well established and the physiological characteristics of many brain components have been successfully defined. Unfortunately, the specific functions of many major brain components are still unknown. Perhaps, even more significantly, the integrated functions and processes whereby the brain effects consciousness, logic-processing, memory storage and recall, and control of body actions remain vague and ill-defined.

As has already been mentioned, the brain exhibits many characteristics of an electronic digital computer. The brain is, of course, much more sophisticated than any current digital computer. In addition, there are acknowledged major differences, primarily in programming and control characteristics. Yet there are, at the detail level, significant similarities between the two. For example, each receives, processes, and transmits information in pulse-coded form. The characteristics of the brain neurons and the electronic control gates

discussed in the preceding chapters are strikingly similar. Moreover, the information storage and retrieval characteristics of the systems are quite analogous.

Numerous information sources contribute to improved understanding of the brain. Results from brain research, clinical observations of mental patients, and human behavioral studies are all extremely useful. These sources include many case studies which show that such characteristics as memory, logic-processing, and emotions are associated with specific areas of the brain.

Much of the available material considered germane to improved understanding of the brain is covered in Chapters 2 and 3. From this information and certain analytical considerations, a conceptual model of the brain has been synthesized and provides the basis for a unified concept of brain functions and processes.

A generalized, computerlike diagram of the conceptual model is shown in Figure 4.1. The model accounts for all major brain functions and identifies the areas of the brain responsible for each. The similarity between the brain and a com-

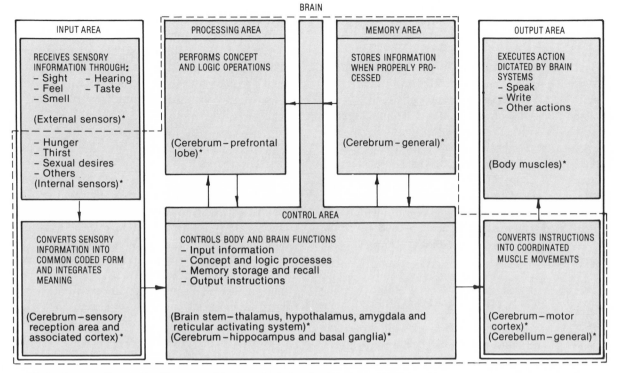

*Notes in parentheses identify areas of brain or body involved.

Figure 4.1 Conceptual model of the brain—functional diagram

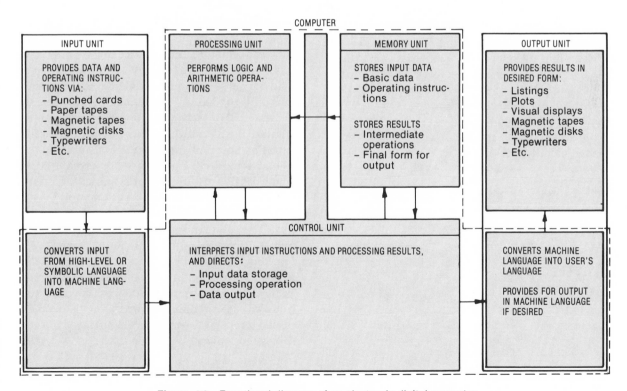

Figure 4.2 Functional diagram of an electronic digital computer

puter can be seen by comparing the conceptual model of the brain in Figure 4.1 with the diagram of the digital computer shown in Figure 4.2.

The processes ascribed to the functional areas of the computer and conceptual model differ in many details, the most important of which is in the method of control. Computer operation is controlled by instructions stored in the memory area by the user. The brain, however, as represented by the conceptual model, develops its own control instructions. Figure 4.1 identifies those areas of the brain postulated to control its operation.

The conceptual model, the bases on which it is postulated, and the unified concept of brain functions and processes are discussed in the following sections.

THE CONCEPTUAL MODEL

The conceptual model includes all those elements of the brain considered pertinent to brain functions and processes. The major elements of the model, their mutual interactions, and interactions with other parts of the body are indicated in a simplified computerlike diagram in Figure 4.1. Figure 4.3 is a more comprehensive conceptual model which emphasizes the anatomical and physiological aspects of the brain. This model indicates how the billions of brain neurons and their associated synapses interact to effect brain functions and processes. It also shows important interfaces and neuronal connections between the brain and its environment.

The postulated model includes 12 functional areas, identified as follows:

> Sensors
> Sensory reception areas
> Association cortex
> Thalamus
> Memory area
> Concept and logic center
> Amygdala
> Hippocampus
> Hypothalamus
> Motor cortex
> Cerebellum
> Reticular activating system

In addition to these areas, the basal ganglia, fornix, and cingulate gyri—elements of the limbic system—provide important interfaces, but none have been assigned separate and critical functions in the unified concept.

Each of the 12 areas listed has a unique function in the model. The specific functions postulated for each area and the interactions between the areas, as shown in Figure 4.3, are discussed below.

SENSORS

Brain functions are influenced by both external and internal sensory inputs. External sensors are those associated with the five senses. Internal sensors are those associated with such sensations as hunger, thirst, sexual desires, and emotions.

Both types of sensors perform the same basic functions. First, they detect sensations from their environment. Second, they convert these sensations, or information, into frequency-coded electrical pulses for further transmission to the brain. In these respects, sensors are analogous to input units of the digital computer.

The external sensors are located outside the brain and provide the brain with information through sight, smell, taste, feel, and hearing.

The internal sensors, located within the hypothalamus,[A][*] have been divided into two categories and designated as internal physiology sensors and emotion sensors (see Figure 4.3). The physiology sensors of interest are those associated with hunger, thirst, and sexual desires. They interface with the blood and glandular systems of the brain and with certain neuronal fibers. In contact with the blood and glandular systems, the sensors detect balance and imbalance in body chemistry as it is affected by hunger, thirst, or sexual desires. These sensors also receive external sensory inputs via the consciousness area.[B] The emotion sensors receive inputs from the amygdala and hippocampus. The resulting sensations are then translated and transmitted to the consciousness area. The resulting emotional conditions may range from aggression to indifference and from pleasure to displeasure. At any particular time, these conditions will depend upon the processing taking place in the brain and the physiological body status relative to hunger, thirst, sex, etc.

---

[*]Superscript letters indicate that a new and perhaps controversial concept is involved. The bases for the concept are discussed in Appendix B, "Bases for the Conceptual Model," under the section designated by the superscript letter.

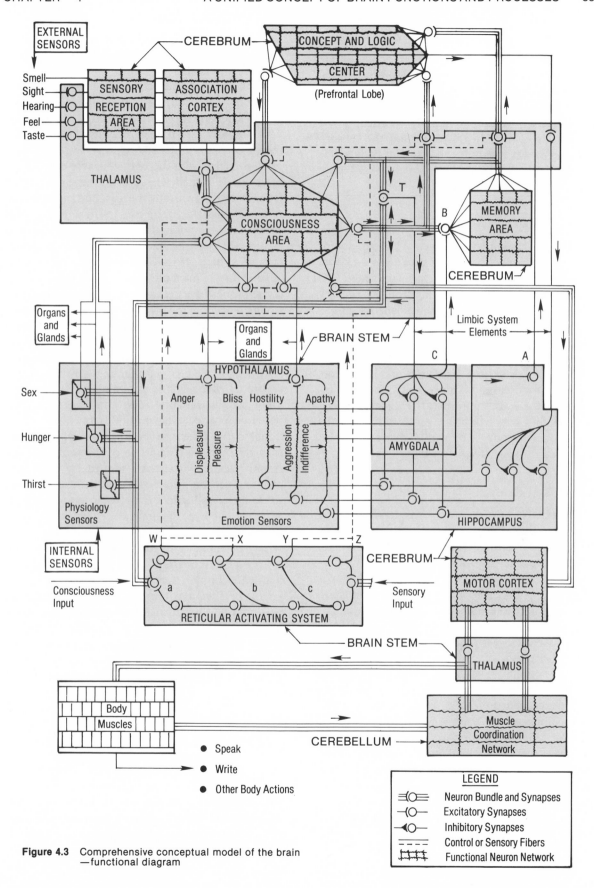

Figure 4.3   Comprehensive conceptual model of the brain
—functional diagram

SENSORY RECEPTION AREAS

For each of the five senses there is a separate sensory reception area located within the cerebral cortex. The primary function of the sensory reception areas is to receive coded information from the respective sensors and transmit it, recoded, to the association cortex. In this operation the sensory reception areas resemble the compiler, utilized as an encoder in digital computer systems (see Figure A.5a, Appendix A).

ASSOCIATION CORTEX

The association cortex covers a large region of the cerebral cortex, involving the parietal, occipital, and temporal lobes. Its primary function is to integrate information arriving from the sensory reception areas. Here the independent sensations of sight, hearing, taste, feel, and smell are integrated into a meaningful whole and passed on to the consciousness area of the thalamus. The association cortex is a fixed-network integrator. Specific input sensations always yield the same integrated results. In this respect the association cortex exhibits characteristics very similar to the "read-only memory" of a digital computer, as discussed in Appendix A (see Figure A.16).

THALAMUS

The thalamus is generally considered to be the control center of the brain. In the unified concept it is also responsible for human consciousness, which is postulated to originate in the consciousness area (see Figure 4.3).

The functions performed by the thalamus are both extensive and complex. Those of major importance to the unified concept, however, are those associated with the consciousness area, the concept and logic center, and the reticular activating system. The latter two areas involve primarily peripheral controls and are discussed later in conjunction with their respective functional areas.

The functions performed by and in conjunction with the consciousness area are crucial to the unified concept. The consciousness area, as shown in Figure 4.3, receives information from the external sensors, internal (physiology and emotion) sensors, memory area, and the concept and logic center. It transmits information to the concept

and logic center, the memory area, and the motor cortex. Through these interactions and processes, the thalamus is able to perform two of its most important functions: it effects control of all brain functions and voluntary body actions; and it presents information to the consciousness level, which at any one time represents the integrated results of brain and body actions. Functions and processes involving the consciousness area of the brain are intitiated whenever inputs are received from any of the various sources, and the information is immediately projected to the memory area. This evokes memory recall; that is, information is returned from the memory area to the consciousness area. If the information or experiences recalled are in harmony with those existing in the consciousness area, calmness prevails in the control network. On the other hand, if the experiences recalled from the memory area differ significantly from those present in the consciousness area, a disturbance is created. The differences, which may also be regarded as representing a problem, are registered as a synaptic potential in a neuron terminal, as illustrated by point T in Figure 4.3. This potential produces an output frequency proportional to the differences between the two sets of information or the magnitude of the problem. The resulting signal passes to the amygdala, hippocampus, and certain synapses within the thalamus. In so doing, it influences the level of emotions generated by the hypothalamus, it regulates operation of the concept and logic center, and it effects final release of instructions for body action. This signal is very important to the unified concept in that it dominates human actions or behavior.

In performing the above functions, brain neurons and their associated synapses accomplish operations very analogous to those performed by decoders, registers, and other logic circuits of the digital computer, such as those illustrated in Figures A.5b, A.8 and A.9.

MEMORY AREA[c]

The memory area is the storage center for all human knowledge. It is generally considered to be located within the cerebral cortex, since that is where most of the brain neurons are. In the unified concept, the memory area is closely associated with both the consciousness area and the concept and logic center. It receives from and returns information to the consciousness area. And, as the source of stored information within the brain, the memory area functions to support the concept and logic center in resolving problems which arise within human consciousness. New concepts or interpretations developed during logic-processing are also stored and retained in the memory area for future use.

According to the unified concept, all bits of information appearing in the consciousness area are passed to the memory area. There, sets of related information bits, called *engrams,* are stored in groups of synapses. This information remains there indefinitely and is dormant until retrieved by a command. Brain memory in this respect is analogous to the "programmable read-only memory" of a digital computer (see Appendix A).

Although in this concept of memory all information entering the memory area is stored permanently as engrams, it is not always readily available for use. It must be retrieved. The retrieval process is therefore an essential feature of the unified concept. Retrieval, or recall, occurs when information entering the memory area from the consciousness area is similar or is in some way related to the previously stored engram. Under these circumstances, the frequencies of the incoming coded information may be sufficiently close to that of the engram to induce excitation and recall.

The ease with which information stored as an engram can be recalled depends upon the processes involved in storage. When several sensory inputs such as sight, smell, hunger, and thirst are involved, there is a wide range of storage frequencies and numerous associated engrams. The potential for recall under these conditions is considerably enhanced over that when only one input, such as sight, is involved. Memory recall ability is improved even more by repeated submission of information to the memory area. This improvement occurs because information that relates to the various engrams is introduced as repetition proceeds and engram interactions result. Engram interactions and the corresponding improvement in recall may be effected by either repeated inputs of sensory information or repetitive processing of information by the concept and logic center. The first condition results simply from repeated exposure to a particular environment. The second occurs when there is a conscious effort to develop memory recall or when a problem arises that is of

sufficient magnitude to activate the concept and logic center. In the second case, the information of concern is processed repeatedly through the concept and logic center, the consciousness area, and the memory area. As this happens, more and more related information is introduced and interactions among engrams are increased. Information stored in this manner is recallable and results in the phenomenon referred to as *long-term memory recall.* Information stored in the absence of interactions between engrams may be available only during the storage process and not subject to later recall. This type of storage results in the phenomenon referred to as *short-term memory recall.*

Thus the brain stores myriads of engrams— some easily recallable, others essentially non-recallable, still others falling somewhere between these two limits. Just where in this span of recallability each engram falls depends upon how storage is effected. Four primary storage processes, each resulting in a particular type of engram, have been identified. These engram types, listed in order of their ease of recall, have been designated as *enate engrams, associated engrams, synthesized engrams,* and *isolated engrams.* The nature and character of these particular engrams are discussed in Appendix B, section C, "Memory Area."

CONCEPT AND LOGIC CENTER[D]

The concept and logic center is the problem-solving portion of the brain. It consists of a complex logic network of neurons that functions much like the central processing unit of a digital computer. It occupies the prefrontal lobe of the cerebral cortex and is closely associated with other parts of the brain. Its most important interactions, however, are directly with the memory and consciousness areas and indirectly with the hypothalamus. Figure 4.3 indicates the various neuronal connections.

The concept and logic center receives information from both the consciousness and memory areas. As outputs, it provides processed information to the consciousness area and a control signal to the hypothalamus via the hippocampus. The primary function of the concept and logic center is to assess the logic and compatibility of information reaching it from the two sources and to transmit the results to appropriate areas.

The process involves a closed-loop operation and is influenced by several functional areas; however, the consciousness and memory areas are of paramount importance. When there is an apparent incompatibility between the information present in the consciousness area and the information (engrams) retrieved from memory, the difference is reflected in the form of a synaptic potential, at point T in Figure 4.3. As discussed previously, this results in a control signal output with a frequency proportional to the difference potential. One path of the signal is through the amygdala and hippocampus areas to that region of the thalamus that controls operation of the concept and logic center. This control signal excites control neurons in the thalamus. They, in turn, initiate processing by the concept and logic center.

The results from this processing are transmitted to the consciousness area. If the differences or apparent differences are successfully resolved, the control signal at point T in the thalamus becomes nil and the concept and logic center ceases operation.

If, however, a logical resolution of the information differences is not forthcoming, the logic circuit operation tends to continue indefinitely, with information passing continuously through the concept and logic center, consciousness area, and memory area. Under these circumstances the thalamus reflects the persisting differences and continues to transmit signals to command continued logic-processing. This will continue until action in some form is initiated to remove the differences or other brain controls intercede.

The concept and logic center also generates a signal while logic-processing is proceeding which indicates progress toward resolving the existing differences. A low-frequency output indicates successful processing; a high-frequency output, lack of success. These effects are discussed later.

AMYGDALA[E]

The amygdala is closely associated with emotion sensations generated within the brain. It is part of the limbic system, which is sometimes called the emotional brain. Located in the temporal lobe of the cerebral cortex, the amygdala has numerous neuronal connections with various functional areas in both the cerebrum and the brain stem. It is an integral part of the basal ganglia.

The primary functions of the amygdala in the unified concept are identified as those related to aggression and indifference. However, there are indications that interactions between the pleasure/displeasure and aggression/indifference centers, via the hippocampus, also occur, and the concept includes this consideration.

The manner in which the amygdala is postulated to perform its roles is illustrated in the conceptual model (Figure 4.3). The amygdala receives signals from the thalamus via elements of the limbic system which indicate the magnitude of the difference between information in the consciousness area and that recalled from the memory area. High-frequency signals indicating large differences are passed through the neuronal network to the hypothalamus, where they evoke an aggressive response. A low-frequency input to the amygdala evokes a response of indifference in the hypothalamus, and intermediate frequencies result in correspondingly proportional responses. In these operations, the neuron synapses function much like the control gates of the digital computer, discussed in Appendix A.

HIPPOCAMPUS[F]

The hippocampus is important to the unified concept because of its effect on emotions, logic-processing, and long-term memory recall. It is a complex system of neuron fibers located in the temporal lobe of the cerebral cortex. Its primary function is to interchange impulses or information between various functional areas of the brain, as illustrated by the conceptual model (Figure 4.3). The hippocampus receives two important input signals and provides two output signals.

One input signal originates in the thalamus and enters the hippocampus by way of the amygdala. This signal leaves the hippocampus after synapsing within the hippocampus and returns to the thalamus, where it effects operation of the concept and logic center.

The other input signal to the hippocampus originates in the processing area of the concept and logic center. By frequency variations, it indicates the success with which information is being processed, as discussed above in the concept and logic center section. The hippocampus directs a signal to different areas of the hypothalamus according to the frequency of the input. A low-frequency input indicating successful logic-processing passes through the neuronal network to the pleasure area. A high-frequency signal resulting from unsuccessful logic-processing passes through the neuronal network and stimulates the displeasure area.

HYPOTHALAMUS[A]

The hypothalamus may be considered the center of human emotions and general well-being. Located in the brain stem immediately below the thalamus, it is connected through neuronal fibers to many of the functional areas of the brain. It exercises control and regulating influences over numerous body functions. Its functions of interest here, however, are those involving the emotions of pleasure and displeasure, aggression and indifference, and the internal body desires related to hunger, thirst, and sex.

In performing these functions the hypothalamus receives stimulating inputs from the amygdala, hippocampus, and the consciousness area. It also senses the desires for food, water, and sex through body-fluid concentrations. It evolves emotions and bodily desires from these inputs and communicates them to the consciousnesss area. It sends stimulating impulses to organs and glands throughout the body. The resulting sensations enter the consciousness area, interact with other inputs, and become an integral part of consciousness. In this way, these sensations affect all brain-related functions. Through their influence on body organs and glands, these sensations also affect such body functions as heartbeat rate, adrenalin flow, and breathing rate.

MOTOR CORTEX

The role of the motor cortex is reasonably well understood. It is the center of all voluntary body movements. Located at the rear boundary of the frontal lobe of the cerebral cortex, its primary neuronal connections are with the consciousness area, body muscles, and the cerebellum. It receives movement instructions via the thalamus and simultaneously sends motion command impulses to appropriate body muscles and the cerebellum.

CEREBELLUM

The principal function of the cerebellum is the coordination of muscular activity. Located behind the brain stem and beneath the occipital lobes of the cerebral cortex, the cerebellum receives and processes all information related to voluntary body movement. Important neuronal connections are indicated in Figure 4.3.

The cerebellum receives two important inputs in performing its primary function. First, it receives from the motor cortex the same impulses sent to the body muscles. Second, impulses produced by the muscle movements are returned to the cerebellum as they occur. Hence, both the command instructions for movement and the results produced by the movement are present almost instantaneously in the cerebellum. The results are recognized by the cerebellum and transmitted to the motor cortex. Body positions are also simultaneously recognized in the consciousness area through the external sensors. This information is likewise communicated to the motor cortex via the consciousness area. These two feedback inputs provide the bases for smooth and precise body movements.

Even so, initial attempts at any new body movements tend to be imprecise. With repetition, however, another important function of the cerebellum becomes evident. It develops and stores a memory of the repeated movements in the neurons. A particular motion, once initiated, is subsequently executed smoothly and precisely almost entirely under the control of the cerebellum. Swimming, bicycling, walking, and other physical skills of the body fall into this category. Such movements become almost automatic and are difficult to change. The type of memory involved here is very analogous to the "programmable read-only memory" storage frequently used in digital control systems and high-speed digital computers (see Appendix A).

RETICULAR ACTIVATING SYSTEM[G]

The reticular activating system is responsible for controlling all levels of consciousness. It is a part of the reticular formation, located at the center of the brain stem. The system consists of numerous short-fibered neurons interconnected to form very elaborate reverberating circuits that are illustrated in simplified form in Figure 4.3.

As indicated by the dashed lines in Figure 4.3, the reticular activating system sends impulses to the thalamus, where synaptic excitation affects sensory inputs, logic-processing, memory storage and recall, and voluntary body movements. In this manner the system controls the levels of alertness or consciousness. Alertness is high when the output frequencies of the reverberating circuits are high, and alertness is low when the output frequencies are low.

The reticular activating system is in a constant state of excitation. The level of excitation is changing continuously, however, depending upon the operating frequencies of the reverberating circuits. These frequencies are determined by stimulations generated by sources both external and internal to the system. The external sources are the various sensors and the consciousness area, each of which supplies varying levels of stimulation. How internal stimulation of the circuits is generated is a bit more subtle. The process involves the fatigue characteristics of synapses in the many reverberating circuits, illustrated schematically in Figure 4.3. The output frequencies are high when the synapses in the reticular activating system are rested and they are stimulated by inputs from the sensors and consciousness area. A high level of consciousness or alertness then exists. But such a condition can exist for only a limited period. The synapses soon fatigue, their ability to provide excitation drops, and output frequencies decrease. An individual becomes less alert as this process continues, then relaxes, and finally falls asleep. The synapses again become sufficiently rested to support wakefulness after an adequate period of sleep. How this operation is effected is described in detail in Appendix B, section G, "Reticular Activating System."

Through the processes just described, the reticular activating system is responsible for the varying levels of human consciousness and the normal 24-hour wake-and-sleep cycle. The system exhibits characteristics quite analogous to those of the synchronous clock in the electronic digital computer in performing the above functions.

THE UNIFIED CONCEPT

The unified concept of brain functions and processes is a comprehensive concept that identifies and accounts for all major brain operations and the resulting human performance.

The significance and the usefulness of the unified concept are most easily conveyed by show-ing how the conceptual model of the brain operates as an integrated system and by illustrating its operation through examples.

SYSTEM OPERATION

The brain receives, stores, and processes information; and in performing these functions, it controls its own operation and all body actions. The conceptual model, Figure 4.3, identifies the functions and illustrates the processes involved.

At the center of all these operations is the consciousness area, which receives information from external sensors, internal sensors, the memory area, and the concept and logic center. It integrates the information and then projects it to both the memory area and the concept and logic center. At the same time, the consciousness area initiates the body actions or behavior essential to personal well-being. That is, it initiates body actions directed toward satisfying individual wants and needs.

The system operates only with binary-coded information. Incoming information is encoded by the various input sensors. Information transfer, logic-processing, and memory storage and recall are also effected in coded form. Human actions or behavior represent the decoded results. Figure 4.4, a special representation of the conceptual model, was devised to more clearly indicate the brain processes and the information flow during operation. The different waveforms on the diagram represent information moving to and from various functional areas of the brain.

Brain system operation is initiated by incoming information from the external and internal body sensors. Sensory information reaches the consciousness area in coded form representing sight, hearing, feel, taste, smell, hunger, thirst, sexual desires, and emotions. These different bits of information are symbolized in Figure 4.4 by waveforms a through f. The information reaches the consciousness area through the many neuronal networks, where the various bits are combined into a meaningful whole. The resulting information is then decoded and projected to the consciousness level in integrated form. The coded results (symbolized by waveform h) are transmitted to the memory area, the concept and logic center, the internal physiology sensors, and the reticular activating system.

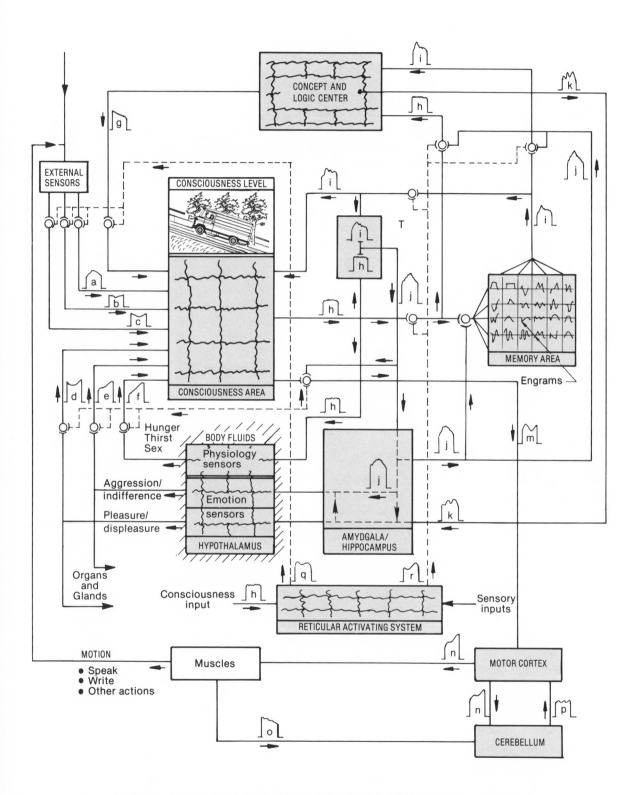

Figure 4.4 Conceptual model of the brain, illustrating the flow of information

Upon reaching the memory area, the incoming information (waveform *h*) induces memory recall. If the incoming information is in harmony with that recalled (evoked engrams indicated by waveform *i*), no further brain activity is initiated. Where the incoming information (waveform *h*) and that recalled (waveform *i*) differ, however, a new signal identified as waveform *j* is generated at point *T*, which initiates several actions. It excites the synapses, which effect body actions identified as appropriate by the consciousness area. It also passes to the amygdala and hippocampus complex, from which it enters the thalamus and activates the concept and logic center, and it enters the hypothalamus, where it excites the emotion sensors. The activated concept and logic center then proceeds toward resolving the differences between the information identified by waveforms *h* and *i*. In the hypothalamus the signal generates aggressive sensations proportional to the waveform frequency and the problem. These results are then transmitted to the consciousness area as indicated by waveform *e*. From there, the aggressive sensations are projected to consciousness level.

As the concept and logic center processes the inputs symbolized by waveforms *h* and *i*, it transmits the results to the consciousness area as indicated by waveform *g*. If the concept and logic center proceeds successfully toward resolving the differences, or solving the problem, a signal symbolized by waveform *k* is generated. This signal then passes through the hippocampus to the hypothalamus, where it stimulates the pleasure area. From there, the resulting sensation is projected to the consciousness area, as indicated by waveform *d*. Decoded, the results are projected to consciousness level as a condition of pleasure.

The above situation changes drastically if the concept and logic center is unable to proceed successfully toward resolving the problem. The pleasure sensation will change to displeasure, and the result at the consciousness level will reflect aggression and displeasure. Various combinations of these two conditions may exist, of course, depending upon the nature of the problem involved. Hence, conditions varying from anger to bliss and from hostility to apathy are possible.

There is an apparent paradox in the brain operations just described. That is, the brain processes that generate both aggression and pleasure are initiated by the same signal: waveform *j* in figure 4.4, which exists only when there is a problem to be resolved. Aggression, as indicated by the conceptual model, results directly from the prevailing problem. Pleasure, on the other hand, depends primarily upon how well the concept and logic center proceeds toward resolving the problem. The fact that aggression and pleasure are related, as indicated here, is consistent with general observations. For example, when people are aggressively and successfully pursuing a goal, they are known to experience pleasure (and happiness).

Other important processes are also occurring in the brain while the operations discussed above are proceeding. Emotion sensations, which are generated in the hypothalamus and projected to the consciousness area, are also transmitted to various organs and glands of the body. This often results in changes in the body functions such as adrenalin flow, digestive processes, and heartbeat and breathing rates. Extensive quantities of related information also pass repeatedly to and are stored in the memory area as the concept and logic center acts to resolve problems. This repetition along with the storage of related information (associated engrams) greatly enhances long-term memory recall. As mentioned earlier, this repetitive process explains why situations involving significant problems and emotions are most easily recalled.

In the brain processes just described, the consciousness area is continuously transmitting commands to body muscles to produce action and aid in problem resolution. Instructions symbolized by waveform *m* in Figure 4.4 pass to the motor cortex, from which they are simultaneously directed to the appropriate muscles and the cerebellum as waveform *n*. The command to the muscles induces action. The cerebellum coordinates the commanded action. Body actions that result from the command are transmitted to the cerebellum as waveform *o*. Here the movements are coordinated, smoothed, and returned to the motor cortex as waveform *p*. The effectiveness of the cerebellum in coordinating the body movements initiated by the motor cortex improves as particular movements are repeated. As reviewed previously, the cerebellum provides memory which is programmed by repetition. It is responsible for such movements as a golfer's swing, the touch of the artist, and the skill of a bricklayer.

The brain is not always in an alert or problem-solving state. Under control of the reticular activating system, it follows a cyclic operation that produces conditions which vary between alert wakefulness and deep sleep, as indicated in Figure B.3 in Appendix B. The reticular activating system receives stimulating inputs from the consciousness area, indicated by waveform h and various sensory inputs. The system projects outputs to the various control synapses within the thalamus and the consciousness area, as symbolized by waveforms q and r.

Normal stimulation from external sources keeps the reticular activating system in various degrees of wakefulness for about two-thirds of each day. After this period, however, fatiguing synapses within the reticular activating system induce sleep. About one-third of each day is required for resting the synapses (sleep) before full awakening returns.

This approximate relationship between wakefulness and sleep may be altered on a temporary basis by added external excitation of the reticular activating system. Special circumstances—excessive pain or serious problems, for example—sometimes act to maintain the reticular activating system in an excited state for more than two-thirds of a day. When this happens, the synapses become overfatigued, the resting-and-fatiguing cycle is upset, and alertness suffers. But when only a few hours are involved, the results are not of major concern, since the synapses adjust to the situation within a day or so. This is the situation that develops when an individual travels across time zones (referred to as *jet lag*). Under these circumstances a certain amount of time is required for the synapses to regain a stable fatigue-and-recovery cycle and permit the return of full alertness.

A much graver condition develops, however, if wakefulness is forced for extended periods of time. Because of the highly fatigued synapses, the brain activity which can be generated by the reticular activating system often falls to the level associated with sleep. And although the individual remains "awake," a dreamlike situation developes which may produce hallucinations or even collapse.

EXAMPLES OF SYSTEM OPERATION

The operating characteristics of the conceptual model can be more clearly illustrated through examples of individual experiences.

Example A: Unexpected Problem

For this example, consider the reaction of a man presented with an unexpected tax problem. A written notification from the Internal Revenue Service states that the taxes due far exceed those paid.

The initial reaction of the individual is one of surprise and hostility toward the tax service. Soon thereafter he begins to question himself. What is wrong? What makes the difference? Who made a mistake? What does it mean to me? He then begins to evaluate the available information. Assume first that the assessment indicates that the IRS made a mistake. When he finds their mistake, his hostility begins to subside. As he successfully works through the problem, a pleasant and satisfied attitude evolves. On the other hand, if he cannot understand their claim for more taxes and he sees no way to resolve the problem, his hostility may be accentuated. If so, an attitude of displeasure and aggressiveness will prevail. In addition, if the problem remains unresolved for several days, the individual may develop insomnia, stomach pains, headaches, erratic pulses, diarrhea, or other physiological disorders.

The brain functions and processes involved in the incident described are obviously very complex, but each can be successfully explained by the unified concept. As indicated in Figures 4.3 and 4.4, information relative to the tax situation enters the individual's brain through sight (written notification). It passes through the sensory area, association cortex, consciousness area, and then to the memory area. Here it evokes an engram (waveform i) that differs significantly from the incoming information (waveform h). In coded form, the message is that there is a major disagreement over the taxes owed the IRS. The difference induces a high-frequency output (waveform j) at the synaptic juncture identified as point T in Figure 4.4. This signal, passing through the amygdala, stimulates the aggression area of the hypothalamus and causes transmission (symbolized as waveform e) to the consciousness area. The resulting aggressive sensation is reflected at the consciousness level as hostility or aggressiveness toward the IRS. While this process is proceeding, the same initiating signal (waveform j) passes through the amygdala and hippocampus areas and activates the concept and logic center.

Regarding the first assumption, in which a mistake was made by the IRS, the logic-processing will indicate such by the signal (symbolized by waveform *g*) passed to the consciousness area. As processing continues toward successful substantiation of the mistake, the concept and logic center transmits a low-frequency signal (waveform *k*) through the hippocampus and to the hypothalamus. This results in stimulation within the pleasure center, and the sensation is transmitted as waveform *d* to the consciousness level. At this point, the individual becomes satisfied. The initial difference between the two sets of information is resolved, and the signal (waveform *j*) which initiated the hostile feeling and activated the concept and logic center disappears.

If it is assumed, however, that the individual cannot understand the claim made by the IRS, the processes within the conceptual model yield a completely different result. Again, the new information results in stimulating the aggression area of the hypothalamus and transmits that feeling to the consciousness level. The concept and logic center is likewise activated. However, the concept and logic center is unable to proceed immediately toward a successful resolution, since no mistake is apparent. The resulting high-frequency output signal passes through the hippocampus and stimulates the displeasure area of the hypothalamus. The displeasure sensations pass to the consciousness area and are reflected at consciousness level. The aggressive and unpleasant attitude will prevail at the consciousness level as long as this condition exists. Other effects may appear if these conditions persist for an appreciable time period. The emotional-sensation signals passing from the hypothalamus to the consciousness area are also projected to various body organs and glands as indicated by arrows. Through neuron excitations these signals may upset the functional balance and cause discomforts identified earlier, such as stomach pains, headaches, and diarrhea. These effects, along with the highly activated concept and logic center, may also stimulate the reticular activating system sufficiently to induce insomnia.

Example B: Memory Recall (Remembering)

The memory storage and recall phenomenon is well illustrated by the processes involved in remembering a person's name. Suppose, for example, the name to be remembered is John Gillette. It may be "committed to memory" either by rote repetition or by consciously associating or relating the name to stored memory information which is easily recalled. For an example of conscious association, assume the individual by coincidence happens to have a long nose. In that case a good association would be *long nose* and *sharp*. Thus, a logical association for this person's name would be *long nose, sharp, razor, Gillette* (a well-known razor manufacturer). This technique of association is well established and is widely employed by memory recall experts.

The concept and logic center plays a major role in memory storage and recall. In addition to performing logic-processing, it transfers information to and from the memory area through the consciousness area. The resulting interactions serve to relate new information to that previously stored, and they thus enhance memory recall. Hence, establishing easy recall (remembering) of a name requires excitations which cause the concept and logic center to function. The name of a stranger alone is hardly adequate to do this. If a name is to be remembered, therefore, it must be associated with a situation where related new information and other stored information are sufficiently different to effect operation of the concept and logic center. During this operation the name may be processed repeatedly through the system to ensure easy recall. The processes involved here can be best illustrated by the example used above. Suppose the individual with the desire to recall a name is a politician. His election to office and his later success depend upon people, and the ability to recall names is important for numerous reasons. Therefore, whenever he meets a constituent who is a stranger, he is presented with a new situation. He cannot be certain of that particular person's support now and in the future. However, stored in his memory is information recognizing the need for everyone's support. As explained earlier, this difference between new and stored information produces a control signal. Among other effects, this signal activates the concept and logic center. The processing necessary for establishing memory recall is thereby initiated. As the operation continues, information associated with all facets of the situation is cycled and recycled through the system effecting both recall and storage. From the recalled information, the concept and logic center utilizes whatever available procedural technique is best suited to enhance memory storage for name recall. In any case, however, repetition of information through the system is provided and the ability to recall names enhanced, whether the person is John Gillette or someone else.

Example C: Physical Skill

The swing of a professional golfer represents a highly developed physical skill and provides a good example for illustration.

Years of effort are generally required to develop a successful golf swing. Aside from physical stature, which varies widely among individuals, two primary factors affect the development of a good golf swing. One is correct knowledge of what constitutes a good golf swing. The other is extensive practice using proper knowledge. Knowledge may be obtained from a book, movie, or a professional golfer, but knowledge can influence the swing only through repetitive practice.

The brain processes involved during the development of a golf swing are indicated by the conceptual model, Figure 4.4. Information on the fundamentals of a good golf swing may be provided to the brain from outside sources by written words, pictures, or spoken words. This information enters the brain and is stored in the memory, as noted previously. Once stored, it is available to

support development of the golf swing. Practice, however, begins only when information entering the consciousness area from the sensory area, memory area, and concept and logic center causes release of instructions for body movement. Instructions to initiate the swing enter the motor cortex area as indicated by waveform m. They are directed simultaneously to the appropriate muscles and the cerebellum (waveform n). Instructions to the muscles command action, and the swing is initiated. As the swing progresses, signals from the muscles indicating their positions are immediately transmitted to the cerebellum (waveform o). Here the initial instructions (waveform n) are compared with the results. The deviations are transmitted back to the motor cortex (waveform p), which modifies the instructions to make corrections to the swing. In this role, the cerebellum acts as coordinator, adding smoothness to the swing. Initially, the swing can be expected to be rough and erratic. The result will be detected by the individual or an observer and communicated to the consciousness area and the memory area. The difference will be assessed and a new practice swing initiated. When errors in the swing are reduced and repetition continues, the cerebellum takes on a more dominating role. It, in effect, develops and stores a program which controls the swinging motion. At this point, the swing becomes essentially automatic and, except for initiation, requires little attention from the consciousness area.

Part 1 Bibliography

ANATOMY, PHYSIOLOGY, AND PSYCHOLOGY

Anthony, Catherine P., and Kolthoff, Norma J. *Textbook of Anatomy and Physiology.* 9th ed. St. Louis: The C.V. Mosby Co., 1975.

Asimov, Isaac. *The Human Brain: Its Capacity and Functions.* Boston: Houghton Mifflin Co., 1963.

Bailey, Ronald H. *The Role of the Brain.* New York: Time-Life Books, 1975.

Berne, Eric. *Games People Play: The Psychology of Human Relationships.* New York: Grove Press, 1964.

Binney, Ruth, and Janson, Michael, eds. *Atlas of the Body and Mind.* New York: Rand McNally & Co., 1976.

Butler, S. T., and Raymone, Robert. *The Brain and Behavior.* Garden City: Anchor Press/Doubleday, Anchor Books, 1977.

Calder, Nigel. *The Mind of Man.* New York: The Viking Press, Inc., 1970.

Carpenter, Malcolm B. *Human Neuroanatomy.* 7th ed. Baltimore: The Williams & Wilkins Co., 1976.

Chaffee, Ellen E., and Greishermer, Esther M. *Basic Physiology and Anatomy.* 3rd ed. Philadelphia: Lippincott Co., 1974.

DeArmond, Stephen J.; Fusco, Madeline M.; and Dewey, M. M. *Structure of the Human Brain.* New York: Oxford University Press, 1976.

Desiraju, T., ed. *Mechanisms in Transmission of Signals for Conscious Behavior.* Amsterdam: Elsevier Scientific Publishing Co., 1976.

Eccles, John C. *The Understanding of the Brain.* New York: McGraw-Hill Book Co., R. R. Donnelly, 1977.

Freud, Sigmund. *A General Introduction to Psychoanalysis.* Translated by Joan Riviere. New York: Washington Square Press Inc., 1965.

Gardner, Weston D., and Osburn, William A. *Structure of the Human Body.* 2nd ed. Philadelphia: W. B. Saunders Co., 1967.

Gray, Henry. *Anatomy of the Human Body.* 29th ed. Edited by Charles M. Gross. Philadelphia: Lea and Febiger, 1966.

Guyton, Arthur C. *Functions of the Human Body.* 4th ed. Philadelphia: W. B. Saunders Co., 1974.

Halacy, Daniel S. *Man and Memory.* New York: Harper & Row, Inc., 1970.

Harris, Thomas A. *I'm OK—You're OK.* New York: Harper & Row, Inc., 1969.

James, Muriel, and Jongeward, Dorothy. *Born to Win.* Reading, Mass.: Addison-Wesley Publishing Co., 1973.

James, William. *The Principles of Psychology.* 2 vols. 1890. Reprint. New York: Dover Publication, Inc., 1950.

Jaynes, Julian. *The Origin of Consciousness in the Breakdown of the Bicameral Mind.* Boston: Houghton Mifflin Co., 1976.

Keirsey, David, and Bates, Marilyn. *Please Understand Me: Character & Temperament Types.* Delmar, Calif.: Prometheus Nemesis Books, 1978.

Kiev, Ari. *A Strategy for Daily Living.* New York: The Free Press, 1973.

King, Barry G., and Showers, Mary J. *Human Anatomy and Physiology.* 6th ed. Philadelphia: W. B. Saunders Co., 1969.

Ornstein, Robert E., ed. *The Nature of Human Consciousness.* San Francisco: W. H. Freeman & Company, 1973.

Maltz, Maxwell, *Psycho-Cybernetics.* Englewood Cliffs: Prentice-Hall, Inc., 1960.

McConnell, James V. *Understanding Human Behavior.* 2nd ed. New York: Holt, Rinehart and Winston, 1977.

Munn, Norman L. *Psychology.* 5th ed. Boston: Houghton Mifflin Co., 1966.

Oatley, Keith. *Brain Mechanisms and Mind.* New York: E. P. Dutton & Co., 1972.

Penfield, Wilder. *The Mystery of the Mind.* Princeton: Princeton University Press, 1975.

Pfeiffer, John E. *The Human Brain.* New York: Harper & Brothers, 1975.

Strughold, Hubertus. *Your Body Clock.* New York: Charles Scribner's Sons, 1971.

Wilber, Ken. *Up From Eden: A Transpersonal View of Human Evaluation.* Garden City: Anchor Press/Doubleday, 1981.

Wittrock, M. C., and others. *The Human Brain.* Englewood Cliffs: Prentice-Hall, Inc., 1977.

Woolridge, Dean E. *The Machinery of the Brain.* New York: McGraw-Hill Book Co., 1963.

COMPUTERS

Boyce, Jefferson C. *Digital Computer Fundamentals.* Englewood Cliffs: Prentice-Hall, Inc., 1977.

Deem, Bill R.; Muchow, Kenneth; and Zeppa, Anthony. *Digital Computer Circuits and Concepts.* Reston: Reston Publishing Co., Inc., 1980.

Diebold, John. *The World of Computers.* New York: Random House, 1973.

Fenichel, R. R., and Weizenbaum, Joseph. *Computers and Computations.* San Francisco: W. H. Freeman & Co., 1971.

Halacy, Daniel S. *Computers: The Machine We Think With.* New York: Harper & Row, Inc., 1969.

Lenk, John D. *Computers for Technicians.* Englewood Cliffs: Prentice-Hall Inc., 1973.

Nikolaieff, George A. *Computers and Society.* New York: H. W. Wilson Co., 1970.

Pfieffer, John F. *The Thinking Machine.* New York: J. B. Lippincott Co., 1962.

Weizenbaum, Joseph. *Computer Power and Human Resources.* San Francisco: W. H. Freeman & Co., 1976.

PART 2

HUMAN MENTAL QUALITIES

It is impossible to reduce civil society to one dead level . . . [because] People differ in capacity, skill, health, strength . . .

POPE LEO XIII

They who say all men are equal speak an undoubted truth, if they mean . . . equal right to liberty, to their property, and . . . protection of the laws. —But they are mistaken if they think men are equal in their station and employments, since they are not so by their talents.

VOLTAIRE

The unified concept of brain functions and processes presented in the preceding chapter delineates each major area of the human brain and identifies the brain's three most important functional characteristics:

- The capacity to store and recall information
- The capacity to perform logic-processing operations
- The capacity to effect human emotions and actions

The unified concept also shows how these three brain characteristics, or capacities, in conjunction with information about environmental experiences, determine what a person is mentally able and willing to do.

The effect of this combination—that is, the interaction between the brain and its environment—is to produce three unique human mental qualities for each person. These qualities are identified herein as follows:

- Knowledge
- Problem-solving capability
- Behavioral characteristics

Every normal human being, of course, possesses knowledge, problem-solving capability, and behavioral characteristics. These qualities, however, differ greatly among individuals. They differ for two reasons: first, each person's brain is a unique entity; and second, no two persons are ever exposed to identical environments.

How the brain is postulated to interact with the environment to effect these three human mental qualities is the subject of the following four chapters. Chapter 5 identifies three discrete and independent brain capacities and shows how they combine with environmental experiences to effect human mental qualities. Chapter 6 defines those brain capacities and environmental experiences responsible for a person's knowledge and problem-solving capability, and it shows how these two qualities combine to make up mental capability. Chapter 7 identifies those brain capacities and environmental experiences that determine human behavioral characteristics. It describes the brain processes that establish human wants and needs and explains how they, in conjunction with environmental experiences, determine human behavior. Chapter 8 shows how human mental qualities combine to produce effective mental capability: that quality which determines the level of mental work a particular person is able and willing to perform.

5

The Nature of
Human Mental Qualities

It is evident that there are two leading factors in producing a man and making him what he is: One, the endowment given at birth; the other, the environment into which he comes.

CATTELL

Human beings, by nature, share many common mental attributes. Every person has the ability to remember experiences, solve problems, and feel and express emotions, for example. Common mental attributes, of course, do not correspond to equal mental qualities. Indeed, human mental qualities are known to differ widely among individuals.

Human mental qualities, as defined here, stem entirely from the brain and its environment. The unified concept of brain functions and processes presented in Chapter 4 is consistent with and supports this premise. Thus, this concept—based on the analogy that exists between the brain and the digital computer—provides a mechanism for examining and understanding the relationships among the brain, the environment, and human mental qualities. Figure 5.1, which is a simplified illustration of the brain-computer analogy, shows these relationships. Here, in computer terms, the brain is analogous to "hardware"; information is analogous to "software"; and human mental qualities are analogous to the computer's "capability" to produce useful results.

Accordingly, it follows that the mental qualities of a particular person depend upon the brain (hardware) characteristics possessed and the information (software) acquired from environmental experiences.

Figure 5.2 delineates the pertinent brain characteristics and indicates how information is acquired from environmental experiences. It also illustrates how the various factors interact to establish a person's knowledge, problem-solving capability, and behavioral characteristics. And it shows how these three mental qualities combine to form two dependent mental qualities defined as mental capability and effective mental capability.

BRAIN CHARACTERISTICS

Like other organs of the human body, the physical and functional characteristics of the brain are influenced by both genetics and age. They are, therefore, subject to wide variations within the population.

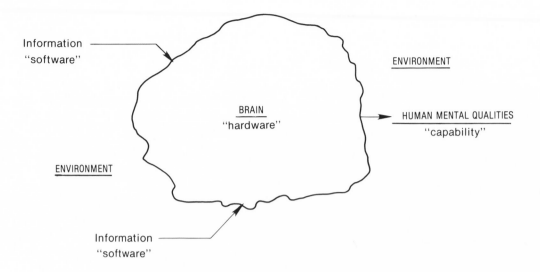

Figure 5.1 Simplified illustration of the brain-computer analogy

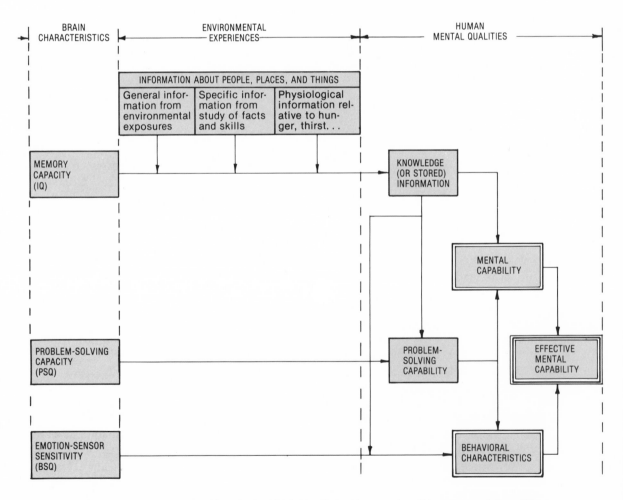

Figure 5.2 Interrelationships among the brain, the environment, and human mental qualities

PHYSICAL BRAIN CHARACTERISTICS

The fact that the anatomy and physiology of the human brain are affected by genetics and age is universally acknowledged. The influence of genetics on the physical characteristics of the brain are readily discernible by the neurosurgeon. This is, of course, as would be expected, since there are billions of neurons and trillions of synaptic connections in the brain. With such a vast number of possible combinations and permutations, it is virtually impossible statistically for any two persons to have identical brains.

Although the fundamental characteristics of a person's brain are fixed by genetics, the brain itself changes continuously with age. During early life, these physical changes are manifested by growth in size of the brain and head. Changes in later life are less obvious but, nevertheless, present. The fact that physical characteristics of the brain change with age is most evident from estimated brain weights. Figure 5.3 shows how brain weight typically varies with age.

FUNCTIONAL BRAIN CHARACTERISTICS

The unified concept identifies 12 different areas of the brain that account for all important brain characteristics. These characteristics manifest themselves in three recognizable and identifiable brain capacities, designated in Figure 5.2 as memory capacity, problem-solving capacity, and emotion-sensor sensitivity.

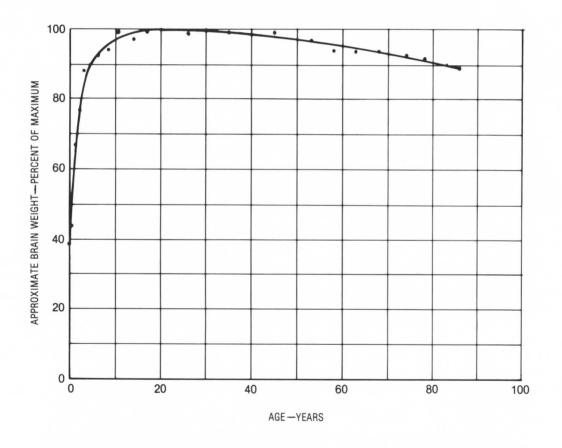

Data from Anatole S. Dekaban and Doris Sadowsky, "Changes in Brain Weights During the Span of Human Life: Relation of Brain Weights to Body Heights and Body Weights," *Annals of Neurology,* 4 (October 1978), p. 349, table 2.

Figure 5.3 Approximate weight of the human brain

These three brain characteristics are unique to each human being. They depend only upon the anatomy and physiology of the brain. And, as indicated earlier, these characteristics differ among individuals because of genetic and age differences. The anatomy and physiology of the brain, as indicated by brain weight, reach their highest levels of physical maturity some time near the age of 20 (see Figure 5.3). Beyond age 20, a slight decrease in brain weight implies corresponding changes in brain anatomy and physiology. Even so, the physical brain, and therefore its functional characteristics, may be considered as fixed quantities during most of adult life.

Memory Capacity

Memory capacity represents the potential of the human brain to store and recall information received from the environment. Thus memory capacity depends upon the arrangement and basic characteristics of the neurons present in those areas of the brain identified as the memory area and the concept and logic center (see Figure 4.3).

Memory capacity, as defined here, is quite similar to that mental characteristic referred to as *intelligence quotient (IQ)*. This important and useful similarity can be best demonstrated by a brief discussion of IQ and how it is measured.

Intelligence quotient, as the term implies, is not an absolute quantity. It is, instead, a relative measure of "intelligence" that shows where a particular person stands within a population. It is important to note that intelligence, as indicated by IQ, has not been precisely defined. One authority states simply that IQ is a score determined by an IQ test.

There are many highly developed testing techniques available for determining a person's IQ. These tests are fundamentally the same, although they differ in detail. All make use of verbal and quantitative test batteries. The verbal battery typically includes vocabulary, verbal analogies, sentence completions, and reading comprehension. The quantitative battery includes rather simple problems in physics and mathematics.

One pertinent feature of these tests is their emphasis on memory. None involve creative problem-solving or problem synthesis. Even the solutions to problems in physics and mathematics require only the use of memorized procedures developed by others. Hence, as determined by such tests, an IQ score is essentially a relative measure of a person's memory capacity—the ability to store and recall information received from the environment.

Despite the similarity between IQ and memory capacity, they are not identical terms. Memory capacity varies with genetics and age and is in a continuous state of change. Intelligence tests are so contructed as to normalize or negate the influence of age. Hence, IQ depends upon genetics only and, for a particular person, is generally regarded as essentially fixed throughout life.

A person's IQ, therefore, does not always correspond to memory capacity. In the case of a child, IQ is only an indication of future memory capacity. That is, the IQ of a child is the memory capacity predicted for that child when his or her brain reaches anatomical and physiological maturity. Figure 5.3 shows that the brain, as indicated by weight, reaches full maturity at about 20 years of age. For several years following maturity there are evidently few changes in brain anatomy and physiology. Thus, during most of an adult's life, it is reasonable to expect that the IQ and memory capacity are essentially equal and fixed quantities. IQ is, therefore, a measure of an adult's memory capacity.

Problem-solving Capacity

Problem-solving capacity, like memory capacity, represents a brain potential. The potential in this case is to process and integrate information and produce creative problem solutions. It depends upon the arrangement and basic characteristics of the neurons located in that region of the brain (the prefrontal lobe of the cerebral cortex) designated as the *concept and logic center*.

The concept and logic center processes and circulates information to and from the memory area of the brain (see Chapter 4). In this operation it influences information storage and recall, or memory capacity. It is the ability to compare, evaluate, and synthesize new concepts and creative problem solutions, however, that establishes the center's problem-solving capacity. This capacity is also responsible for those mental qualities referred to as *judgment, foresight,* and *creativeness*.

Problem-solving capacity is independent of other brain capacities. Since, like memory capacity, it depends only upon the anatomy and physiology of the neurons present in a specific area of the brain, it is convenient to define this capacity in similar terms. Accordingly, this capacity is designated here as the *problem-solving quotient (PSQ)*.

Emotion-sensor Sensitivity

Emotion-sensor sensitivity is that brain characteristic that determines how an individual responds to the various processes performed by the brain. It depends primarily upon the arrangement and basic characteristics of the neurons located in those regions of the brain stem referred to as the *limbic system* (the emotional brain). As is indicated in Figure 4.3, these regions receive signals that indicate the magnitude of the problems being processed by the brain and the success with which their resolution is being pursued. These signals enter the limbic system and terminate in the emotion sensors of the hypothalamus. The results produced—in the form of aggression or indifference, pleasure or displeasure, and corresponding human actions (or behavior)—depend upon the characteristics of the limbic system in general and the sensitivity characteristics of the emotion sensors in particular.

Emotion-sensor sensitivity, like other brain capacities, is an independent quality. It depends only upon the anatomy and physiology of the limbic system. In this respect it is also similar to memory capacity (or IQ) and can therefore be defined in similar terms. Since emotion-sensor sensitivity is so closely related to human actions or behavior, the quality representing this capacity is designated here as *behavioral-sensitivity quotient (BSQ)*.

The Character of Brain Capacities

Determining quantitative values for the three brain capacities—memory capacity, problem-solving capacity, and emotion-sensor sensitivity—is currently not possible. However, the general character of each of these capacities can be inferred by reference to known brain characteristics.

Since each brain capacity depends upon the arrangement and basic characteristics of the neurons located in specific regions of the brain, it is reasonable to conclude that the three capacities have similar characteristics. The similarity between an adult's memory capacity and IQ has already been noted. For an adult, therefore, it follows that the general character of each of the

three brain capacities can be regarded as analogous to IQ. Figure 5.4 shows a typical IQ distribution curve along with postulated curves for PSQ and BSQ.

The typical IQ distribution curve, the Stanford-Binet intelligence scale, is shown in Figure 5.4*a*. This curve is based on extensive IQ testing results and analyses, in which the mean value of the test results was arbitrarily normalized about a value of 100. The resulting curve is, in statistical terms, normal about the mean value with a standard deviation of 16. In more useful terms, this means that 500,000 persons out of every 1 million in a particular population have an IQ of 100 or above; 160,000 persons per million have an IQ of 116 or greater; and only 23,000 persons out of every 1 million have an IQ of 132 or above.

Comparable distribution curves postulated for PSQ and BSQ are given in Figure 5.4*b* and *c*. The basis for these two curves is the scientific logic which indicates that the arrangement and basic characteristics of the neurons present in the related regions of the brain vary in the same statistical manner as those responsible for IQ and that PSQ and BSQ can be identified on the same relative scale as IQ.

ENVIRONMENTAL EXPERIENCES

The brain, like the computer, requires information in order to operate and perform its many functions. The required information is provided from life experiences and comes from both the existing environment and previous environmental experiences (stored in the memory area). In terms of importance, however, the latter is by far the more significant.

The memory area acquires and retains vast quantities of information even at an early age. These quantities, of course, continue to increase as a person grows older and is exposed to more and varied experiences.

The influences of these ever-increasing quantities of information on human capabilities is continuous but does not depend only on the quantity stored. It depends a great deal on the quality of the environment and on the stage of life when the information is stored: early, intermediate, mature, or advanced age. How the environment experienced during different stages of life influences

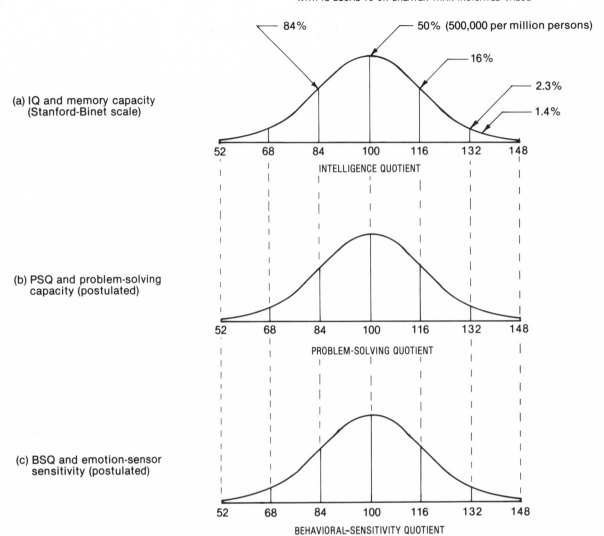

Figure 5.4 Distribution of brain capacities within the adult population

important human mental qualities is shown in Table 5.1.

EARLY AGE

Early-life experiences are known to be crucial to the future well-being of any individual. The unified concept supports this important observation.

During the early phases of life, the anatomy and physiology of the brain and its associated sensors are in a rapid state of change. The magnitude of these changes may be implied by the change in brain weight shown in Figure 5.3, but just how they influence brain capacities is not known. However, it is obvious that the various sensors, as well as the memory area and the concept and logic center, are affected.

The following observations relative to information acquisition and storage during early life therefore appear to be reasonable. First, information acquired by underdeveloped sensors and stored in the underdeveloped memory area lacks completeness and fidelity. Second, the underdeveloped concept and logic center provides a minimum of problem-solving capacity and contributes

Table 5.1 Age and environmental influences

AGE		NATURE OF INFORMATION STORED IN MEMORY		ADULT HUMAN MENTAL QUALITIES MOST INFLUENCED
Stage of life	Years*	Primary source	Dominating characteristics	

Early	0 to 6	General observations
		– human actions
		– material surroundings
		  • physical things
		  • taste
		  • comfort
		  • etc.
			Random information
			
			Unchallenged information
			– accuracy
			– moral quality
			
			Low fidelity information
			(underdeveloped brain)
				Behavioral charac-
				teristics
				- prejudices
				- ethics
				- motivation
				- interpersonal
				  relationships

Intermediate	6 to 18	General observations – human actions – material surroundings Formal education	Organized information – formal training Challenged information (compared with experiences) Improved fidelity information (increased brain develop- ment)	Knowledge
Mature	18 to 70	General observations Formal education Work experiences	Organized information – formal training – job training Challenged information (compared with experiences) High fidelity information (mature brain)	Knowledge Problem-solving capability
Advanced	70 +	General observations Work experiences	Less challenged and lower fidelity information (brain deteriorioration)	All

*Nominal range

little to memory recall (storage of associated engrams).

Irrespective of the quality of information stored in the memory area during early life, this information exerts a significant influence on the future of every human being, since information from a wide range of environmental experiences is acquired. These experiences, as indicated in Figure 5.2, provide a wide spectrum of information about people, places, and things which is stored in the memory area in numerous engrams. These engrams play a very important role when recallable (associated engrams), because, according to the unified concept of brain functions and processes, they become the standards to which new incoming information is compared. They therefore determine whether an individual's reactions to new experiences (or problems) are favorable or unfavorable.

The most important engrams stored during this early age period are those acquired through observations of human actions that reveal such characteristics as integrity, responsibility, confidence, and morality plus all the physical things identified by the five senses.

Witnessing the actions of people results in engrams that affect such later-life human characteristics as prejudices, ethics, motivation, interpersonal relationships, and happiness. Childhood exposures to physical things such as landscapes, sounds, climatic conditions, foods, orders, and physical activities result in engrams that determine what an individual regards as pleasant sensory inputs.

By the age of 6 years the child has stored engrams from experiences that affect each of the items discussed above. And these remain with the individual throughout life, except in rare instances. The child's brain, of course, stores other information at this time, but any significant quantity of information necessary for personal success related to such subjects as sciences, history, geography, and law is generally stored later in life and usually with considerable effort.

INTERMEDIATE AGE

Intermediate age, that period of life between 6 years and adulthood, is a transitional and very complex phase of life. The brain ostensibly approaches and reaches its highest level of maturity during this period, and it reaches its maximum weight (see Figure 5.3). For most individuals, improvements in problem-solving ability and memory fidelity are readily observable.

Intermediate age is the most difficult period of life for many persons. The unified concept can be used to illustrate why. According to this concept, brain processes and the resulting human behavior are affected by each of the following: recallable information (associated engrams) stored in the memory area, new information entering the memory area, and the success of the concept and logic center in resolving differences between the two.

Information stored in the memory area during early life may be desirable or undesirable, since environmental experiences are not always perfect. Also, as suggested in the preceding section, the immature brain and associated sensors tend to induce adverse influences. The underdeveloped concept and logic center may enhance information storage that is neither consistent nor logical, and the immature memory area may contribute to storing low-fidelity information. Stored information of this type is extensive, much of it is recallable (associated engrams), and it remains in the memory area indefinitely.

According to the unified concept, new information entering the memory area evokes the related engrams present. If the new and the stored information differ, the concept and logic center is activated to resolve the difference. The results produce human actions or behavior.

The just-described brain processes are continuous throughout life. But the situation during the intermediate age is unique with respect to both the conditions encountered and the results produced. The brain effects more accurate problem-solving (or logic) operations as it approaches maturity, and it stores information that is much higher in fidelity. The new information enters the memory area, where related engrams are evoked and the processes to resolve differences begin. But the conditions are highly complex. The more mature concept and logic center not only perceives the basic differences between new information and that evoked from the memory area; it also responds to the lack of logic and accuracy present in previously stored information. The concept and logic center is seldom able to resolve all these differences expeditiously. According to the unified concept, such conditions produce a corresponding period of unpleasantness, which tends to distract the consciousness area of the brain away from other subjects. As a result, individuals of intermediate age often lack the interest necessary for acquiring and storing the new information essential for future success.

During this period, early-life engrams are not replaced by new ones when new experiences are added to the memory area. Instead, new engrams are added. Some engrams stem from sensory information provided by the environment. Others are synthesized by the concept and logic center. In any case, engrams stored during this period are less easily evoked than those stored earlier, because they are related to fewer engrams. As a result, early-life engrams tend to dominate human behavior during this period of life.

MATURE AGE

The process of comparing new experiences with previously stored engrams continues throughout the individual's life. At some point in time a majority of the most pertinent environmental exposures are complete and a new period, defined here as the mature age, begins. By this time the brain has reached maximum maturity and a period of personal development begins. Emphasis is on gathering and storing information relative to material things which provide for human health and well-being. The concept and logic center plays a dominating role at this age, and individual actions are generally more logical than emotional. Mature associated engrams or synthesized engrams instead of early-life engrams, usually dominate in instances when logic-processing prevails. These provide the bases for comparing incoming information, and a mature and logical response results. Even during the mature age, however, exposure to certain adverse information may occur too suddenly to allow adequate logic-processing. A highly emotional response may result if adverse information is compared only with related early-life engrams.

There is apparently no way for even a mature person to eliminate adverse early-life engrams. Even so, certain emotionally packed experiences may serve to produce strong engrams which essentially negate those from early life. For example, experiences such as the death of a loved one or a religious conversion have been known to drastically change an individual's emotional responses to specific adverse experiences.

ADVANCED AGE

People often experience a loss in ability to store and recall information (lose memory capacity) as they approach old age. This is completely consistent with the unified concept of brain functions and processes. Innumerable neuronal fibers in the brain extend via the thalamus to those regions identified as the concept and logic center and the memory area. These fibers, which are essential to memory storage and recall, tend to deteriorate with age. For example, one authority has reported that half of the neuronal population in the frontal cortex of a 90-year-old man are nonfunctional. The adverse effects of advanced age are also indicated by the brain-weight curve shown in Figure 5.3, which shows that the typical brain at age 80 retains only 90 percent of its maximum weight.

HUMAN MENTAL QUALITIES

When the brain of a human being is supplied with information from environmental experiences, it possesses unique mental qualities. Those qualities of interest have been designated here as *knowledge, problem-solving capability, mental capability, behavioral characteristics,* and *effective mental capability*. In combination, these mental qualities account for all human actions or behavior and, therefore, control an individual's life accomplishments. Figure 5.2 shows the relationship that exists between the five different mental qualities, and it illustrates how each one is derived from different brain capacities and environmental experiences.

The knowledge a person possesses is determined by the inherited memory capacity of the brain and the environmental experiences to which that person has been exposed.

Problem-solving capability represents the combined influence of the problem-solving capacity of the brain and the problem-solving skills or procedures stored as knowledge in the memory area.

Mental capability depends upon the two preceding qualities: knowlege and problem-solving capability. It simply represents the combined influence of both.

Behavioral characteristics are those human qualities produced by the combined influence of knowledge, problem-solving capability, and emotion-sensor sensitivity characteristics.

Effective mental capability is the sum total of all human capabilities. It depends upon both mental capability and behavioral characteristics. Mental capability determines what a person is able to accomplish mentally. Behavioral characteristics determine how effectively mental capability is used. Thus, effective mental capability determines what a person is mentally able and willing to do.

6

Mental Capability

Knowledge and wisdom* far from being one,
Have ofttimes no connexion. Knowledge dwells
In heads replete with thoughts of other men;
Wisdom in minds attentive to their own.

WILLIAM COWPER

Mental capability, as defined in the preceding chapter, is one of the most significant of the human mental qualities. It is a recognizable quality with a specific and definitive meaning. Very simply, it is that capability which permits an individual to recognize, define, and solve problems of varying degrees of complexity. In this context, *problem* is used in a general sense and applies to any situation that requires brain processes to resolve a particular question. By this definition, the challenges presented by such diverse tasks as writing reports, making mathematical calculations, and designing an aerospace system are regarded as problems.

Because it encompasses so many important brain characteristics and environmental experiences, mental capability perhaps more than any other mental quality determines what an individual can accomplish in life. An understanding of mental capability is, therefore, an essential prerequisite to a clear understanding of the human

being. The unified concept of brain functions and processes, which makes use of an analogy between the brain and computer, provides a basis for this understanding. Figure 6.1 illustrates this analogy.

The computer characteristics and operating processes that determine computer capability are discussed in Chapter 3. How memory capacity and processing capacity of a computer combine with information supplied by the user to effect computer capability is illustrated in Figure 6.1a. An analogous illustration, Figure 6.1b, shows how a person's memory capacity and problem-solving capacity combine with information from environmental experiences to effect his or her mental capability. From this analogy comes a new and important factor not previously defined: mental *capacity*. How this factor relates to the other factors that determine a person's mental *capability* is indicated in Figure 6.2. Its specific characteristics and contributions to the understanding of human mental qualities are discussed later.

From the above review, the usefulness of the brain-computer analogy in understanding mental

*Wisdom depends upon problem-solving capability.

58

capability is readily apparent. It provides a basis—the computer—for examining and understanding those elements of the brain responsible for mental capacity; and it illustrates how mental capacity combines with environmental experiences to determine mental capability.

MENTAL CAPACITY

Mental capacity is a quality unique to every human being, because it depends upon two unique brain capacities: memory capacity and problem-solving capacity. Described in Chapter 5, the nature of these two brain capacities is summarized as follows:

o Memory capacity represents the capacity (potential) of the human brain to store and recall information received from the environment. This definition of memory capacity is analogous to IQ; and memory capacity and IQ are considered to be identical quantities for an adult.

o Problem-solving capacity represents the capacity (potential) of the brain to process and integrate information and produce creative problem solutions. Because of its nature, problem-solving capacity exhibits genetic characteristics like those of memory capacity, or IQ. Accordingly, it is designated in similar terms, that is, PSQ.

Since mental capacity is a composite of memory capacity (IQ) and problem-solving capacity (PSQ), it inherently exhibits many similar characteristics. For example, it is subject to the same type variations among individuals as are IQ and PSQ. Also, it is essentially a fixed quantity for any particular adult.

Viewed in this perspective, mental capacity places an upper limit on what a particular person can accomplish in life. Perhaps even more importantly, this concept emphasizes that a person's success in life is greatly influenced by the integrated characteristics of two independent brain capacities, IQ and PSQ.

GENERAL OBSERVATIONS

The fact that IQ alone is an inadequate measure of mental capacity is well documented. Lack

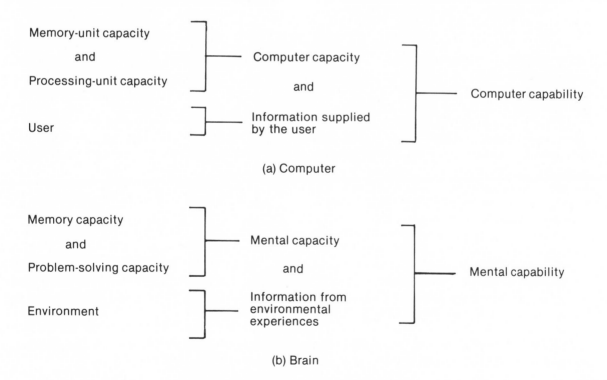

Figure 6.1 Computer-brain analogy

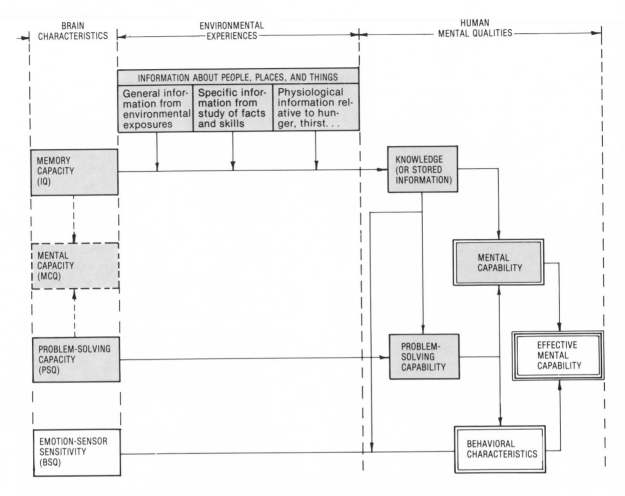

Figure 6.2 Relationships of factors that influence mental capability

of correlation between IQ test scores and academic performance is legend. There is even less correlation between IQ test scores and on-the-job performance. Examination of intelligence tests clearly indicates why they are inadequate for measuring mental capacity. They are, as discussed in the preceding chapter, oriented toward measuring memory capacity, which is the capacity to store and recall information received from the environment. Even the physical and mathematical problems included in these tests require using only memorized procedures for solutions. Few, if any, of the test questions require creative problem-solving or problem synthesis.

PSQ, the other component of mental capacity, has not been recognized or explored by psychologists. Its existence, however, is well known by those faced with complicated problems that yield only to logical reasoning and sophisticated syn-

theses. This brain capacity manifests itself in the ability to resolve problems that require the integration of numerous and complex variables into a meaningful and useful form.

Since IQ and PSQ are independent of each other, individuals with high PSQ may or may not have a high IQ. A high IQ, of course, enhances problem-solving proficiency by providing more readily available information to support the process. Because each capacity is independent of the other, however, the probability of a person's possessing high levels of both capacities is statistically low.

The fact that PSQ, as defined here, is independent of IQ is well borne out by experience. This experience shows that few individuals with exceptionally high IQs are able to synthesize complex problems, direct the activities of a multifaceted organized effort, or write clearly and concisely on complex subjects. This apparent ambiguity often frustrates the manager, who is unable to understand why the most "intelligent" employees are frequently the least able at problem-solving. This characteristic is, of course, not a recent discovery. It has been recognized by men of eminence for centuries.

I have hardly ever known a mathematician who was capable of reasoning.

PLATO

A strong memory is generally coupled with infirm judgment.

MONTAIGNE

We sometimes see fools possessed of talent, but never of judgment.

LA ROCHEFOUCAULD

Intelligence obscures more than it illuminates.

ISRAEL ZANGWILL

The most learned are often the most narrow-minded men.

HAZLITT

They who have read about everything are thought to understand everything, too, but it is not always so;

reading furnishes the mind only with material of knowledge; it's thinking that makes what we read ours.

W. CHANNING

These remarks, unscientific though they are, suggest that human mental capacity does in fact consist of two separate and independent capacities: one involving memory, the other logic.

THE BRAIN-COMPUTER ANALOGY

The brain-computer analogy provides the basis for a meaningful definition of mental capacity in terms of IQ and PSQ.

In this analogy, as indicated above, IQ and PSQ correspond functionally to computer memory capacity and processing unit capacity, respectively. These characteristics (in an adult) are also like those of the computer in another important way: each is essentially fixed in capacity. Hence, the mental capacity of an adult in terms of IQ and PSQ can be represented in the same manner as computer capacity (see Chapter 3, Figure 3.4). Figure 6.3 shows such a representation.

Figure 6.3*a* illustrates the resulting relationship where IQ and PSQ are defined in similar units, with mental capacity as a parameter. This relationship between brain capacities is the same as

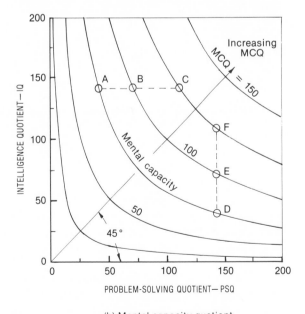

(a) Mental capacity

(b) Mental capacity quotient

Figure 6.3 Mental capacities: relationships between IQ, PSQ, and MCQ

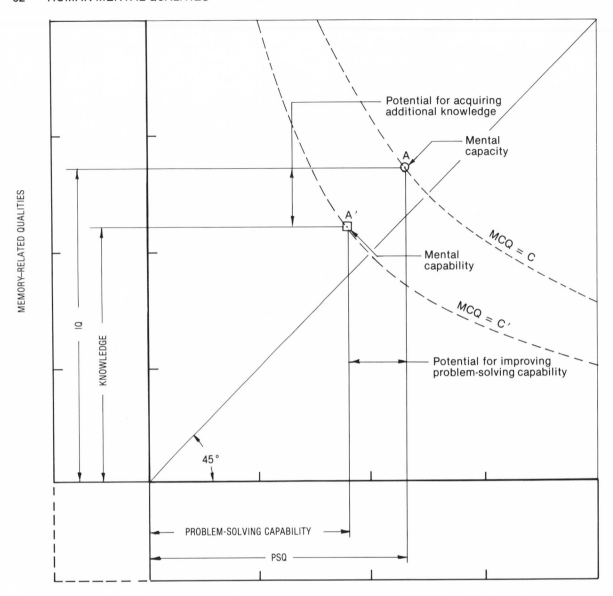

Figure 6.4 Mental capability

that shown for the computer in Chapter 3, where computer capacity is expressed as a function of the product of memory unit capacity and processing unit capacity. However, a slightly different definition of brain memory capacity is used. The product of the two brain capacities IQ and PSQ yields a number that is too large and cumbersome for practical use, so for convenience mental capacity is expressed here as the square root of the product of IQ and PSQ. The resulting term, for consistency with IQ and PSQ, has been designated *mental capacity quotient (MCQ)*. Figure 6.3b indicates the resulting relationships among MCQ, IQ, and PSQ.

Numerical values are used in Figure 6.3 only to enhance clarity of the illustration; they have no quantitative significance. Indeed, only one of the quotients, IQ, can be determined quantitatively, and the relationships between the three quotients have not been rigorously defined. Nevertheless, these relationships are useful. They not only indicate that both IQ and PSQ are influencing factors but also provide the basis for greater insight and understanding of mental capacity.

For example, the reason that IQ is not an adequate indicator of a person's potential for school or on-the-job success is conveyed by the relationships implied in Figure 6.3*b*. As illustrated, a specific IQ may or may not accompany a high MCQ. A wide range of MCQs is indicated among individuals represented by points *A, B,* and *C,* even though the IQ of each individual is the same.

This figure also shows that a high IQ, although desirable, is not a requirement for a high MCQ. More specifically, individuals represented by points *D, E,* and *F* have the same mental capacity as those represented by points *A, B,* and *C,* respectively, but with drastically lower IQs. These results are possible, of course, only because of the higher PSQs associated with persons represented by points *D, E,* and *F*.

The capacity relationships shown in Figure 6.3 are not suggested as being rigorous. But they are significant and useful. Based on the brain-computer analogy discussed earlier, these relationships show results consistent with documented observations. They, therefore, provide the basis for a systematic and logical approach toward improved understanding of mental capacity and the human being.

MENTAL CAPABILITY

The human brain, like the computer, acquires capability when supplied with information. Again, for any particular person this mental capability depends upon his or her mental capacity and environmental experiences.

Chapter 3 shows that computer capability depends upon the combined capacities of its memory and processing units, the information available, and the efficiency of the computer pro-

gramming. Since neither information storage nor process programming is ever perfect, computer capability is always less than computer capacity.

Similarly, it is reasonable to conclude that the mental capability of the human brain is always less than mental capacity. Unfortunately, in the absence of definitive values for memory capacity and problem-solving capacity, neither mental capacity nor mental capability can be assessed in quantitative terms. Even so, mere recognition of such relationships is helpful in developing an understanding of mental capability.

This understanding is enhanced by separately examining the interaction between the environment and a person's mental capacities (IQ and PSQ). Figure 6.2 indicates how the brain and environmental experiences combine to produce human mental qualities. More specifically, a person's IQ in combination with environmental experiences determines that person's level of knowledge. And a person's PSQ in combination with information acquired through environmental experiences is responsible for that person's problem-solving capability.

The relationships between brain capacities and human mental qualities are illustrated in Figure 6.4, which expresses the general relationships between IQ, PSQ, and MCQ. Point *A* in the figure represents the mental capacity of a particular person in terms of IQ, PSQ, and MCQ. Point *A'* represents the mental capability of that person in comparable units designated as knowledge and problem-solving capability. Since mental capacity is always greater than mental capability, there is an ever-present potential for a person to improve his or her mental capability (both knowledge and problem-solving capability). The degree to which a person's mental capability approaches the limiting value of mental capacity is determined by behavioral characteristics. How this influence is effected is discussed in subsequent chapters.

7

Behavioral Characteristics

No child is born a criminal; no child is born an angel; he is just born.
SIR SIDNEY SMITH

The hand that rocks the cradle is the hand that rules the world.
W. R. WALLACE

Human resources, like material resources, are valuable only when properly and effectively used. The presence of mental capability is not sufficient to assure the success of an individual. Appropriate behavioral characteristics are also necessary.

Behavioral characteristics are simply the human actions that result when information enters the brain, evokes engrams, and initiates brain processes. Thus, human behavior is influenced by both environmental experiences and inherited brain characteristics. Figure 7.1 identifies those brain characteristics and environmental experiences that determine behavioral characteristics. As will be seen later, each of these factors plays a crucial role in human behavior.

The importance of human behavioral characteristics to an individual's overall performance capability has long been recognized by managers and leaders. And in recent years, widespread investigations have contributed much to improved understanding of these important characteristics. Even so, the findings are general and somewhat superficial, and their practical value is limited.

The unified concept of brain functions and processes defined in Chapter 4 provides a basis for a more fundamental and useful understanding of these characteristics.

The brain processes postulated by the unified concept account for all human behavioral characteristics. In addition, they provide a basis for greater insight and improved understanding of the most important and observable manifestations of human behavior: motivation, interpersonal relationships, and happiness and frustration.

POSTULATED BRAIN PROCESSES

The brain processes postulated to effect human behavior are initiated when information entering the memory area evokes information stored as engrams that differs from the incoming information. Many different brain circuits are affected when this happens, as indicated in Chapter 4 and illustrated in Figures 4.3 and 4.4. Immediately upon initiation, a signal is passed through the amygdala to the hypothalamus, where the emotion sensors located in the aggression and indifference area of the brain are stimulated. The resulting sensation is then transmitted to the consciousness area. The concept and logic center is also activated at the same time and begins processing information directed at resolving the differences. During this process, the concept and logic center generates another signal which indicates its relative success toward a logical resolution of the differences. This signal then passes to the hypothalamus, where it stimulates the emotion sensors that produce pleasure and displeasure sensations.

These sensations are continuously transmitted to the consciousness area, where they reflect the desirable and undesirable conditions represented by information entering the brain from different sources. In response, the consciousness area automatically initiates body actions, or behavior, to bring about more desirable conditions (increased pleasure or decreased displeasure). Since the emotional conditions present at the consciousness level at any particular time depend upon the information entering the consciousness area, body actions adequate to change these emotional conditions must be sufficient to modify incoming information. The results of physical actions may be transmitted to the brain by either internal or external sensors. Changing the input of these sensors to the brain alters the processing results, changes emotion-sensor stimulations, modifies the sensations transmitted to the consciousness area, and directs further body action as is appropriate.

The information which enters the consciousness area from both the memory area and the con-

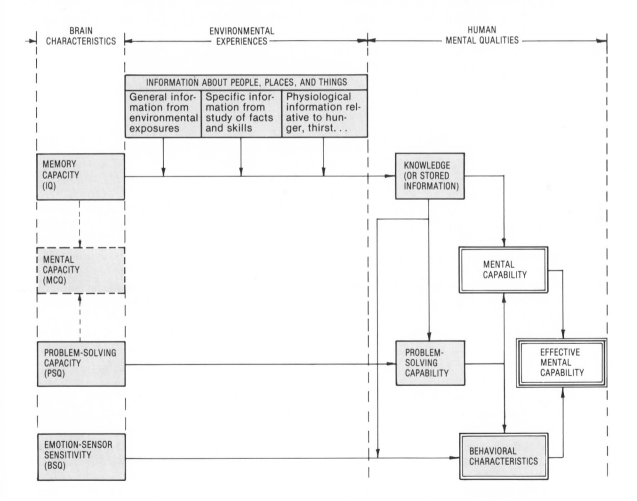

Figure 7.1 Relationships of factors that influence behavioral characteristics

cept and logic center also affects the brain processing results and human behavior. These are not completely independent sources, however, since each is activated indirectly and uses information initially supplied by either the internal or external sensors.

The brain processes and associated behavioral characteristics, as postulated above, depend upon the following:

- Information which enters the brain through the various sensors
- Information stored in the brain as memory engrams
- Problem-solving capacity of the concept and logic center
- The sensitivity of the emotion sensors (located in the hypothalamus)

The first two items depend upon present and past environmental exposures and are therefore subject to change with time. The last two are genetically determined and remain essentially fixed throughout most of the adult life. Accordingly, the behavior of any particular individual is affected only by the existing and past environmental exposures.

These precepts lead to a very important observation: Since at any specific time, memory engrams, problem-solving capacity, and the sensitivity of the emotion sensors are fixed, the behavior of a particular individual is determined only by information which enters the brain from the environment.

The above discussion clearly shows that an individual can willfully exercise only limited control over behavior at any particular time. When exposed to a set of sensory inputs, the resulting brain processes, emotion-sensor stimulations, and human behavior are essentially predetermined. At a later time, however, the same individual's behavioral response to identical inputs may differ. The reason for this difference is basic. Memory engrams change as new information is added from the environment. Thus, if these new engrams are evoked later by an identical environmental exposure, the brain processes will produce different results, and behavioral responses will then change accordingly. Also, the behavior of another individual exposed to the same sensory inputs will necessarily differ, since no two persons possess identical brain characteristics and past experiences (memory engrams).

The lack of control which the unified concept indicates an individual can exercise over his or her behavior may be disturbing to some. However, it is consistent with the consensus of numerous authorities and learned observers. Many eminent persons, for example, have suggested that an individual's behavioral characteristics are virtually fixed during early-life experiences and change little thereafter.

Nearly all human activity is programmed by an ongoing script dating from early childhood, so that the feeling of autonomy is nearly always an illusion...
ERIC BERNE

It is easy to train the mind while it is still tender.
SENECA

The direction in which education starts a man will determine his future life.
PLATO

Discipline your son in his early years while there is hope. If you don't you will ruin his life.
SOLOMON, PROVERBS 19:18

Brain processes responsible for human behavior are postulated to take place at the subconscious level. The results, however, appear at the consciousness level as emotions—aggression or indifference, and pleasure or displeasure. The intensity of these emotions varies over a wide range, and they become manifest in what are commonly referred to as individual wants and needs. Thus, human wants and needs may be regarded as initiators of the brain processes that produce feelings of aggression or indifference and of pleasure or displeasure. They are, therefore, directly responsible for every body action.

Typical of the vast number of human wants and needs are desires for food, water, sex, an automobile, a college degree, a house, a big office, friends, and admirers. The list is essentially limitless. And of course, not all can be simultaneously satisfied. To accommodate this situation, the brain is postulated to function according to a predetermined priority based on the relative importance of the specific wants and needs to the individual's overall well-being.

Human wants and needs which command the

highest priority are those related to physical survival. Next in order are those associated with comfort and convenience, and these are followed by wants and needs for creative achievements. These three categories of human wants and needs, therefore, constitute an ordered hierarchy, or priority, according to the relative importance of each to the individual's overall well-being. The fact that different human wants and needs command different priorities over an individual's actions is well established from observations. These observations are in consonance with the brain functions and processes postulated by the unified concept.

The priority associated with any specific set of human wants and needs is determined by the magnitude of the signal which initiates brain proc-

esses, as defined by the unified concept. The intensity of this brain process-initiating signal may be large or small. Its magnitude depends upon the character of the information entering the memory area and the characteristics of the evoked engrams.

Brain process-initiating signals may be generated by different combinations of information sources and memory engrams. Behavior in response to wants and needs in each category, however, is affected only by signals generated by certain combinations of information sources and engrams. The postulated relationships between the different brain process-initiating sources and the wants and needs in each category are illustrated in Figure 7.2. Some typical specific wants and needs are also listed.

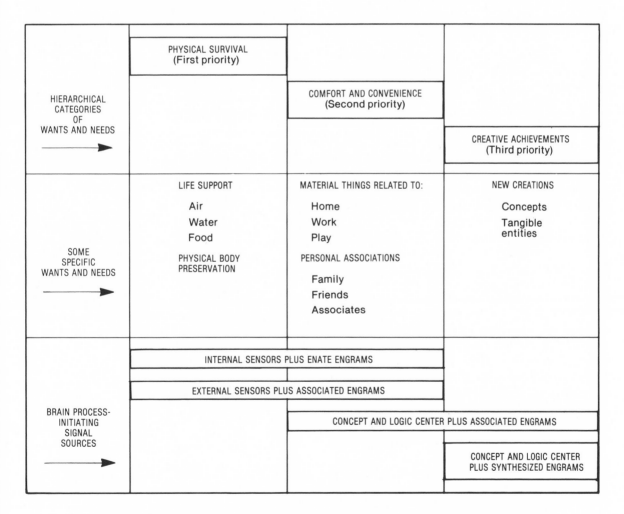

Figure 7.2 The hierarchy of wants and needs, and brain process-initiating signal sources

That a hierarchy of wants and needs exists is apparent from everyday observations of human behavior. The brain processes and operations postulated to account for the various human behavioral characteristics are discussed below.

PHYSICAL SURVIVAL

As the highest priority category of wants and needs, physical survival implicitly includes all those wants and needs related to life support and physical body preservation. Wants and needs which involve physical survival are unique in two respects: they are initiated only by "strong" brain process-initiating signals, and they can be satisfied only by physical body actions.

Specific Wants and Needs

The most obvious and basic wants and needs associated with physical survival are life support (such as food and water) and physical body preservation. When physical survival is challenged, the brain operates on a first-priority basis to produce the body actions or behavior necessary to assure survival.

Initiating Sources

Human behavior directed toward physical survival may be initiated by either of the following brain process-initiating sources: internal physiology sensors plus enate engrams or external sensors plus associated engrams.

INTERNAL PHYSIOLOGY SENSORS
PLUS ENATE ENGRAMS

The internal physiology sensors constantly monitor the body conditions with respect to needs for life-supporting substances such as food and water. When deficiencies develop, the sensors pass signals to the consciousness area and then to the memory area, where enate engrams are evoked. The difference between the sensory information and the evoked enate engrams initiates brain processes. Small differences may result in slight discomfort and constrained behavior. When these differences are sufficient to threaten survival, however, they dominate all other process-initiating signals. These signals then initiate appropriate behavior.

The physiology sensor plus enate engram characteristics responsible for initiating brain processes are essentially fixed quantities: sensor characteristics are established genetically; enate engrams, which relate to hunger, thirst, etc., are subject to little if any change during life.

The internal physiology sensors' signals are unaltered by brain processes. When strong, these signals coupled with the fixed, yet easily evoked, enate engrams account for the high priority of the wants and needs associated with physical survival.

EXTERNAL SENSORS
PLUS ASSOCIATED ENGRAMS

When a threat of bodily destruction exists, the situation is detected by external sensors (responsible for the five senses) and is passed to the consciousness area and then to the memory area. The resulting action of the individual depends upon the associated engrams evoked. If no previous experience relative to the threatening condition is stored in the memory, little action will take place. On the other hand, aggressive action will result if an associated engram indicates a serious situation exists. Hence, the actions of a particular individual to satisfy wants and needs for physical body preservation depend upon the existing environmental situation plus past environmental experiences (associated engrams).

Operations

When an individual's survival is threatened, the brain process-initiating signals are extremely strong and dominate control of brain operations. The aggression area of the hypothalamus is highly stimulated, causing immediate and aggressive actions. At the same time the concept and logic center is activated.

The concept and logic center is hopelessly challenged when the brain processes are initiated by internal physiology sensor inputs plus evoked enate engrams. Although activated, it cannot satisfy the needs for water or food through logic-processing. As a result, the concept and logic center generates a signal which passes to and stimulates the displeasure area of the hypothalamus. The resulting condition is one of extreme activity and great displeasure. Under such circumstances the individual may run, fight, or even kill to ensure survival.

The situation is only slightly different when external sensor inputs plus greatly differing associated engrams are involved. The initiating signal is again strong, the aggression area is highly stimulated, and the concept and logic center is activated. Also, as before, no amount of logic-processing can change the difference between the existing conditions of the environment and the danger indicated by the evoked associated engram. In a like manner, both aggression and displeasure are present, as is the potential desire to run, fight, or kill.

There is, however, one important and significant difference between the two process-initiating sources associated with physical survival. The difference stems from the nature of associated engrams. The external sensory information which evokes engrams indicating danger may also evoke other engrams. When a moral issue or a loved one is involved, personal danger may not dominate human behavior. For example, a person may accept death to save the life of a loved one.

COMFORT AND CONVENIENCE

When wants and needs for physical survival are satisfied, the brain processes and related body actions are directed toward providing the individual with comfort and convenience. The wants and needs in this category are enormous. The sources of information and engrams which combine to initiate the brain processes are numerous and varied. Appropriately, therefore, very complex behavior occurs as the individual responds to the variety of results produced by the brain.

Both physical actions and logic-processing play important roles in satisfying wants and needs for comfort and convenience. Physical actions are directed toward changing (or improving) the external situation and, hence, improving the sensory input information. Logic-processing by the concept and logic center is directed at resolving any apparent incompatibility between incoming information and the engrams evoked from the memory area. If the concept and logic center is successful in resolving the apparent differences between the information from the two sources, wants and needs (and aggressiveness) are reduced. This success, in keeping with the unified concept, can produce pleasure sensations at the consciousness level. Within this hierarchical category, therefore,

there is always a potential for pleasure. The only requirement is that the concept and logic center function successfully toward resolving differences (or problems) as they arise.

Specific Wants and Needs

Wants and needs for comfort and convenience are extensive, involving both material things and human associations.

Material things are those primarily associated with the physical environment, things which exist at home, work, and play. Some of the most common include the following:

• Home: house, household furnishings, automobile, clothes, and food
• Work: office space, furnishings, parking space, and expense account
• Play: facilities (playgrounds, etc.), equipment, and skills

Human associations are those interactions which develop with family, friends, and associates. The wants and needs for personal interactions differ greatly among both individuals and groups. Love, support, communication, and competition are typical of these specific wants and needs.

Initiating Sources

Behavior directed toward comfort and convenience may be initiated by any of the following combinations of input sources and engrams: internal physiology sensors plus enate engrams; external sensors plus associated engrams; or concept and logic center plus associated engrams.

INTERNAL PHYSIOLOGY SENSORS
PLUS ENATE ENGRAMS

These are the same factors involved in the initiation of processes when physical survival is threatened. The difference is the intensity of the sensor signals that indicate the level of wants and needs. When slight hunger or thirst exists and does not threaten survival, for example, only discomfort is manifested at the consciousness level. This condition would not, therefore, be expected to prompt overt aggressiveness.

EXTERNAL SENSORS
PLUS ASSOCIATED ENGRAMS

Information from the external sensors plus the

evoked associated engrams provides the initiating signals for most brain processes.

External sensors provide current information from the surroundings. Associated engrams represent extensive records of the past, having been stored throughout life. However, those stored during the early years are very crucial to behavior. In these early years, children are exposed to most aspects of material things and personal associations that they will experience during life. Information which enters the memory area at this early age is often inaccurate and low in fidelity. Even so, many of the engrams stored are readily recallable, since the same or related experiences are repeated numerous times.

The material things to which the child is exposed determine which related engrams are stored. That is, the home, clothes, foods, and automobiles to which a child is exposed form associated engrams which represent recallable knowledge of the material environment. These experiences subsequently determine an adult's behavior toward related matters.

The personal associations the child experiences produce associated engrams that establish behavior toward people. A child growing up in an environment where love, integrity, self-respect, respect for others, and fair play are exhibited will store corresponding engrams; a child raised in the opposite type of environment will store the opposite kind of engrams.

Associated engrams which relate to both people and things become the standards against which new information and experiences are compared. The resulting differences establish the magnitude of wants and needs and, accordingly, initiate behavior directed toward achieving comfort and convenience.

CONCEPT AND LOGIC CENTER PLUS ASSOCIATED ENGRAMS

The logic-processing of information (problem-solving) within the concept and logic center generally produces information that is different from that previously available. This information, like that from sensory sources, evokes related associated engrams when it arrives at the memory area. The result is additional brain process-inititiating signals. This process may be the most important one performed by the human brain. In addition to providing new brain-initiating signals, the process brings logic to diverse bits of incoming and memory-evoked information. The resulting newly evoked engrams then provide additional information for use in further logic-processing.

Operations

Brain operations which function to satisfy wants and needs for comfort and convenience differ in two important aspects from those associated with physical survival. First, the magnitude of the brain process-initiating signal for comfort and convenience is lower. Accordingly, the physical actions resulting from stimulating the emotion sensors are less aggressive. Second, the concept and logic center can and does influence brain operations. Utilizing its logic-processing (or problem-solving) capacity, the concept and logic center functions to assess the meaning of differences between the incoming information and the evoked engrams. As brain logic-processing proceeds, more engrams are evoked by related information from the newly evoked engrams. Each time a new set of engrams is evoked, further brain processing and corresponding behavioral actions take place. This process continues until either the initial wants and needs are satisfied or a compromise is reached between the initial wants and needs and the existing conditions. Because of the large number of engrams present in the memory area, there is always a high probability of successful logic-processing. Therefore, an increase in pleasure, or at least a decrease in displeasure, is always a possibility when wants and needs for comfort and convenience are involved.

There are billions of associated engrams in the memory area of the adult brain, which constitute the sum total of the recallable information acquired from the environment. Many of these engrams represent factual information about such subjects as art, science, literature, and government. Others, however, consist of random bits of information about the same subjects which are stored as received, regardless of correctness. Also, engrams representing repeated observation of human characteristics such as integrity, promptness, work and play habits, joyfulness, and friendliness are stored without interpretation. Likewise, information about physical surroundings such as the taste and sight of food, natural scenery, weather conditions, living quarters, and transportation modes become associated engrams simply by repeated exposure.

All these engrams influence the brain processes associated with comfort and convenience. As a result, extensive and complex functional operations of the brain are involved in detecting and satisfying wants and needs for comfort and convenience.

The role of the associated engrams in human behavior cannot be overemphasized. These engrams influence a large percentage of all brain operations and behavioral responses to some degree. If an individual has experienced desirable environmental exposures with respect to information accuracy, human activities, and natural surroundings, then associated engrams reflect those experiences. Under such circumstances the individual's behavior will be inclined to be favorable. On the other hand, less desirable environments will be reflected adversely in the individual's behavior.

A simplified illustration will serve to show how the brain is postulated to operate when exposed to a situation involving wants and needs for comfort and convenience. First, consider an individual whose environmental exposures include the following:

• A conscientious, dependable, and hardworking family
• Friends and neighbors with greater material possessions
• Nominal economic means and financial frugality
• Religious training and high integrity

Under these circumstances, the resulting associated engrams can be expected to reflect these traits: work responsibility; appreciation for better material things; and a high regard for money, honesty, and integrity. Thus, any information entering the brain that is at variance with any of these engrams will initiate appropriate brain processes and behavioral responses.

For example, if this individual experiences difficulties in getting to work on time because of maintenance problems with his automobile, certain brain processes will be set in motion. That is, his current experiences are different from the evoked engrams, which reflect work responsibility. The brain operations that follow can best be described by referring to the unified concept and the associated conceptual model shown in Figures 4.3 and 4.4.

The information relative to late arrival at work enters the memory area from the consciousness area and evokes engrams related to work responsibility. The difference between the two initiates operation of the concept and logic center and causes stimulation of the aggression area of the emotion-sensitive hypothalamus. The concept and logic center begins logic-processing directed toward resolving the difference. This exposes the memory area to additional information as the operation proceeds, and additional associated engrams are evoked. The emotion stimulations are projected to the consciousness area at the same time, where they initiate behavioral responses to aid in resolving the problem. The results of these actions also produce new inputs to the consciousness area and still other associated engrams are evoked from the memory area. This continuous and iterative type of process either proceeds until a resolution is reached or a higher-priority situation diverts the brain.

The individual's behavior during the brain operations just described, as well as the final resolution of a problem, depends upon the associated engrams evoked and the problem-solving capacity of the concept and logic center. Based on the information available, the concept and logic center will operate to establish possible solutions, and the final resolution will depend upon the many associated engrams involved. If a new automobile is considered as a solution, for example, the engrams may affect the resolution as follows: The appreciation for material things places emphasis on high quality and perhaps an expensive automobile, whereas prior exposure to financial frugality directs action toward lower cost. And the integrity-related engrams prevent dishonest acts in obtaining a car.

Although the operations and processes involved appear random, they are very systematic. As each successive associated engram is evoked, systematic logic-processing is initiated and behavioral responses begin. Progress toward resolution is indicated by stimulation of the pleasure or displeasure and the aggression or indifference areas. The process continues, always moving in a direction tending to increase pleasure or decrease displeasure. The operations cease when additional processing fails to increase pleasure or decrease displeasure, even though the wants and needs may not be completely satisfied. Generally, the result is a compromise between the new information and that evoked as associated engrams.

CREATIVE ACHIEVEMENTS

Human wants and needs for creative achievements arise only after physical survival is assured and when wants and needs for comfort and convenience are minimal. When these conditions prevail, little physical action is necessary, and the concept and logic center is free to operate primarily with internal information. It is under these conditions that the individual is most able to perform creative functions.

Specific Wants and Needs

Wants and needs for creative achievements are unique in that they arise only when physical body wants and needs are nil and they appear as the desire to create new concepts or tangible entities. The brain processes responsible for these wants and needs stem from the incompatibility of information stored in the memory area. When these incompatibilities are identified through the brain processes, the concept and logic center begins processing to resolve the differences. Successful resolutions of the differences results in new concepts or in the development of new tangible entities.

Initiating Sources

The mental activity responsible for creative achievements may be initiated by either of the following brain process-initiating sources: the concept and logic center plus associated engrams, or the concept and logic center plus synthesized engrams.

CONCEPT AND LOGIC CENTER PLUS ASSOCIATED ENGRAMS

All information resulting from logic-processing in the concept and logic center passes to the consciousness area and then enters the memory area, evoking related engrams which supply additional information to the concept and logic center for further processing. When undisturbed by higher-priority signals, the brain processes continue, creating new concepts and ideas for tangible entities through logic-processing operations.

CONCEPT AND LOGIC CENTER PLUS SYNTHESIZED ENGRAMS

Information from the concept and logic center that enters the memory area also evokes synthesized engrams. The process is the same as that involved in evoking associated engrams. The only difference is that synthesized engrams are often stored with less-related information and are usually more difficult to evoke. In fact, most synthesized engrams are assumed to be evoked only by information from the concept and logic center.

Operations

The brain operations responsible for creative achievements involve primarily the concept and logic center and the memory area. The role of the concept and logic center is to compare and rearrange information until wants and needs which can be satisfied by new concepts or ideas for tangible entities are met. The memory area is the major source of information for the creative achievements. Indeed, at any particular time the information immediately available from the environment is too small to be significant to the creative process. Thus, the brain processes responsible for creative achievements operate almost entirely on information from the memory area. The operation, however, must first be initiated by information from sensory sources. But once initiated, operations continue until new concepts or ideas are evolved or higher-priority operations intervene.

Upon initiation, the information entering the memory area evokes associated engrams. The concept and logic center compares the information evoked from engrams with that entering the memory area for logic and compatibility. The result enters the memory area and evokes additional engrams, either associated or synthesized. The operation repeats itself over and over. New results, like new sensory information, evoke additional engrams, and logic-processing continues until a logical resolution is reached, progress toward a resolution ceases, or the process is interrupted by higher-priority inputs.

There is no threat to physical survival under the conditions just described, and the wants and needs for comfort and convenience are essentially satisfied. As a result, the primary brain activities are those that are internally, or self-, sustained by the interactions between the concept and logic center and the memory area. Such brain processes, if successful, lead to the creation of new concepts and ideas for tangible entities. As is the case during all brain operations, successful logic-processing by the concept and logic center causes stimulation of the pleasure area of the hypothalamus and produces a pleasure sensation at the consciousness level.

In the absence of physical wants and needs, the dominating brain processes may produce long periods of either pleasure or displeasure. When pleasure results, the individual may experience one of the most pleasant aspects of life. On the other hand, when displeasure results, the experience may be correspondingly unpleasant.

MOTIVATION

Motivation, as the term is generally used, refers to actions which cause a body or system to move. As it is used here, motivation is an identifiable behavioral characteristic which arises when an individual is exposed to certain environmental conditions that initiate a sequence of brain processes that culminate in human actions.

The ability to assess and influence human motivation is an essential quality of any successful manager or leader. Yet few managers and leaders have acquired an adequate understanding of this important characteristic. The reasons are obvious. Motivation involves very sophisticated brain processes which are not sufficiently well-understood to be used in a fundamental and practical manner.

The unified concept, along with the postulated brain processes discussed in the preceding section, provides for much greater fundamental understanding and permits considerable insight into human motivation. From this concept, the factors which affect motivation level are easily identified, and their effect on the motivation of people is readily apparent.

MOTIVATION FACTORS

Motivation, as a manifestation of human behavior, is influenced by the same factors as are all behavioral characteristics. It therefore stems from

wants and needs. Accordingly, there exists a hierarchy of motivation levels, designated here as *high, nominal,* and *low.* These levels correspond respectively to wants and needs for physical survival, comfort and convenience, and creative achievements. They occur, therefore, as follows:

o *High* levels of motivation result when life is threatened.

The necessary action is physical; the desire is to live; and success is measured by survival.

o *Nominal* levels of motivation exist when the opportunity to enhance comfort and convenience is present.

The necessary actions involve both physical activity and brain logic-processing. The desire is for improved comfort and convenience. Successful physical action results in greater comfort and convenience, while successful logic-processing produces pleasurable experiences during the activity; lack of successful physical action and logic-processing produces the opposite result.

o *Low* but very important levels of motivation may exist even when all physical desires are satisfied.

The necessary action involves only mental activity. The desire stems from the apparent incompatibility between evoked memory engrams and results produced by the concept and logic center. Success in resolving these differences results in new concepts or ideas for tangible entities. The accompanying logic-processing produces a situation favorable to pleasurable sensations. The lack of successful logic-processing, on the other hand, produces unpleasant sensations.

The hierarchical motivation levels, along with the factors which contribute to each of the different levels, are summarized in Figure 7.3.

The influence of the various factors on the three motivation levels is illustrated graphically in Figure 7.4. This figure shows how motivation level may vary among individuals, represented by *A, B,* and *C.* It also indicates how the motivation level of different individuals may be influenced by the existing environment, memory engrams, problem-solving capacity (or logic-processing capacity), and emotion-sensor sensitivity.

From these and earlier observations, the following comments relative to individual motivation are pertinent:

o When the physical survival of a particular individual is involved, the resulting *high* level motivation is dominated by the existing environment, memory engrams, and emotion-sensor sensitivity characteristics. The influence of problem-solving capacity is nil.

o When only the comfort and convenience of an individual are involved, the resulting *nominal* level of motivation is influenced by all the four factors.

o When only creative achievements are involved, the *low* level of motivation is determined by memory engrams, emotion-sensor sensitivity, and problem-solving capacity. The influence of the existing environment is minimal, requiring only that needed for initiating the mental process.

o Many of the factors which determine individual motivation are fixed by heredity. Only those that are influenced by the environment are subject to any appreciable change.

MOTIVATION CONTROL

As is clear from the preceding discussion, the amount of control that can be exercised over human motivation is quite limited, since memory engrams are determined by past experiences and since problem-solving capacity, memory capacity, and emotion-sensor sensitivity are fixed by heredity. Thus, environmental changes offer the only promise for motivation control.

An environment which presents a threat to physical survival is the surest and simplest way to assure human motivation. Also, conditions which present a threat to comfort and convenience are almost certain to induce motivation. The deliber-

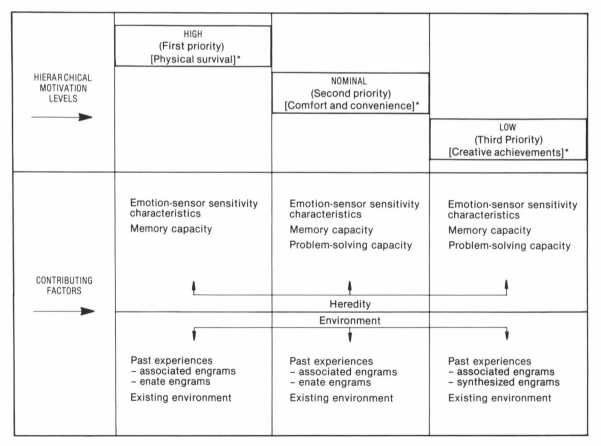

*Hierarchical categories of wants and needs

Figure 7.3 Motivation levels and contributing factors

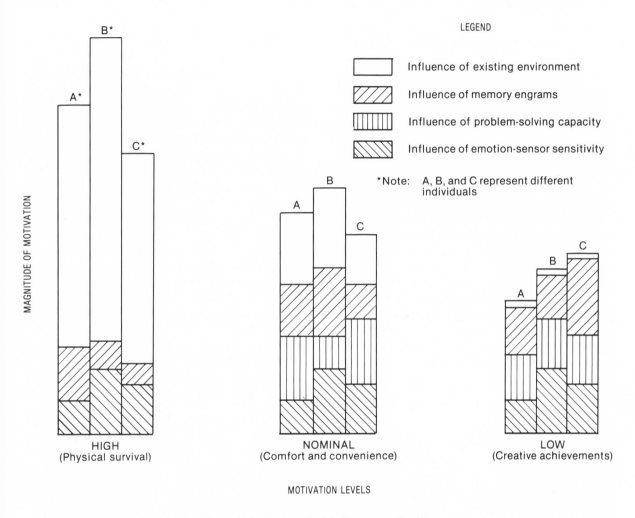

LEGEND

☐ Influence of existing environment

▨ Influence of memory engrams

▥ Influence of problem-solving capacity

▧ Influence of emotion-sensor sensitivity

*Note: A, B, and C represent different
individuals

MAGNITUDE OF MOTIVATION

HIGH
(Physical survival)

NOMINAL
(Comfort and convenience)

LOW
(Creative achievements)

MOTIVATION LEVELS

Figure 7.4 Factors that influence motivation

ate use of either of these techniques to control motivation is, obviously, undesirable. In fact, their use over a period of time renders them ineffective and counterproductive. No competent person in a free economic society will work long under such circumstances.

A much more desirable approach to motivation is to create environmental conditions that promise greater human comfort and convenience and also permit the pursuit of creative achievements. Unfortunately, these conditions are often difficult to produce. The unified concept of brain functions and processes, however, provides the basis for a logical approach.

As previously noted, motivation is postulated to begin when information enters the memory area and evokes engrams that differ from the incoming information. The resulting action (or motivation) is automatic and is directed so as to increase pleasure and decrease need for action. Hence, motivation control for a particular individual resolves itself simply to controlling the information which enters the memory area from the environment and to modifying the engrams previously stored in the memory area.

Considerable influence can be exercised over the environment at any particular time and, hence, the information entering the memory area. The engrams evoked from memory may be controlled by this means and motivation effected. It may in fact be possible, although not necessarily practical, to dominate human actions by controlling information entering the brain via the various sensors.

When evoked by incoming information, every memory engram representing past experiences influences human motivation to some degree. Thus, gaining control of human motivation by modifying or adding memory engrams is reasonable and feasible. However, because of the almost limitless number of memory engrams present in the adult brain, the overall effect of such an effort will be small at best. Nevertheless, changes are possible and often desirable and useful. Such changes may be made by adding new engrams through the various sensors, adding information to previously stored engrams, or evolving synthesized engrams in the concept and logic center.

The idea that stored memory engrams can be used to control motivation is a significant and familiar precept. Viewed in this way, the engram may be regarded as a *goal,* as the term is used by the behavioral scientists. It, therefore, explains fundamentally why well-established goals (engrams) are so strong and effective in motivating people.

INTERPERSONAL RELATIONSHIPS

Interpersonal relationships are unique manifestations of human behavioral characteristics. They reflect the ability of individuals to work harmoniously and effectively with each other. Few other human characteristics are as crucial to an individual's success in life.

Interpersonal relationships are closely associated with human motivation in that they are manifested in human actions. Whether such relationships are favorable or unfavorable is determined by essentially the same factors that determine motivation. Environmental experiences and emotion-sensor sensitivity characteristics are primary among these factors. And each of these affects, in some way, every personal interaction.

ENVIRONMENTAL EXPERIENCES

Environmental experiences have a significant influence on interpersonal relationships because they determine what information is available to an individual. Thus, they determine which memory engrams are stored and whether they are correct/incorrect or desirable/undesirable (relative to the accepted criteria of society).

Memory engrams influence interpersonal relationships in two important ways: they provide the knowledge necessary for problem-solving and they interact with the brain processes that produce human actions or behavior. This latter influence is the one of primary interest here. It is this influence of memory engrams that results in those human characteristics referred to as *ethics* and *prejudices.* These characteristics are important in interpersonal relationships because they influence, to some degree, the outcome of every personal interaction.

Ethics

Ethics reflect an individual's concept of right and wrong. They stem from the early childhood environment and change little thereafter. Hence, an individual exposed as a child to an environment where deceit, personal exploitation, and lack of self-respect are prevalent is likely to develop distorted concepts of right and wrong. If so, the resulting low ethical standards may become a lifetime burden. On the other hand, individuals reared in an environment where Judeo-Christian ethics are practiced tend to develop more desirable concepts of right and wrong. Early exposure to the Ten Commandments plus the moral and ethical teachings of Christ encourage an individual to develop high integrity, self-respect, and respect for others. These latter characteristics are generally recognized as being synonymous with high ethics.

Prejudices

Prejudices are in reality irrational opinions based on random information. Prejudices are not rare. Indeed, few people are entirely free of prejudices. As a product of early life, these traits tend to remain with an individual throughout life.

Prejudices are troublesome because they are attitudes held by individuals about people, places, things, and situations for which there are no factual bases. The most detrimental prejudices, and those of interest here, are associated with people. Typical prejudices involve such items as color of skin, race, creed, sex, age, and even birthplace. For example, a person may feel that women are poorer automobile drivers than men. Another individual may believe that people from Italy tend to be criminals. There is no basis for such feelings or beliefs, but a lack of a logical foundation does not change the attitude of these individuals.

Prejudices may be strong or weak, depending on the environment of childhood exposures. Again, a Judeo-Christian environment tends to minimize undesirable prejudices, whereas an atmosphere of hate and mistrust encourages the growth of adverse prejudices. In any case, however, each individual is destined to live with certain prejudices.

EMOTION-SENSOR SENSITIVITY CHARACTERISTICS

Emotion-sensor sensitivity characteristics play a major role in interpersonal relationships. A highly sensitive characteristic may induce an individual to act immediately and irrationally at the first indication of any kind of problem. Favorable interpersonal relationships may not be possible under such circumstances, even when desirable environmental exposures have been experienced. Successful personal interactions may not be feasible either when the emotion sensors of the persons involved are abnormally insensitive. Fortunately, for most individuals these characteristics fall between two extremes. Whatever the characteristics, however, they greatly influence interpersonal relationships.

PERSONAL INTERACTIONS

Because of the many factors which influence interpersonal relationships, the potential for disagreement or discord is always present in any personal interaction. Generally speaking, such disagreements and discords are minimal in situations where the persons involved have similar early-life experiences and favorable emotion-sensor characteristics. Under these circumstances the parties can usually resolve problems and differences in a logical and amicable manner. Considerable time may be needed before a logical and mutually satisfactory resolution can be achieved, however, if these capabilities differ significantly. Whether time is available for a logical resolution depends upon the magnitude of the problem and the emotion-sensor sensitivity of the individuals involved. If the sensitivities are great, discord is certain to develop. When such discords do arise, emotions instead of logic usually prevail and,

under these circumstances, individual ethics and prejudices tend to dominate the interaction.

An individual's ethics may either aid or hinder interpersonal relationships. Ethics built on high integrity, self-respect, and respect for others tend to minimize discord. On the other hand, ethics which encourage exploiting, belittling, and using others to gain unfair advantage promote intense discord.

Prejudices almost never have a beneficial effect on interpersonal relationships. Since prejudices are strongly held opinions which cannot be supported by facts or logic, any challenge to these immediately provokes emotions. Hence, interaction between individuals involving prejudices is almost certain to result in unfavorable interpersonal relationships.

In summary then, it can be stated that keeping discussions on a plane of logic is an absolute necessity if desirable interpersonal relationships are to be maintained. Once emotions enter a discussion, interpersonal relationships will inevitably suffer. When this happens, only patience by one or both sides can prevent the discussion from falling into the emotional stage. Whether patience can be exercised under such conditions depends upon the individuals involved.

The importance of controlling emotions and exercising patience during personal interactions has long been recognized by persons of eminence:

The greatest remedy for anger is delay.

SENECA

When angry, count to ten before you speak; if very angry, count to a hundred.

JEFFERSON

He that can have patience, can have what he will.

FRANKLIN

Considering all the complex interaction involved in working with people, it is inconceivable that harmonious interpersonal relationships will always be present. Nevertheless, the problems of interpersonal relationships will be minimal among those with similar environmental experiences and favorable emotion-sensor sensitivity characteristics.

HAPPINESS AND FRUSTRATION

As commonly used, the words *happiness* and *frustration* represent diametrically opposite emotional conditions that are periodically experienced by everyone. These conditions are closely related to those defined as *pleasure* and *displeasure* in terms of brain processes as postulated by the unified concept. In this context, however, neither happiness nor frustration is related to specific wants and needs. Instead, each results from brain processes directed toward satisfying wants and needs. Successful processing produces pleasure. Unsuccessful processing produces displeasure.

The relationships that exist between happiness and pleasure or between frustration and displeasure are not precise. Certainly, a single short period of pleasure does not produce happiness; nor does a single short period of displeasure produce frustration.

Happiness and frustration generally refer to conditions that persist over an appreciable time span, that is for hours or days. On the other hand, pleasure and displeasure conditions produced by brain processes often exist for periods of only seconds or minutes. Thus, repeated periods of pleasure or displeasure are necessary to produce corresponding conditions of happiness or frustration. When periods of pleasure predominate, the net effect produces happiness; periods dominated by displeasure produce frustration. The level of happiness or frustration produced depends upon the degree by which either pleasure or displeasure dominates the emotion sensations produced by brain processes.

Happiness and frustration stem from the same brain processes that produce other behavioral characteristics. They are, therefore, affected by the same factors delineated previously:
• Information which enters the brain through the various sensors
• Information stored in the brain as memory engrams
• Problem-solving capacity of the concept and logic center
• The sensitivity of the emotion sensors, which are located in the hypothalamus
The first two factors depend upon environmental exposure and are subject to change with time. The last two factors are genetically determined and are subject to little change throughout life. Each affects happiness and frustration in specific ways.

Every brain process is initiated by sensory-input information. The degree by which the input information differs from the engrams it evokes determines what brain processes follow. Pleasure results if the problem can be successfully pursued by the concept and logic center, and a potential for happiness exists. On the other hand, displeasure and perhaps frustration will result if differences indicated cannot be resolved by either physical action or logic-processing.

As previously emphasized, the information stored in the memory engrams has two important effects. First, it determines what information is available to support processing by the concept and logic center. Second, it determines the content of engrams evoked by incoming information. The difference between these establishes the magnitude of the brain process-initiating signal.

Successful resolution of the differences between input information and evoked memory engrams depends upon the logic-processing capacity of the brain. Since this capacity differs among individuals by inheritance, a situation which causes frustration for one person could result in happiness for another. Hence, there is a significant relationship between logic-processing capacity and the happiness or frustration that results.

The sensitivity characteristics of the emotion sensors, like those of any organic element, are different for every individual. Therefore, the happiness or frustration experienced by different individuals can be expected to differ accordingly.

HAPPINESS

Happiness is undeniably the most desirable state of being that is experienced by humans. Beyond this statement, happiness is difficult to describe. Yet, through use of the unified concept, certain important observations can be made that greatly enhance our understanding of happiness:

o The happiness of a particular individual can be willfully influenced only by controlling information entering the brain. That is, happiness can be deliberately affected only by controlling the memory engrams stored and the input information which evokes the stored engrams. (All other factors that affect happiness are fixed by heredity.) Thus, while happiness cannot be controlled directly, it can be influenced by information management.

o The inherited logic-processing capacity (or problem-solving capacity) of the brain has a major effect on individual happiness. The greater the capacity to resolve differences between new incoming information and stored information, the greater the potential for happiness.

o The inherited sensitivity characteristics of the emotion sensors in the hypothalamus exert a significant influence on an individual's happiness. They affect how the sensors respond to stimulations produced by the various brain processes.

o Happiness is transient in character; it is fleeting. It exists only when logic-processing is proceeding successfully toward the resolution of a difference or a problem. Happiness never lingers after a problem is resolved since no stimulating signal exists.

o Happiness can exist only when brain processes produce longer periods of pleasure than displeasure. In the hierarchy of wants and needs this requirement precludes the category of physical survival, as well as those wants and needs which involve severe discomfort and inconvenience. Happiness is possible when wants and needs involve comfort and convenience, however, if the conditions are such that the brain processes are directed toward improving a relatively comfortable and convenient condition.

o The greatest potential for prolonged happiness exists during the pursuit of wants and needs for creative achievements. Here, all other wants and needs for physical survival are satisfied and the wants and needs for comfort and convenience are nil. Under these conditions long periods of successful logic-processing are possible and most likely.

The above observations are new and unique only in that they stem from the unified concept of brain functions and processes developed in this book. Many of these same observations have been made over the centuries by poets, philosophers, statesmen, and other distinguished professionals.

Action may not always bring happiness; but there is no happiness without action.

DISRAELI

Now happiness consists in activity: such is the constitution of our nature: it is a running stream, not a stagnant pool.

J. M. GOOD

Happiness is not steadfast, but transient.

EURIPIDES

Happiness is not a reward—it is a consequence.

R. G. INGERSOLL

We are happy when we are growing.

W. B. YEATS

[Happiness is] a state of mind in which our thinking is pleasant a good share of the time.

DR. JOHN A. SCHINDLER

Always have the next goal in the back of your mind, since the most satisfaction comes from pursuing a goal, not simply from achieving it.

ARI KIEV

FRUSTRATION

While difficult to define, frustration is easy to recognize. The direct opposite of happiness and a highly undesirable state of being, it is produced by the same brain processing network that produces happiness. It arises when brain logic-processing and body actions are unable to proceed successfully under the conditions imposed. The unified concept shows why this occurs and provides the basis for the following observations:

o The frustration experienced by a particular individual can be willfully influenced only by controlling the information entering the brain. That is, it can be deliberately affected only by controlling the memory engrams stored and the input information which evokes the stored engrams (all other factors affecting frustration being fixed by heredity). Thus, while frustration cannot be directly controlled, it can be minimized by information management.

o Frustration may exist at any hierarchical level of wants and needs. It is almost inevitable when the environment imposes a threat to physical survival or induces severe discomfort or inconvenience. At high levels of wants and needs it results when differences between the information entering the memory area and that evoked cannot be resolved. Thus, the greatest potential for frustration exists when the quantity of information stored in the memory area exceeds the brain's logic-processing capacity (or problem-solving capacity). It may be caused by either unusually low problem-solving capacity or a high memory capacity. In either case, more differences exist between the incoming information and that evoked from memory than can be expeditiously resolved.

o The inherited emotion-sensor sensitivity characteristics of the hypothalamus play a major role in frustration. They determine how the emotion sensors respond to stimulations produced by the various brain processes.

o Frustration is experienced by everyone to some degree. When short-lived, it produces no ill effects. The effects can be serious if it persists, however, introducing difficulties generally referred to as psychological.

8

EFFECTIVE MENTAL CAPABILITY

Wise men are instructed by reason;* men of less understanding by experience;†
the most ignorant by necessity.‡

CICERO

Those brain characteristics and environmental experiences that determine a person's mental qualities were treated in detail in the preceding chapters. As a matter of convenience and to enhance fundamental understanding, mental capability and behavioral characteristics were discussed separately and considered as independent qualities. In reality, there is considerable interaction between different human mental qualities. Figure 8.1 shows how the combined influence of the human mental qualities, discussed earlier, form the integrated quality identified as effective mental capability: the quality which determines the level of mental work a person is able and willing to perform.

Unfortunately, there is currently no way to measure effective mental capability. Nevertheless, there is a general understanding of the many factors involved and how they influence this important quality. This understanding, while highly subjective, is significant and provides a viable basis

for assessing a person's effective mental capability. The considerations, interpretation, and postulations involved in such an assessment are discussed in the following paragraphs.

HUMAN MENTAL QUALITIES

Figure 8.1 identifies all those factors that contribute to human mental qualities. The interrelationships between the various mental qualities are shown, and the mergence of mental capability and behavioral characteristics into a single composite quality, effective mental capability, is indicated.

As has already been emphasized, the factors that effect a person's mental qualities exhibit very complex characteristics, and none of them have ever been measured. Even so, much is known about their mutual relationships. Figure 8.2, which is based on the concepts and fundamental considerations presented in earlier chapters, illustrates these relationships.

The mental capacity (MCQ) of a particular individual is identified by point A in Figure 8.2, and the corresponding levels of IQ and PSQ are indicated. The mental capability of the same in-

---

*Reason: related to problem-solving capability.
†Experience: related to knowledge.
‡Necessity: related to survival and comfort (behavioral characteristics).

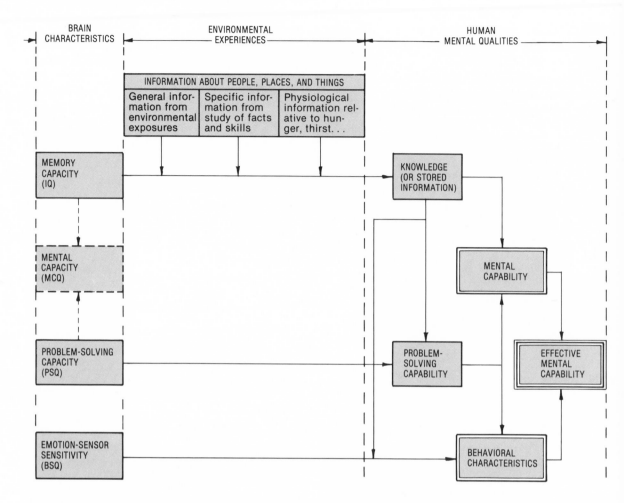

Figure 8.1 Relationships of factors that influence human mental qualities

dividual is symbolized by point A'. Since environmental experiences are never perfect and complete, mental capability is always less than MCQ. Accordingly, knowledge is less than IQ and problem-solving capability is less than PSQ. Thus, as shown in the illustration, there is an ever-present potential for acquiring more knowledge, increasing problem-solving capability, and enhancing mental capability.

An individual's mental capability (knowledge and problem-solving capability) is never fully used, because it depends upon another imperfect human quality: behavioral characteristics. How behavioral characteristics combine with mental capability to establish an individual's effective mental capability is symbolized by point A'' in Figure 8.2.

Figure 8.2 is a useful vehicle for illustration only; it has no quantitative significance. It merely shows how a number of complex factors combine and interact to produce effective mental capability. And it suggests the following pertinent conclusions:

o MCQ, as fixed by IQ and PSQ, limits what a person can accomplish in life.

o MCQ and environmental experiences determine what mental capability (knowledge and problem-solving capability) a specific person possesses at any particular time.

o Behavioral characteristics determine how effectively a person uses his or her mental capability. Thus, the combination of these two factors establishes a person's effective mental capability and, therefore, what he or she is mentally able and willing to do.

Although these conditions are based on a new concept—the unified concept of brain functions and processes—they are in general agreement with everyday observations. For example, it is a well-accepted fact that mental capacity, as indicated by memory capacity and problem-solving capacity, differs among individuals and influences what each person can accomplish. There is also general agreement that education (knowledge) and the

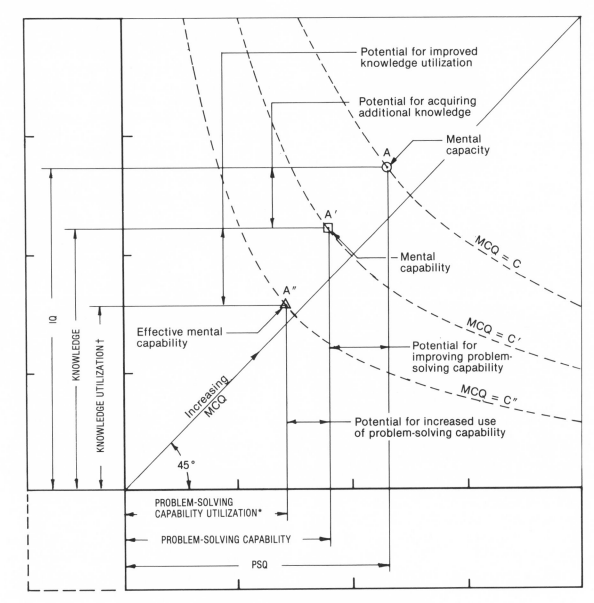

*Problem-solving capability utilization resulting from behavioral characteristics

†Knowledge utilization resulting from behavioral characteristics

Figure 8.2 Effective mental capability

ability to solve problems (problem-solving capability) influence how well a person can perform in society.

The influence of behavioral characteristics on a person's capabilities is most clearly manifested in two characteristics: motivation and interpersonal relationships. These characteristics are reflected in the desire and effectiveness with which an individual acquires information from the environment. But more importantly, they determine how well an individual uses the knowledge and problem-solving capability available.

The fact that motivation and interpersonal relationships are major contributors to a person's success in life is well supported by observations of successful historical figures:

Motivation

Genius is one percent inspiration and ninety-nine percent perspiration.

EDISON

If people knew how hard I work to get my mastery, it would not seem so wonderful.

MICHELANGELO

Nothing in the world can take the place of persistence. Talent will not; unrewarded genius is almost a proverb. Education will not; the world is full of educated derelicts. Persistence and determination alone are omnipotent.

COOLIDGE

We can do anything we want to do if we stick to it long enough.

HELEN KELLER

All the genius I have is merely the fruit of labor.

HAMILTON

Interpersonal Relationships

He that does good to another, does good also to himself;

SENECA

Good nature is stronger than tomahawks.

EMERSON

A successful man is he who receives a great deal from his fellowman.

EINSTEIN

Never . . . one person can make success. It takes a number of them merging into a perfect whole.

MARIE DRESSLER

Kindness is the golden chain by which society is bound together.

GOETHE

POSTULATED RELATIONSHIPS

The factors that influence effective mental capability were delineated in the preceding section, their interactions postulated, and the resulting relationships illustrated. Though general in character, these results provide for much improved insight into the meaning and significance of human mental qualities.

Even greater insight and understanding are possible through a closer and more detailed examination of the variables involved. To pursue this approach in a fundamental way, it is convenient to identify the factors and their relationships as

Effective mental capability

$$= f \left[\left(\begin{array}{c} \text{inherited brain} \\ \text{characteristics} \end{array} \right) \left(\begin{array}{c} \text{environmental} \\ \text{experiences} \end{array} \right) \right]$$

$$= f \left[(IQ, PSQ, BSQ)(Emi, Emps, Ebx) \right]$$

$$= f \left[(IQ, Emi)(PSQ, Emps)(BSQ, Ebx) \right] \quad (8.1)$$

where the terms are defined as follows:

f is a functional coefficient.

IQ is a "brain capacity" factor indicating the capacity of a person's brain to store and recall information.

PSQ is a "brain capacity" factor indicating the capacity of a person's brain to process and integrate information and produce creative problem solutions.

BSQ is a "brain capacity" factor indicating how a person will respond to various environmental experiences and results produced by brain processes.

Emi is an "environmental" factor indicating the quality and duration of a person's environmental experiences which, in conjunction with IQ, determines one's knowledge.

Emps is an "environmental" factor indicating the quality of a person's environmental experiences which, in conjunction with PSQ, determines one's problem-solving capability.

Ebx is an "environmental" factor indicating the nature of a person's environmental experiences which, in conjunction with BSQ, determines one's behavioral characteristics. Unlike Emi and Emps, Ebx is a combination environmental factor whose value depends upon two other environmental factors, defined as Ebmo and Ebip, where Ebmo represents the influence of the environment on a person's motivation, Ebip represents the influence of the environment on a person's interpersonal relationships, and Ebx is the mean value of the two factors. That is,

$$Ebx = \frac{Ebmo + Ebip}{2}$$

As written, the above equation has no quantitative significance. With the exception of IQ, none of the brain capacity factors have been defined explicitly. And none of the environmental factors can be directly measured. Nevertheless, enough is known about the basic characteristics of each variable to support a fundamental examination and, hence, provide a greater understanding of the factors responsible for effective mental capability.

INHERITED BRAIN CHARACTERISTICS

The brain capacity factors IQ, PSQ, and BSQ are the most basic contributors to effective mental capability. Fixed by inheritance, these factors place an upper limit on a person's mental qualities and, therefore, control what that person can accomplish in life.

Since each of the brain capacity factors is determined by different combinations of the same basic component (the neuron), it is reasonable to expect that they are independent of each other but exhibit similar basic characteristics. Careful consideration of the variables involved indicates that such is indeed the case. The nature of these brain characteristics is reviewed in Chapter 5. The postulated distribution of each brain capacity factor among individuals is shown in Figure 5.4.

The postulation that IQ, PSQ, and BSQ are independent and exhibit similar characteristics leads to a very important observation relative to the

distribution of human mental qualities within the population: a high value of one factor is, statistically, unlikely to be accompanied by a high value of another. This observation is based on the simple law of probability, which states that the probability that two or more events will occur simultaneously is the product of their separate probabilities.

For illustration, consider the following examples: From Figure 5.4a, the probability that any individual randomly selected from the population will have an IQ of 100 or more is 0.50. Stated another way, half of the people (or 500,000 individuals out of every 1 million) have an IQ of 100 or more. However, the probability that a randomly selected individual from the population will have all brain capacity factors (IQ, PSQ, and BSQ) equal to 100 or more is considerably lower. Specifically, this probability is $0.5 \times 0.5 \times 0.5$, or 0.125. Thus, 12.5 percent of the people (or 125,000 of every 1 million) have all three brain capacity factors equal to 100 or more. The number of individuals whose brain capacity factors are equal decreases dramatically as the capacity factor levels increase. For example, about 14,400 individuals per million have an IQ, PSQ, or BSQ of 135 or more, while the number of persons for which all three quotients are at the 135 level or more is less than 3 per million ($0.0144 \times 0.0144 \times 0.0144 = 0.00000299$, or 2.99 per million).

Figure 8.3 shows, in summary form, how the number of individuals with brain capacity factors at or above a certain level decreases as the factor level increases. It also shows how the number of individuals with all three brain capacity factors equal to or above a particular value is affected by capacity levels.

The relationships shown in Figure 8.3 are based on greatly simplified assumptions of brain characteristics. Even so, these statistical relationships do have meaning. They indicate how brain capacities of individuals vary within the population, both singly and in combination. But more importantly, they show that, for any individual, the higher the value of any single factor (say, IQ), the greater is the probability that the value of the other factors will be lower.

ENVIRONMENTAL EXPERIENCES

Inherited brain characteristics, as defined by the factors IQ, PSQ, and BSQ, place an upper

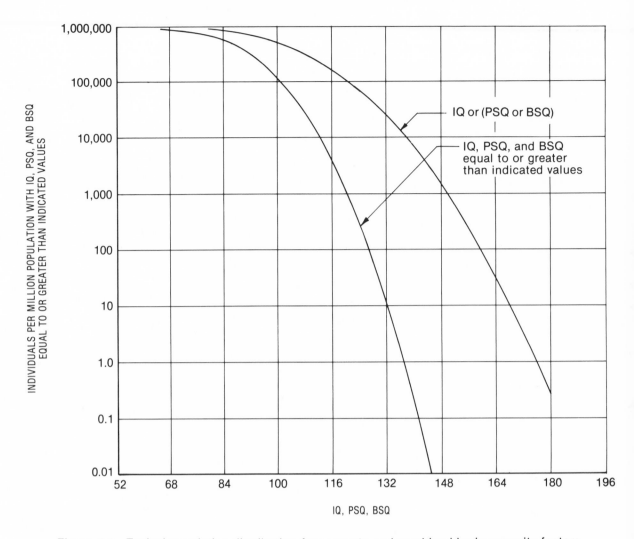

Figure 8.3 Typical population distribution for separate and combined brain capacity factors

limit on the effective mental capability of every person. Environmental experiences, as identified by the factors Emi, Emps, and Ebx, determine how closely a person's effective mental capability approaches its limits.

There is currently no way to define the influence of environmental experience on human capabilities in quantitative terms. However, there is considerable appreciation for the effects of various types of environments on the quality of information that enters the brain. The influence of exposure time (or age) on the quantity of information stored in the brain is also well recognized, since it relates to all human mental qualities. More specifically the following observations are generally accepted by psychologists, behavioral scientists, and others in the field:

• The influence of environmental exposures on a person's knowledge and problem-solving capability, expressed here in terms of Emi and Emps, is greatest during the midteens and twenties.

• The influence of the environment on a person's behavioral characteristics, expressed here in terms of Ebx (Ebmo and Ebip), is greatest during the first years of life (0 to 6 years).

Figure 8.4 indicates the relationship described and illustrates, in a general way, how the factors Emi, Emps, Ebmo, and Ebip are influenced by age and the type of environmental exposure.

Although qualitative in character, the relationships shown in Figure 8.4 illustrate the relative importance of environmental experiences to effective mental capability. As is apparent in Equation 8.1, environmental experiences represented by Emi,

Emps, and Ebx (Ebmo and Ebip) can exert dominating influences. They, in fact, determine how well an individual can use the brain capacities symbolized by IQ, PSQ, and BSQ.

Figure 8.4 shows that each of the environmental factors may vary between the extremes of 0 and 1.0. Each is essentially zero at birth, but they increase with age and environmental experiences and approach a value of 1.0 under the most favorable conditions. Under the least favorable conditions they may approach a value significantly less than 1.0. The most likely values are logically those that fall in between. Environmental factor values are, of course, subject to wide variations. Yet for each person at a particular age the factors are essentially fixed quantities.

EFFECTIVE MENTAL CAPABILITY

Effective mental capability, as defined here, is expressed by Equation 8.1 in terms of brain capacity factors and environmental factors.

The brain capacity factors are represented by numerical quantities whose values correspond to a person's IQ, PSQ, and BSQ. The mean value of each factor is 100 for the population as a whole, but each varies widely among individuals, as shown in Figure 5.4.

The environmental factors, unlike the brain capacity factors, are represented by relative quantities. Their values, varying between 0 and 1.0, depend upon the quality and duration of the environmental exposures for any particular person. Defined in this manner, the environmental factors (Emi, Emps, and Ebx) may be regarded as coefficients to the brain capacity factors (IQ, PSQ, and BSQ). Thus, Equation 8.1 may be restated so that each factor is a "composite," including the combined influence of inherited brain capacity and environmental experience. It would thus read:

Effective mental capability

$$= f\left[(IQ \times Emi)(PSQ \times Emps)(BSQ \times Ebx)\right] \quad (8.2)$$

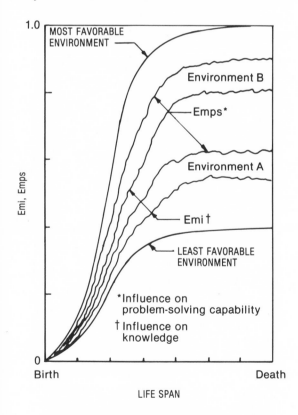

(a) The influence of environment and age on mental capability

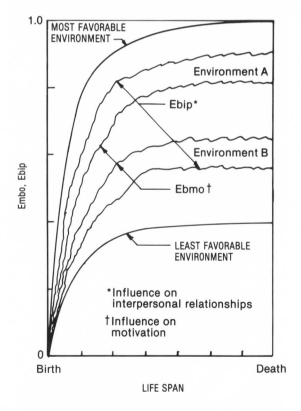

(b) The influence of environment and age on behavioral characteristics

Figure 8.4 Influence of environment and age on environmental factors

where

IQ × Emi represents knowledge, dependent on inherited brain capacity (IQ, or memory capacity) and the information provided from the environment.

PSQ × Emps represents problem-solving capability, dependent on inherited brain capacity (PSQ, or problem-solving capacity) and the problem-solving skills or procedures acquired from environment.

BSQ × Ebx represents behavioral characteristics, dependent on inherited brain capacity (BSQ, or emotion-sensor sensitivity) and the influence of the environment on motivation and interpersonal relationships.

This equation, like Equation 8.1, has no quantitative significance. But it does indicate what is needed for quantitative evaluation: The terms representing knowledge, problem-solving capability, and behavioral characteristics must be defined in quantitative and consistent units, and the relative influence of the three capabilities must be established.

None of the above three terms can be quantitatively determined at present, nor can their relative influence on effective mental capability be precisely defined. There is considerable understanding of the variables that make up these composite factors, however, and this understanding provides a fundamental basis for estimating the value of each composite factor.

Unfortunately, there is no way to fundamentally examine the relative influences of knowledge, problem-solving capability, and behavioral characteristics on effective mental capability. But the information available gives adequate bases for reasonable postulations. In Equation 8.2, for example, qualitatively consider the influence on the different capabilities. Knowledge is absolutely essential; little can be done without it. Problem-solving capability is important; success in life often depends upon how well a person is able to solve problems as they arise. Behavioral characteristics are clearly crucial, because personal achievements are closely associated with a person's behavioral qualities, as reflected by motivation and interpersonal relationships.

Each of the above mental qualities is obviously important. But there is no basis for claiming one to be more or less influential than the other. To the contrary, any of the three qualities may dominate, even among persons of eminence. For example:

The eminence of John Quincy Adams, the sixth president of the United States, must be attributed primarily to the vast quantities of information (knowledge) he was able to accumulate and use. (His IQ was estimated at 165.) He was not a successful planner or problem-solver, as indicated by his inability to get programs passed by Congress. He was not a popular president, and he was decisively defeated in his campaign for a second term.

Thomas Edison unquestionably gained eminence from his creative ability (problem-solving capability). He certainly was not an intellectual with vast knowledge. His personal relationships with contemporaries were never highly favorable; he had few close friends.

George Washington's eminence obviously stemmed primarily from his ability to work with and influence people (behavioral characteristics). He was not an intellectual. He apparently possessed considerable problem-solving capability, but even this can be considered as only a secondary contributor to his eminence.

From the information currently available, it is therefore reasonable to consider that the relative influence of each of the three mental qualities on effective mental capability is essentially the same.

If, in fact, each of the composite factors in Equation 8.2 exerts an influence proportional to its value, the product of the three terms is an acceptable way to define their combined influence. This product (which is usually a six- or seven-digit number) is too cumbersome for practical use as an expression of effective mental capability. It is therefore convenient to express the relationship (and, hence, effective mental capability) in terms of a cube root of the product and state the relationship as follows:

Effective mental capability

$$= \sqrt[3]{(IQ \times Emi)(PSQ \times Emps)(BSQ \times Ebx)} \quad (8.3)$$

or stated in more literal terms,

Effective mental capability

$$= \sqrt[3]{knowledge \times \frac{problem\text{-}solving}{capability} \times \frac{behavioral}{characteristics}}$$

$$(1.1)$$

The significance of these two equations is readily apparent. In summary form, they identify the factors and show the relationships that exist among a person's mental qualities. In so doing, they provide a basis for determining a person's effective mental capability—a measure of what an individual is mentally able and willing to do at any particular time in life.

SUBSTANTIATING OBSERVATIONS

Effective mental capability is unquestionably the human being's most valuable asset. Despite its importance, however, concerted attempts at measuring it have met with little success.

Probably the first significant effort directed toward quantitatively defining mental capability was that of the French psychologist, Alfred Binet. His interest was in defining an objective method for determining how French public school classes could be best structured to accommodate both fast-and slow-learning pupils. The experiment was successful to some degree. The first battery of IQ tests came from his work.

More extensive and elaborate psychological and IQ tests for measuring human intelligence and abilities have been developed since then. These methods are used extensively by both industries and universities as a basis for selecting employees and students. Although useful, these methods cannot be regarded as highly successful. Their principal value is a statistical one. That is, a group of persons selected on the basis of high IQ do better school work on the average than those selected on a random basis. IQ tests can give very misleading results, however. For example, many individuals who score high on IQ tests do very poorly both in school and on the job. At the same time, many individuals who score low on IQ tests do well in school and on the job.

Therefore, IQ is obviously not a viable measure of effective mental capability. This conclusion is completely consistent with the unified concept, which includes IQ (memory capacity) as only one of the elements responsible for effective mental capability.

The inadequacy of IQ as a measure of effective mental capability is generally recognized by experts in the field, and many studies and observations contribute to this conclusion. Even so, good documentation of results is sparse. Studies of the subject typically provide carefully determined IQ scores, but they seldom include a satisfactory measurement of an individual's accomplishments or success in life. Hence, useful comparisons between IQ and success are essentially nonexistent. One exception to this observation is the work by Dr. Catharine Morris Cox,§ in which the relative eminence and IQ of 300 geniuses were reported. These results, plus observation of other unique characteristics of geniuses, indicate that factors other than IQ certainly influence what a person accomplishes in life.

DOCUMENTED STUDIES OF GENIUSES

The study of geniuses directed by Dr. Cox was conducted as follows:

Two hundred and eighty-two geniuses that lived between the years 1450 and 1850 were selected for the study and ranked according to relative eminence. Rank was established according to the space allotted to each in selected biographical dictionaries and encyclopedias. The final selection excluded eminent persons who were members of royalty and those for whom evaluation information was insufficient.

Estimates of IQ were independently made by three educators proficient in the field of psychological testing, and the results were averaged. The estimates included all the information that could be collected on each individual, and covered two periods of each subject's life: from birth to 17 years and from 17 to 26 years of age.

Summary of Data

The significant results from this study of geniuses have been summarized and included in Figures 8.5 through 8.7 and in Table 8.1. Fifteen of the geniuses ranked as the most eminent are listed in Figure 8.5, along with early- and later-life IQ estimates and the vocation in which each achieved eminence. Figure 8.6 is a list of geniuses who span the range of eminence. This list consists of geniuses whose rank of eminence falls at intervals of 25, interspersed with others considered to be of special interest.

The spread of estimated early-life IQ among

§Catharine M. Cox, *The Early Mental Traits of Three Hundred Geniuses,* vol. 2, *Genetic Studies of Genius,* 5 vols. (Stanford: Stanford University Press, 1926).

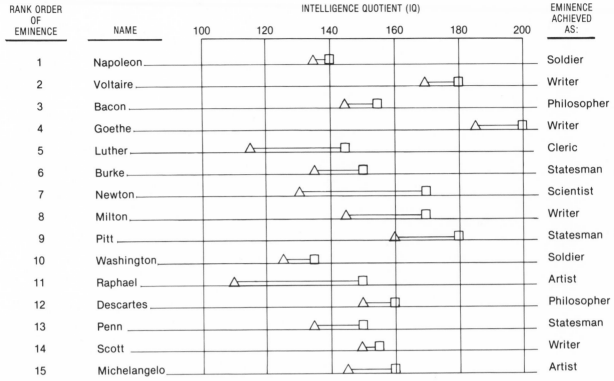

RANK ORDER OF EMINENCE	NAME	INTELLIGENCE QUOTIENT (IQ)	EMINENCE ACHIEVED AS:
1	Napoleon		Soldier
2	Voltaire		Writer
3	Bacon		Philosopher
4	Goethe		Writer
5	Luther		Cleric
6	Burke		Statesman
7	Newton		Scientist
8	Milton		Writer
9	Pitt		Statesman
10	Washington		Soldier
11	Raphael		Artist
12	Descartes		Philosopher
13	Penn		Statesman
14	Scott		Writer
15	Michelangelo		Artist

Estimated IQ based on achievements during two periods of life:

△   Birth to 17 years of age
□   17 to 26 years of age

From Catharine M. Cox, *The Early Mental Traits of Three Hundred Geniuses,* vol. 2, *Genetic Studies of Genius,* 5 vols. (Stanford: Stanford University Press, 1926), table 12A.

Figure 8.5 The estimated IQ of 15 eminent geniuses

the 282 eminent geniuses studied by Dr. Cox ranged from 100 to 190. The distribution is shown in Figure 8.7.

In general, there is an appreciable difference between the IQ estimated for the two periods of each subject's life. These figures differ more in some vocations than others. The variations are shown in Table 8.1.

Interpretation and Analysis of Data

Superficially, the results from the study of geniuses present a very confusing picture. The lack of correlation between IQ and relative eminence is pronounced. The variations in estimated early- and later-life IQs are appreciable, and the suggested reason for this variation is not adequately substantiated.

The results become more meaningful, however, when viewed in light of the unified concept.

They are consistent with the various postulated brain functions and processes, and they provide a supporting base for the unified concept, as well as for the associated concept of effective mental capability.

IQ AND EMINENCE CORRELATION

The lack of a meaningful and useful correlation between eminence and IQ is readily apparent from Figures 8.5 and 8.6. This is as would be expected, however, since IQ is only one of the factors influencing effective mental capability (or eminence).

EARLY- AND LATER-LIFE IQ ESTIMATES

The variations between the estimated early-life and later-life IQs of the geniuses are appreciable. In most cases, the later-life IQ estimate is the greater of the two (one exception is John S. Mill,

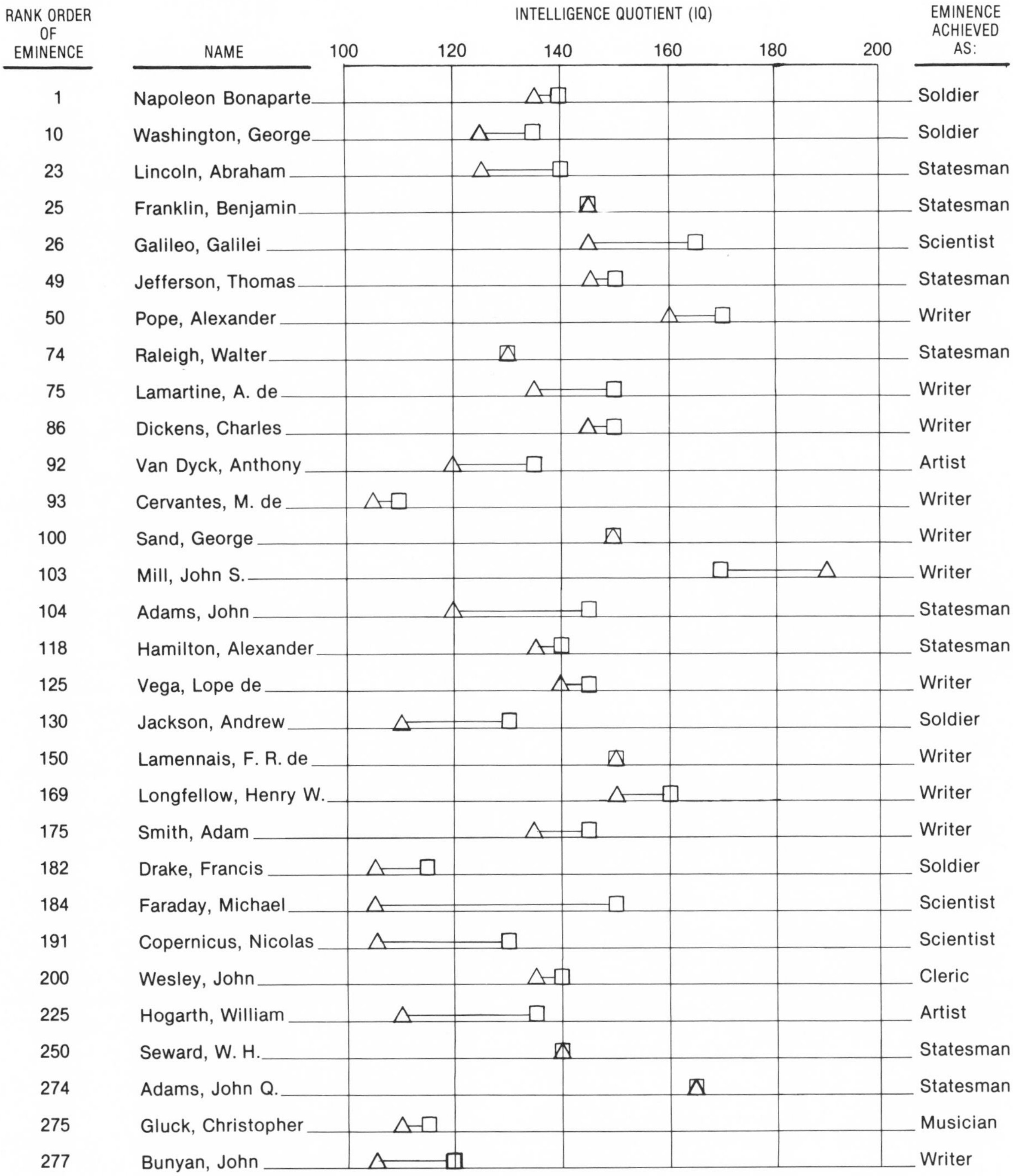

INTELLIGENCE QUOTIENT (IQ)

RANK ORDER OF EMINENCE	NAME	EMINENCE ACHIEVED AS:
1	Napoleon Bonaparte	Soldier
10	Washington, George	Soldier
23	Lincoln, Abraham	Statesman
25	Franklin, Benjamin	Statesman
26	Galileo, Galilei	Scientist
49	Jefferson, Thomas	Statesman
50	Pope, Alexander	Writer
74	Raleigh, Walter	Statesman
75	Lamartine, A. de	Writer
86	Dickens, Charles	Writer
92	Van Dyck, Anthony	Artist
93	Cervantes, M. de	Writer
100	Sand, George	Writer
103	Mill, John S.	Writer
104	Adams, John	Statesman
118	Hamilton, Alexander	Statesman
125	Vega, Lope de	Writer
130	Jackson, Andrew	Soldier
150	Lamennais, F. R. de	Writer
169	Longfellow, Henry W.	Writer
175	Smith, Adam	Writer
182	Drake, Francis	Soldier
184	Faraday, Michael	Scientist
191	Copernicus, Nicolas	Scientist
200	Wesley, John	Cleric
225	Hogarth, William	Artist
250	Seward, W. H.	Statesman
274	Adams, John Q.	Statesman
275	Gluck, Christopher	Musician
277	Bunyan, John	Writer

IQ scale gridlines: 100, 120, 140, 160, 180, 200

Estimated IQ based on achievements during two periods of life:

△ Birth to 17 years of age

□ 17 to 26 years of age

From Catharine M. Cox, *The Early Mental Traits of Three Hundred Geniuses*, vol. 2, *Genetic Studies of Genius*, 5 vols. (Stanford: Stanford University Press, 1926), table 12A.

Figure 8.6 The estimated IQ of selected geniuses

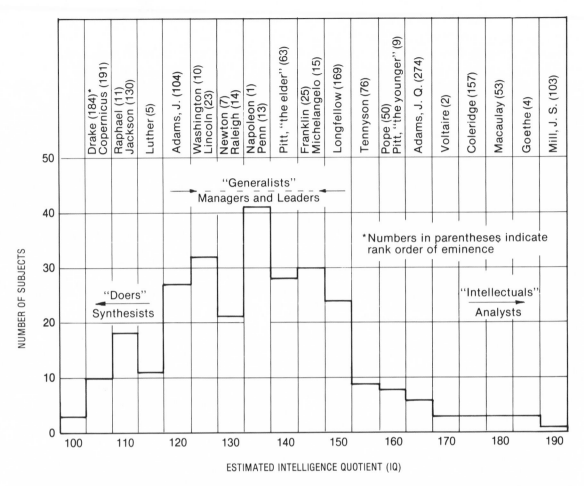

From Catharine M. Cox, *The Early Mental Traits of Three Hundred Geniuses,* vol. 2, *Genetic Studies of Genius,* 5 vols. (Stanford: Stanford University Press, 1926), table 12A.

Figure 8.7   IQ distribution of 282 geniuses

see Figure 8.6). The investigators attributed these differences to insufficient data for early-life evaluations. This explanation is, at best, lacking in rigor considering the number of subjects involved over the 400-year time period. Perhaps a more acceptable explanation involves the interpretation of the information used in evaluating IQ for each of the two life periods. More specifically, the information needed for estimating IQ from personal achievements is better defined for children than adults, and experience in making such estimates is much greater. It follows, therefore, that IQ estimates from early life should be the more accurate.

One reason why early-life achievements may be more closely associated with IQ than later-life achievements is indicated by the unified concept. Brain processes during early life are primarily those associated with storing information, according to this concept. Problem-solving capability becomes a significant factor in effective mental capability only after adequate information is stored in the memory area. The rate and, hence, the quantity of information stored before a specific age depends upon IQ. Thus, early-life accomplishments can be generally attributed to IQ, or learning rate. That is, such accomplishments as learning several languages, reading Plato, and learning mathematics at early ages indicate the presence of IQ, but little more.

From these observations it is concluded that

the early-age estimates of IQ may represent reasonable assessments of ability to receive, store, and recall information. It may also be concluded that the later-age IQ estimates are too high, because they include accomplishments which in many cases stem from problem-solving capacity and from the opportunity to make use of favorable behavioral qualities.

The information summarized in Table 8.1 lends credence to these suppositions. Note the differences between the early- and late-life IQ estimated as a function of vocational groups. There is essentially no change between the average of the two IQ levels for artists, revolutionary statesmen, writers, and philosophers. But there are considerable differences in the estimates for soldiers, musicians, religious leaders, statesmen, and scientists.

Several pertinent observable characteristics are associated with subjects in the first four groups on the list. These include rapid learning capacity, high level of communication ability, little problem-solving capacity, and inexact or nonrigorous work results. Also, accomplishments in these fields generally depend upon memory capacity, or IQ. Hence, accomplishments evaluated at both early- and later-ages should provide a good indication of IQ.

The recognized characteristics associated with subjects in the last five groups listed in Table 8.1, however, are considerably different. Rapid learning is not essential, considerable problem-solving effort is involved, and work results must be exact or rigorous to be useful. Hence, in these groups, accomplishments appear to depend greatly upon problem-solving capacity and emotion-sensor sensitivity (behavioral qualities), the influence of which appears later in life than does IQ.

EMINENCE AND EFFECTIVE MENTAL CAPABILITY

Eminence as determined in the work reported above is admittedly not precise. Yet it provides a relative measure of individual accomplishments with which few would disagree. Defined in this way, eminence corresponds directly with effective mental capability. In view of this correspondence, the following equation appears appropriate:

Eminence level = effective mental capability

$$= \sqrt[3]{(IQ \times Emi)(PSQ \times Emps)(BSQ \times Ebx)}$$

Despite its lack of rigor, this equation serves to enhance comprehension and the meaning of eminence and effective mental capability. The equation indicates why there is no meaningful relationship between IQ and eminence. Five independent variables other than IQ are involved: two other basic brain capacity factors and three environmental factors.

Table 8.1 Variations in estimated IQ of geniuses between early and later life, according to groups

GROUP	AVERAGES OF ESTIMATED INTELLIGENCE QUOTIENTS (IQ)		
	Ages: 0–17	Ages: 17–26	Average differences
Artists	120–135	120–135	0
Revolutionary Statesmen	140–155	140–155	0
Writers	140–155	140–155	0
Philosophers	140–155	140–155	0
Soldiers	110–115	120–125	10
Musicians	120–135	140–155	20
Religious Leaders	120–135	140–155	20
Statesmen	120–135	140–155	20
Scientists	120–135	140–155	20

From Catharine M. Cox, *The Early Mental Traits of Three Hundred Geniuses*, vol. 2, *Genetic Studies of Genius,* 5 vols. (Stanford:Stanford University Press, 1926), figure 3.

The specific influence of these other five variables is, of course, unknown. However, considering the accomplishments of the geniuses involved, we must assume that the environmental experiences represented by the three environmental factors were in most cases relatively favorable. This being so, only two variables, PSQ and BSQ, must account for the lack of correlation between IQ and eminence. That this conclusion is reasonable can be supported by analyses and observations.

For purpose of analysis, consider three of the most eminent men: namely, Napoleon, Voltaire, and Luther, who are ranked 1, 2, and 5, respectively, in the Cox study (see Figure 8.5). First, within the accuracy with which eminence can be determined, these men must be considered to be equally eminent. Second, a review of their life histories shows that each had excellent education opportunities and generally favorable life environments. The environmental effects are considered to be functionally equivalent, therefore. Furthermore, since their eminence is based on a lifetime of accomplishments, it is appropriate to assume that in each instance the environmental factors approach unity. Under these conditions, the equation which represents the eminence level of the three geniuses can be written as follows:

Eminence level

$$= \sqrt[3]{IQ \times PSQ \times BSQ}$$

when each of the environmental factors (Emi, Emps, and Ebx) approaches a value of 1.0.

From Figure 8.5, the IQ levels of the three geniuses are as follows: Luther, 115; Napoleon, 135; and Voltaire, 170. Since each of the geniuses is assumed to have reached about the same level of eminence, considerable variations in PSQ and BSQ are implied by the equation relationships. This implication is supported by recorded information about the three men. The important personal characteristics of each, which are indicators of IQ, PSQ, and BSQ, are summarized in Table 8.2.

Considering—as previously assumed—that all environmental factors were favorable, one can make the following pertinent observations:

o Napoleon's eminence stemmed from a well-balanced combination of memory capacity, problem-solving capacity, and emotion-sensor sensitivity.

o Voltaire's eminence resulted primarily from memory capacity, or IQ. The low ranking of his historical writing indicates lack of problem-

Table 8.2 Observed personal characteristics which relate IQ, PSQ, and BSQ

BRAIN CAPACITY FACTORS	NAPOLEON	VOLTAIRE	LUTHER
IQ (Memory capacity)	Intelligent, but not brilliant Special aptitude in mathematics and history	Prolific, brilliant, and witty writer of poems, drama, philosophy, etc.	Well educated, but not brilliant
PSQ (Problem-solving capacity)	Brilliant military strategist and proficient at complex maneuvers	Best writings are philosophy, drama, poems, etc. that do not require exactness Historical writing, where accuracy is important, ranked low by critics	"The Ninety-Five Theses," directed against the Catholic Church initiated the Protestant Reformation
BSQ (Emotion-sensor sensitivity)	Persistent in carrying out decisions Adored and respected by his men	Quarreled frequently with noblemen and associates Had no close followers	Most popular professor at the University of Wittenberg Strongly supported by students

solving capacity—that is, the ability to comprehend accurately and to put complex issues into perspective. His frequent quarrels with others and lack of close followers imply unfavorable emotion-sensor sensitivity.

○ Luther's eminence evidently stemmed from his emotion-sensor sensitivity and his influence over others. However, his comprehension of the social and religious issues of his time and his action in preparing "The Ninety-Five Theses" reflects considerable problem-solving capacity. In any case, these latter two characteristics overshadow his memory capacity, or IQ.

The influence of the various personal characteristics can be more fully appreciated if viewed in terms of the relationships indicated in the eminence equation. For example, assume that the IQ, PSQ, and BSQ characteristics possessed by Napoleon were balanced, or equal, as indicated above. Since his IQ was estimated at 135, the equation yields

Eminence level

$$= \sqrt[3]{135 \times 135 \times 135} = 135$$

Thus the eminence of Napoleon, as well as that of Luther and Voltaire, is represented by the value 135. Since the eminence of all three men is considered to be the same, the equation can be restated as follows:

Eminence level

$$= \sqrt[3]{IQ \times PSQ \times BSQ} = 135$$

Therefore, when IQ levels are known, the combined effects of PSQ and BSQ can be assessed. If for simplicity it is assumed that the latter two factors are equal, the resulting values for each of the men are as follows:

Brain capacity factors

	Napoleon	*Voltaire*	*Luther*
IQ	135	170	115
PSQ	135	120*	146*
BSQ	135	120*	146*

---

*Assumed to be equal (statistically the most probable).

These values are in general agreement with the observable characteristics of the three men identified in Table 8.2. As such they add support to, and indicate the usefulness of, Equation 8.3:

Effective mental capability

$$= \sqrt[3]{(IQ \times Emi)(PSQ \times Emps)(BSQ \times Ebx)}$$

Only three of the top-ranking geniuses were considered in the above analysis and interpretation. The general applicability of the results, however, is further supported by a general review of the 25 geniuses identified in Figure 8.7.

Note that in this figure, high IQ levels are associated primarily with philosophers and writers (also called "intellectuals" and "analysts"), whose work deals mainly with abstractions. This kind of effort requires extensive knowledge and, therefore, high IQ. But problem-solving capability and favorable behavioral characteristics are not essential. These qualities do not generally exist among "intellectuals." Men included in this category are Mill, Goethe, Macaulay, and Voltaire.

At the lower end of the IQ spectrum are the creative geniuses (also called "doers" and "synthesists"). Their work is characterized by identifiable and useful results. Success requires proficiency at problem-solving, either technical or political. Memory capacity is important, of course, but in this instance it plays a tertiary role. Geniuses in this category include Drake, Copernicus, Raphael, Jackson, and Luther.

At the midpoint of the IQ spectrum are the "generalists," the true leaders and managers. These are the individuals with nearly equal mental qualities: knowledge (related to IQ), problem-solving capability (related to PSQ) and behavioral characteristics (related to BSQ). The geniuses in this category include Penn, Pitt "the elder," Washington, Lincoln, and Napoleon (see Figure 8.7).

GENERAL OBSERVATIONS ABOUT EMINENT PERSONS

The observation that success does not depend upon IQ alone, as illustrated by the concept of effective mental capability, is not a new revelation. The fact that many individuals of eminence did poorly in school (sometimes an indication of low IQ) is well known. For example, the following list of school failures compiled by the British pediatrician Ronald S. Illingworth was published in the May/June 1975 issue of *Learning: The Magazine for Creative Teaching*. (Pitman Learning, Inc., 19 Davis Drive, Belmont, CA 94002).

Poor spellers:	Yeats, Shaw
Poor mathematicians:	Franklin, Picasso, Adler, Jung
Expelled from school:	Einstein, Dali, Poe, Shaw, Shelley, Osler, Paderewski, Röntgen, Whistler
Bottom of class:	Edison
Dreamer:	Gauguin
"Dull and inept":	Watt
"Idiot":	Rodin
Mentally slow:	Einstein
Shows no promise:	Lincoln, Henry Ford, Faraday

PART 3

PERSONNEL SELECTION

There is something that is much more scarce, something finer far, something rarer than ability. It is the ability to recognize ability.

ELBERT HUBBARD

Men are not to be judged by their looks, habits and appearance; but by the character of their lives and conversation, and by their works.

L'ESTRANGE

Personnel selection is in concept a very simple process, involving three basic steps: first, determining the human mental qualities required for performing the job at hand; second, estimating the mental qualities of selected candidates; and third, selecting the candidate whose mental qualities best match those required for the job.

A framework for defining a person's human mental qualities is provided in the preceding chapters. The problem is that there are currently no definitive methods for measuring human mental qualities or for defining job requirements in terms suitable for effecting the comparison and selection process.

The character of human mental qualities, however, has been defined and the variables that influence each have been identified. Thus, by using selected information about a particular person, it is possible to estimate the level of his or her knowledge, problem-solving capability, and behavioral characteristics. It is also possible to define the requirement for any particular job in terms of the same mental qualities. How the value of these mental qualities can be determined and used in the personnel selection process is the subject of the following chapters.

Chapter 9, "Job Requirements," presents a simple and unique approach to stating job requirements in terms of human mental qualities.

In Chapter 10, "Estimating Procedures," methods for estimating quantitative values for a person's mental qualities are presented and illustrated.

Chapter 11, "Information Collection," identifies the information needed in estimating values for a person's mental qualities. It also defines the formats, techniques, and procedures best suited for use in collecting the information required.

In Chapter 12, "The Personnel Selection Process," the factors and special considerations involved in making final personnel selections are identified and discussed.

9

Job Requirements

It is surprising that so few people recognize the seemingly obvious fact that intelligent [personnel] selection is predicated on the knowledge of what to look for in an applicant.

RICHARD A. FEAR

Defining the human mental qualities required for success in a particular job is the first and perhaps the most crucial step in selecting personnel. It is also difficult and, therefore, often neglected.

The most common approach to defining job requirements is the so-called job description, which attempts to define in detail the functions to be performed. A job description is useful, of course, and it certainly affords a good starting point. But its value is limited when the jobs involved are those requiring higher levels of effective mental capability. This situation arises because specific task requirements for these types of jobs change so rapidly that detailed job descriptions quickly become obsolete.

A more fundamental approach is needed, and the concept of effective mental capability provides a framework for such an approach. To use this approach one needs only to define the following:

1. Specific vocation
2. Required level of effective mental capability
3. Required distribution of human mental qualities (or composite factors) that con-

stitute effective mental capability

Definition of item 1, specific vocation, depends upon the product or service supplied by the organization. Naming the vocation inherently establishes whether the need is for, as examples, an aerodynamicist, a nuclear physicist, or a nurse. Items 2 and 3 require special considerations. Item 2 depends upon the general complexity of the job to be performed. Item 3 is more specific. It requires that the needed levels of knowledge, problem-solving capability, and behavioral characteristics be defined in quantitative terms.

EFFECTIVE MENTAL CAPABILITY

Since the level of effective mental capability needed to perform successfully in a particular type of job or activity is directly related to its complexity, it is convenient to identify the requirements in these terms. Accordingly, seven job categories covering a broad spectrum of complexities and capability requirements have been defined and designated as follows: (1) basic study and research, (2) applied research and development, (3) professional service, (4) semiprofessional service, (5) skilled work, (6) semiskilled work, and (7) routine work.

JOB CATEGORIES

The job categories identified herein generally correspond to those widely used by others. The difference is that emphasis is placed on the type of effort involved rather than on the specific vocation.

Basic Study and Research

Basic study and research, as defined here, refers to the effort directed toward exploring and investigating the unknown. Success in this type of work requires the highest level of effective mental capability. Persons in this category are those capable of achieving international eminence or near-eminence. They include scientists, writers, philosophers, statesmen, soldiers, or others who contribute valuable new ideas, concepts, philosophies, discoveries, and inventions.

Applied Research and Development

Applied research and development refers to activities directed toward the discovery, development, and practical use of new ideas, concepts, philosophies, etc., including those stemming from basic study and research. Success in this category requires a very high level of effective mental capability, though this level is somewhat lower than that needed for basic study and research.

Professional Service

Professional service consists of that effort exercised in providing service in highly technical areas such as law, physics, medicine, and engineering. This category requires no new concepts, discoveries, or developments. Instead, it involves applying and using known technology and techniques. It requires an effective mental capability only slightly below that required for successful applied research and development work.

Semiprofessional Service

Semiprofessional service refers to that specialized service which directly supports the functions of those engaged in professional service. Pharmacists, draftsmen, secretaries, stenographers, and bookkeepers are included in this category. This service requires an effective mental capability significantly above average, but below that required for professional service.

Skilled Work

Skilled work involves that effort requiring the use of highly developed procedural techniques which are established by others. An effective mental capability well above average is required for learning and applying these procedures.

Semiskilled Work

Semiskilled work consists of those tasks requiring nominal skill. It can be done by persons possessing an average level of effective mental capability.

Routine Work

Routine work requires no significant or specific skill. It involves routine procedures that are often repeated in the process of completing a task. A less-than-average level of effective mental capability is needed for success in this type work.

REQUIREMENTS FOR EACH JOB CATEGORY

Attempts to define the level of effective mental capability or the overall mental capability for a particular job have, in the past, met with little success. The reason is fundamental: the techniques and procedures for defining and assessing a person's effective mental capability are simply inadequate.

Experience shows that psychological test scores have only limited value as indicators of effective mental capability. In a general way, however, these tests do provide statistically significant results.

Both the limitations and significance of psychological test results are apparent from Table 9.1. The wide range of scores applicable to each of the vocations listed shows clearly why psychological test results provide an inadequate measure of a person's effective mental capability. The overlap in scores between vocations is too great to provide any meaningful selection criteria. On the other hand, the mean IQ scores appear to vary systematically according to the recognized complexity of the vocation.

The difficulties which arise in analyzing these data stem from the fact that the accomplishments of individuals within any one of the vocational groups are not defined. They could conceivably vary according to psychological test scores. Experience indicates, however, that such is not necessarily the case. For example, Chapter 8 concluded that there is little correlation between a person's IQ score and life accomplishments, and the IQ scores of certain eminent geniuses were shown to vary between 100 and 190.

Also in Chapter 8, the effective mental capability of Napoleon (ranked as the most eminent of the geniuses in the study) was placed at a level of 135. Since this value represents the highest level of eminence, the effective mental capability of the other eminent persons should be correspondingly lower. This condition is in fact implied by definition. However, since the accomplishments of each of the geniuses was adequate to effect the ranking of eminent, the differences in their effective mental capabilities must be regarded as relatively small. Accordingly, it is reasonable to assume that the effective mental capability levels of the emi-

nent geniuses studied approach the same level: approximately 135.

In conjunction with the level of effective mental capability assigned to eminent geniuses, one observation is very significant and useful. As is shown in Table 9.1, this value (135) is the same as the mean IQ value for all the geniuses involved.

This result is not a coincidence. Instead, as indicated below, it represents a fundamental relationship. As such, it provides the basis for establishing the effective mental capability level associated with the various vocations and specified job categories. In the case of the 282 geniuses (see Chapter 8), whose environmental exposures were assumed to be the most favorable possible in a career, Equation 8.3 reduces to

Effective mental capability

$$= \sqrt[3]{IQ \times PSQ \times BSQ} = 135$$

Obviously, there are infinite combinations of IQ, PSQ, and BSQ which can produce the effective mental capability of 135; the range of variation of

Table 9.1 IQ scores for various vocational groups

VOCATIONAL GROUPS	RANGE OF IQ SCORES	MEAN VALUE OF IQ SCORES
Eminent geniuses*	100-190*	135*
Professionals		
Civilian professionals	—	132‡
Army draftees (engineers, lawyers, accountants)	97-143†	122†
Semiprofessionals		
Pharmacists, bookkeepers	76-146†	116†
Skilled workers		
Electricians, machinists	51-142†	108†
Slightly skilled workers		
Welders, auto mechanics	58-141†	101†
Unskilled workers		
Laborers, lumberjacks	40-136†	96†

*From Catharine M. Cox, *The Early Mental Traits of Three Hundred Geniuses*, vol. 2, *Genetic Studies of Genius*, 5 vols. (Stanford: Stanford University Press, 1926), table 12A.

†From T. W. and M. S. Harrell, "Army General Classification Test Scores for Civilian Occupations," *Educational and Psychological Measurements*, 5 (1945) 229-239. (IQ values converted to Stanford-Binet IQ scales, standard deviation of 16).

‡From Donald M. Johnson, "Application of the Standard-Score IQ To Social Statistics." *The Journal of Social Psychology*, 27 (1948) 217-227.

each is limited, however. Figure 8.7 shows the range of IQ variation for the 282 geniuses, and it also shows that the variation is approximately normal about the value of 135. No such information is available for PSQ and BSQ. Because of the similarity in the physiological characteristics of the brain elements represented by IQ, PSQ, and BSQ, it is reasonable, however, to postulate that PSQ and BSQ have mean values and distribution characteristics identical to those of IQ (see Figure 8.3). Thus, for the specific conditions identified above, the mean values of IQ, PSQ, and BSQ are postulated to be essentially equal, at a value of 135.

The above conditions are unique because the influence of the environment has been assumed to be ideal. When it is not ideal (as is usually the case), the effective mental capability level of those individuals performing successfully in any particular job category no longer corresponds to the mean IQ value of that population. For example, if the mean IQ, PSQ, and BSQ values of the group are equal but the environmental exposures are less than the most favorable, the mean IQ (and PSQ and BSQ) value will be greater than the effective mental capability of the group. But, even then, the mean IQ value provides useful information. It identifies the *potential* effective mental capability

of the group: the capability level that the group can attain through additional and appropriate environmental exposure of members.

The use of the mean IQ value as the *potential* effective mental capability of the members is not always appropriate. Its use is applicable only when there is assurance that the mean values of PSQ and BSQ are equal to the mean IQ value. For instance, the procedure is not applicable where group members were initially selected on the basis of IQ *only*—independent of effective mental capability. The distribution of IQ about its mean value may or may not be normal under these circumstances, but on a statistical basis, the mean value of PSQ and BSQ would certainly not be equal to the mean value of IQ.

Nevertheless, in most large groups representing a particular vocation in which the members are functioning satisfactorily, it is reasonable to assume normal distributions and equal mean values for IQ, PSQ, and BSQ. A summary of the available data regarding the IQ of various vocational groups is presented in Table 9.1. In addition, Figure 9.1 shows the distribution of IQ scores of three vocational groups. These data provide the basis for establishing the levels of effective mental capability needed for successful performance in each of the vocations identified.

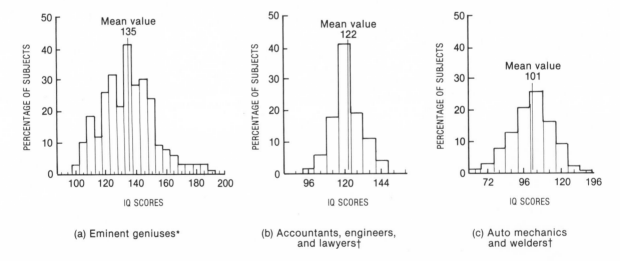

(a) Eminent geniuses*

(b) Accountants, engineers, and lawyers†

(c) Auto mechanics and welders†

*From Catharine M. Cox, *The Early Mental Traits of Three Hundred Geniuses,* vol. 2, *Genetic Studies of Genius,* 5 vols. (Stanford: Stanford University Press, 1926), table 12A.

†From T. W. and M. S. Harrell, "Army General Classification Test Scores for Civilian Occupations," *Educational and Psychological Measurements,* 5 (1945) 229-239. (IQ values converted to Stanford-Binet IQ scales, standard deviation of 16).

Figure 9.1   Distribution of IQ scores for different vocational groups

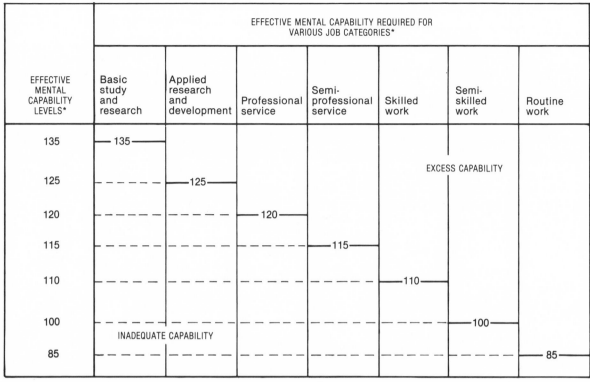

*Effective mental capability = $\sqrt[3]{(IQ \times Emi)(PSQ \times Emps)(BSQ \times Ebx)}$

Figure 9.2 Effective mental capability required for various job categories

Utilizing all the considerations discussed above and the effective mental capability levels associated with each of the vocations identified in Table 9.1, one can approximate the effective mental capability required for each of the job categories defined earlier. These values are presented in Figure 9.2

DISTRIBUTION OF HUMAN MENTAL QUALITIES

The level of effective mental capability required to do a job is an essential part of any job definition; but it is not sufficient. The required distribution of human mental qualities must also be defined. Equation 8.3, restated as follows indicates why:

Effective mental capability

$$= \sqrt[3]{(IQ \times Emi)(PSQ \times Emps)(BSQ \times Ebx)}$$

(8.3)

where

IQ × Emi represents knowledge

PSQ × Emps represents problem-solving capability

BSQ × Ebx represents behavioral characteristics

It is clear from this relationship that numerous combinations of these human mental qualities can provide a particular level of effective mental capability. It is equally clear that the specific functions a person is best suited to perform—that is, analysis, synthesis, supervision, or management —depend upon which of the human mental qualities are dominant. Accordingly, an acceptable job requirement must identify the desired human mental qualities.

A suitable way to state this requirement is in terms of the functional specialists required—that is, analysts, synthesists, supervisors, or managers—where the most favorable attributes of each of these specialists are as defined below:

Analysts

- Large quantities of applicable knowledge
- Capacity to acquire additional knowledge at a rapid rate
- Ability to analyze available knowledge using known procedures

Synthesists

- Capacity to interpret the meaning of knowledge and observations in a logical and useful manner
- Ability to develop new and innovative concepts needed for complex problem-solving when no procedures exist

Supervisors

- A high sensitivity to human wants and needs
- An understanding of human mental qualities (knowledge, problem-solving capability, and behavioral characteristics)

Managers

- A near-equal distribution of human mental qualities

Table 9.2 Functional specialists and dominating human mental qualities

Functional Specialist	Dominating human mental qualities		
	Knowledge ($IQ \times Emi$)	Problem-solving capability ($PSQ \times Emps$)	Behavioral characteristics ($BSQ \times Ebx$)
Analyst	×		
Synthesist		×	
Supervisor			×
Analyst/ Synthesist	×	×	
Supervisor/ Analyst	×		×
Supervisor/ Synthesist		×	×
Manager	×	×	×

Within a population there are, of course, many individuals who can perform more than one functional specialty. This is because the distribution of human mental qualities is such that two of these qualities are often dominant; that is, two are frequently greater than the nominal, or average, of the three. Thus, a job requirement may call for a person who is able to perform in one or more

Table 9.3 Typical distribution of human mental qualities among functional specialists within a group whose effective mental capability is 135

FUNCTIONAL SPECIALISTS	HUMAN MENTAL QUALITIES		
	Knowledge $IQ \times Emi$	Problem-solving capability $PSQ \times Emps$	Behavioral characteristics $BSQ \times Ebx$
Manager	135	135	135
Analyst	170 140	115 133	126 132
Synthesist	115 132	170 140	126 133
Supervisor	126 133	115 132	170 140
Supervisor/ Analyst	140 138 155	126 115 115	140 155 138
Supervisor/ Synthesist	126 115 115	140 138 155	140 155 138
Analyst/ Synthesist	140 138 155	140 155 138	126 115 115

functional specialty areas. The various functional specialists and the dominating human mental qualities associated with each are identified in Table 9.2.

Table 9.3 shows typical composite factor values (mental qualities) associated with each of the functional specialists at an effective mental capability of 135.

STATEMENT OF JOB REQUIREMENTS

The job requirements, or personnel needs, can be very simply stated once they are established. For example, if the need is for an aerodynamicist (performance) to work as a synthesist in an applied research and development organization, the job requirements may be stated as follows:

Vocation: Aerodynamicist (performance)
Job category: Applied research and development (effective mental capability = 125)
Functional specialist: Synthesist
                                        or optionally

Knowledge $(IQ \times Emi)$	$= 122$
Problem-solving capability $(PSQ \times Emps)$	$= 135$
Behavioral characteristics $(BSQ \times Ebx)$	$= 120$

10

Estimating Procedures

It is a fine thing to have ability, but the ability to discover ability in others is the true test.

ELBERT HUBBARD

The yardstick for measuring men is other men.

ANONYMOUS

Chapter 8 defines a framework for estimating a person's overall capability, or effective mental capability, in terms of three human mental qualities; that is,

Effective mental capability

$$= \sqrt[3]{(IQ \times Emi)(PSQ \times Emps)(BSQ \times Ebx)} \quad (8.3)$$

Within this framework, the estimating process resolves itself into one of estimating quantitative values for a person's knowledge, problem-solving capability, and behavioral characteristics in terms of three brain capacity factors and three environmental factors.

As established previously, the three brain capacities—represented by IQ, PSQ, and BSQ—are essentially fixed genetically and are subject to little change during a person's life span. The environmental factors—Emi, Emps, and Ebx—are, on the other hand, in a continuous state of change. Hence, the composite factors—$IQ \times Emi$,

$PSQ \times Emps$, and $BSQ \times Ebx$—(and, therefore, a person's effective mental capability) are also continuously changing.

The qualitative influence of environmental changes on the composite factors can be easily identified. The values of these factors vary from near zero at birth to some maximum value in later life, with the upper limits imposed by inherited brain capacities and the quality of the environmental exposures. The influence of the environment on the composite factors is very great in early life (see Figure 8.4). In later life, however, this influence diminishes considerably and the composite factors approach their maximum values.

Establishing quantitative values for the composite factors is significantly more challenging. Very complex relationships are involved, since each factor is influenced by both inherited characteristics and environmental exposures. There are elegant techniques for measuring IQ, a component of the composite factor that represents knowledge. So-called achievement tests have also been developed for measuring a person's knowledge of specific subjects. Similar techniques can presumably be developed for measuring other brain capacity factors, environmental factors, and composite factors. However, numerical values for these factors can only be estimated at the present time. Just how accurately each can be estimated has not been determined, but indications are favorable. By studying selected works of a child, for example, educators who are authorities in psychological testing can make a reasonable estimate of the child's IQ (see Chapter 8). Using similar techniques, educators can also approximate a person's relative knowledge of a particular subject.

In view of these observations and the nature of the variables involved, it is logical to assume that, with appropriate information, each of the composite factors in Equation 8.3 can be estimated with reasonable confidence. The information sources deemed to be the most useful in estimating values for the various factors in Equation 8.3 are identified in Figure 10.1. It lists the various sources and indicates, with rectangular boxes, the factor each information source helps to define. Each source provides information that can be interpreted in terms of one or more of the brain capacity, environmental, or composite factors. The variables involved are numerous, however, and the basic information is largely qualitative. Hence, the estimating process is essentially one of converting qualitative information into quantitative factor values.

By definition, those factors making up effective mental capability represent quantitative terms whose numerical values are expressed in relation to a fixed reference base: the population as a whole. Accordingly, estimating values for the various factors requires interpreting qualitative information and relating it to this reference base. The character of the various factors and the conditions corresponding to the reference base of each are defined and discussed below.

Brain capacity factors (IQ, PSQ, and BSQ) represent quantitative terms that define a person's brain capacities in relation to others in the population, where the mean value of each factor is 100 and the standard deviation is 16.

Environmental factors (Emi, Emps, and Ebx) represent quantitative terms that define the relative influence of environmental exposures on human mental qualities, where the reference base for each factor is the most desirable environmental exposure possible.

Composite factors (IQ $\times$ Emi, PSQ $\times$ Emps, and BSQ $\times$ Ebx) represent numerical quantities that define a person's knowledge, problem-solving capability, and behavioral characteristics in relation to others in the population. The reference base for each factor is the most desirable human actions or the highest level of accomplishments possible within the population.

Each of the selected sources in Figure 10.1 provides information that is useful in assessing one or more of the various factors. Only one factor (IQ) can be determined with any degree of precision, however. The other factors can be estimated, but the task is not simple. Different types of factors are involved, and applicable information available for evaluating purposes is both unique and qualitative. The estimating process, therefore, requires careful analysis and interpretation of the available data plus considerable insight and judgment by the evaluator.

Procedures for determining values for each factor have been established to assure both the greatest possible estimating accuracy and consistency between evaluators. These procedures obviously involve numerous assumptions, many of which are very logical and easily justified; yet some are highly judgmental. Procedures based on such assumptions are of course lacking in rigor, but they are nevertheless useful for several reasons:

• They provide for a logical and systematic approach to estimating numerical values for those factors that determine human mental qualities.

• They assure maximum accuracy in estimating the values of the different factors by allowing necessary assumptions and information interpretations to be made at the most fundamental level where understanding is greatest.

• They permit more accurate estimates of human mental qualities and, therefore, effective mental capability than is possible with any other known method.

These procedures allow many of the factors to be estimated using information from several independent sources. For a number of reasons, the estimated factor values will not always agree. For

SELECTED INFORMATION SOURCES	BRAIN CAPACITY FACTORS			ENVIRONMENTAL FACTORS				COMPOSITE FACTORS			
						Ebx				BSQ x Ebx	
	IQ	PSQ	BSQ	Emi or Emi-e*	Emps	Ebmo	Ebip	IQ x Emi	PSQ x Emps	BSQ x Ebmo	BSQ x Ebip
Early Family-Life Experiences											
Stability							□				
Social and economic status				□		□					
Religion							□				
Discipline and work						□					
Extracurricular Activities											
Organization and group activities										□	
Individual activities and hobbies					□				□		
Written communications					□				□		
Education Programs											
Psychological tests	□										
High school	□			□				□		□	
College	□			□				□			
Advanced study	□										
Work Experiences											
Analyst				□				□	□		
Synthesist					□				□		
Supervisor										□	□
Observed Personal Qualities											
Knowledge								□			
Problem-solving capability									□		
Behavioral characteristics										□	

*See Figure 10.4

Figure 10.1 Selected information sources and the factors they help to define

example, certain procedures are inherently more accurate than others. Also, the accuracy of the information available from the different sources is subject to wide variation. Even so, each assessed value is often useful in the evaluation process. But in the final analysis, the most valid factor values depend upon the accuracy of the particular procedure used and the adequacy of the information available.

The specific procedures established for estimating the various factor values are presented in the following paragraphs, which illustrate the estimating process, define the assumptions, and discuss the bases for each assumption.

BRAIN CAPACITY FACTORS

As stated previously, IQ is the only one of the three brain capacity factors that can be measured.

The Stanford-Binet intelligence test is the most widely used method for measuring IQ. In this method, the reference base is established at 100, which is the projected mean score of all persons in the population.

There are many other techniques for measuring a person's "intelligence." In fact, those tests generally designated as psychological tests are, in reality, intelligence tests. Perhaps the best known of these are the Scholastic Aptitude Test (SAT) and the American College Testing Program (ACT), which were developed to aid colleges in selecting their students from graduating high school seniors.

Both the SAT and ACT scores represent measures of intelligence, but they differ from IQ in two important ways. First, the mean score used as a reference base is that of college-bound high school seniors (not that of the entire population). Second, each method uses a unique quantitative scale of measurement. To be useful in evaluating a person's effective mental capability, therefore, the SAT or ACT score must be converted to an equivalent IQ score. The relationships that permit such a conversion are presented in Figure 10.2. These relationships were derived using information obtained from the following sources:

- Stanford-Binet IQ test standardization norms, as updated in 1972
- Correlation between the combined SAT (verbal plus math) scores and composite ACT scores based on results from several colleges which use both testing programs
- SAT scores determined in a national high school testing administered to high school juniors in October 1974
- National average SAT scores for college-bound high school seniors (1975-1976) (the 1974-1975 junior class)
- National high school enrollment and composition of classes for the year of 1974-1975*

Since IQ is a statistical factor, there is no theoretical limit to its value. Of the 282 geniuses reported in Chapter 8, however, only one was estimated to have an IQ as high as 190 on the Stanford-Binet intelligence scale, and only five were estimated to have an IQ of 180 or above. On this scale, an IQ of 180 corresponds to five standard deviations (five sigma), a level associated with less than three individuals in 10 million.

*Data from the United States Department of Health, Education, and Welfare, Education Division, National Center for Education Statistics, *Digest of Education Statistics,* 1979, pp. 14, 15, 47, and 64.

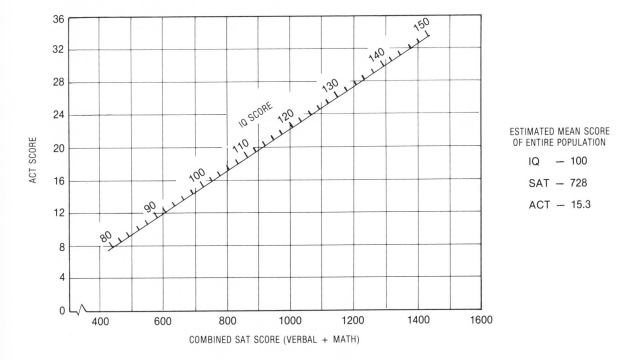

ESTIMATED MEAN SCORE
OF ENTIRE POPULATION

IQ   — 100

SAT — 728

ACT — 15.3

Figure 10.2 Approximate relationships of SAT, ACT, and IQ scores

Thus, in a realistic sense, an IQ of 180 (a standard deviation of five sigma) may be reasonably established as a practical maximum value.

Although there are currently no techniques for measuring the brain capacity factors PSQ and BSQ, they are postulated to exhibit characteristics similar to those of IQ. Figure 10.3 shows the postulated distribution of these factors within the population.

ENVIRONMENTAL FACTORS

None of the factors (Emi, Emps, and Ebx) representing the influence of the environment on a person's knowledge, problem-solving capability, and behavioral characteristics can be systematically measured. Nevertheless, each factor can be estimated using information from selected sources and a suitable evaluation procedure.

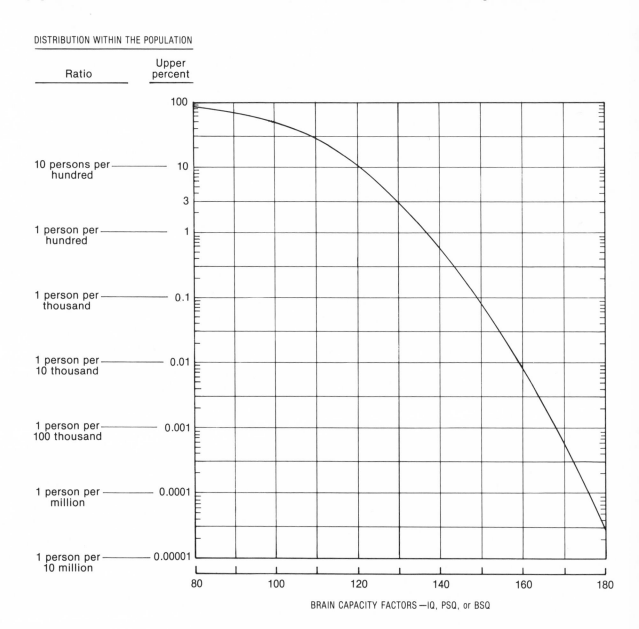

Figure 10.3 Distribution of brain capacity factors

By definition, environmental factors represent the quality of environmental exposures in terms of their influence on a person's knowledge, problem-solving capability, and behavioral characteristics. When an exposure provides the most favorable influence possible, its quality is represented by an environmental factor of unity (Emi, or Emps, or Ebx = 1.0). Those experiences that supply less influential exposures are, of course, represented by correspondingly lower environmental factor values.

The procedures established for estimating environmental factor values involve two basic steps: First, the conditions that represent the most favorable environment possible—for each environment factor—are identified for each of the selected information sources (Figure 10.1). Second, information from the selected sources is used to estimate environmental factor values by comparing the observed conditions with the most favorable environment possible. Thus, the evaluation process becomes one of interpreting the quality of a person's environmental exposures relative to the most favorable possible and then defining the results in numerical values.

Emi (INFLUENCE OF THE ENVIRONMENT ON KNOWLEDGE)

The environmental exposures that have the greatest influence on a person's knowledge are those associated with early family-life experiences, education programs, and work experiences.

Early Family-Life Experiences

The social and economic environment in which a child is reared has a pronounced effect on the knowledge he or she acquires during childhood. And it often has a lifelong influence.

In early life, the child acquires knowledge from exposure to family members and friends, as well as from exposure to diverse experiences both inside and outside the home. Knowledge is acquired almost subconsciously during this period, and in later life this knowledge is manifested in a person's vocabulary, speech, writing, and general information about such subjects as the arts, science, and geography.

Thus, children growing up in the most affluent families begin life with a decided advantage, whereas those growing up in poverty have a corresponding disadvantage. Of course, most common childhood environments are somewhere in between these two extremes.

The influence of early-life experiences on a person's knowledge is well recognized by authorities, but it cannot be easily quantified. Moreover, its ultimate effect depends a great deal on the environmental experiences that follow. For example, the influence of a person's childhood environment, favorable or unfavorable, is reduced or negated by attending schools that provide highly favorable environments for acquiring knowledge.

Because of the close interrelationships between early-life experiences and subsequent education programs, it is advantageous to consider both simultaneously. Techniques for assessing both these influences are included in the following section on education programs.

Education Programs

Formal education programs, by design, present favorable environments for acquiring knowledge. Just how favorable, of course, depends upon the duration of school exposure and school quality (where *quality* refers to the capacity to supply knowledge).

The duration of exposure to education programs generally depends upon the level of work completed, with the doctoral program at an accredited university representing the most favorable environment. Programs directed toward lesser degrees are proportionally less favorable, depending upon their duration.

The quality of a school is more difficult to assess. Many factors are involved. The most obvious are faculty, facilities, economics, and social conditions. Unfortunately, the specific influences of these factors are much too complex to be interpreted in terms of school quality. But there is a more basic and useful way to view school quality: the average intelligence level of the students attending. Intelligence level, as used here, refers to the qualities measured by any of the following:

• Intellegence Quotient (IQ) score
• Scholastic Aptitude Test (SAT) score
• American College Training Program (ACT) score

The basis for defining school quality in this manner is apparent. Parents with high intelligence levels generally appreciate the value of education and, therefore, make special effort to provide the best possible resources—faculty and facilities—for their children's elementary and high school education. With respect to colleges, those with the greatest economic resources usually establish the highest intelligence requirements, and students with the highest SAT and ACT scores tend to select these colleges. Thus, in general, if not universally, the average SAT or ACT scores of the students in a school reflect its quality (defined as capacity to supply knowledge).

Considering the factors discussed above, one can establish relationships and approximations that permit a consistent and relative assessment of a school's influence on the acquisition of knowledge. The variables involved and the relationships presumed to represent the influence of school duration and quality are shown in Figure 10.4.

SCHOOL DURATION

The relationships used to express the influence of exposure duration are based primarily on the formal education programs completed. The duration associated with each is as follows:

- Elementary school: 8 years
- High school diploma: 4 additional years
- Bachelor's degree: 4 additional years
- Master's degree: 1 additional year
- Doctor's degree: 2 to 3 additional years (nominal, not actual, requirement)

Accordingly, exposure to a formal education program which ends in completing a doctor's degree is considered to represent the most favorable duration.

Education, of course, does not end with a college degree. Yet the specific professional knowledge a person acquires by the time of graduation represents a significant portion of what he or she will acquire during a career. Here the doctoral program is considered to represent 85 percent of the most favorable exposure possible, relative to career duration. According to the time spent in each, other school programs are estimated to be proportionately less influential. The environmental factors, designated as Emi-sd and estimated to correspond to the duration of different education programs, are presented in Figure 10.4a.

SCHOOL QUALITY

The relationships developed to aid in assessing school quality are based on the large quantities of information available from both the SAT and ACT programs.

Essentially every American college has for many years required student scores from either the SAT or ACT program as a prerequisite for admission. Therefore, one of these scores is usually available for most every college student and recent graduate. From these, it is possible to define the average SAT or ACT scores of students from almost any high school or college and, hence, to establish the relative quality of their schools.

The quality of American colleges—as indicated by the average combined SAT or the composite ACT scores of the freshman classes—covers a wide spectrum. According to the results reported in *Peterson's Annual Guide to Undergraduate Study 1979,*[†] the combined average SAT scores of freshman classes entering college ranged from about 600 to slightly more than 1400. These scores, according to Figure 10.2, correspond to IQ values of 92 and 148, respectively.

The relationship that exists between the average IQ (or SAT) score and the environmental quality (designated by the factor Emi-sq) of a class is not at all clear. However, the coordinates of two unique points in the relationship can be defined: Emi-sq is 1.0 for a class whose average IQ score is 180 (established as the maximum IQ score); and Emi-sq is 0.50 for a class whose average IQ score is 100 (mean value for the population). The shape of the curve connecting these two points is, of course, unknown. But it can be approximated through careful consideration of the variables involved.

By definition, the relative quality of a particular school environment, as represented by Emi-sq, is applicable to all members of the population. In other words, it is assumed that any student attending a school with an average environment (class-average IQ score of 100) will be exposed to half (Emi-sq = 0.50) of the information he or she would be exposed to in a class with an average IQ score of 180 (Emi-sq = 1.0).

There are, however, very few students with the basic brain capacity to take full advantage of a

†Published by Peterson's Guide, Princeton, New Jersey

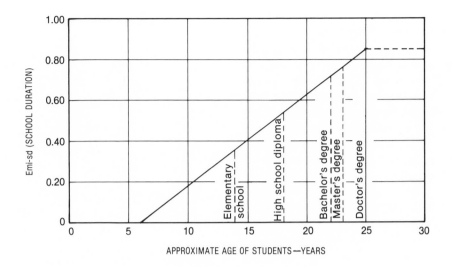

(a) Influence of school duration

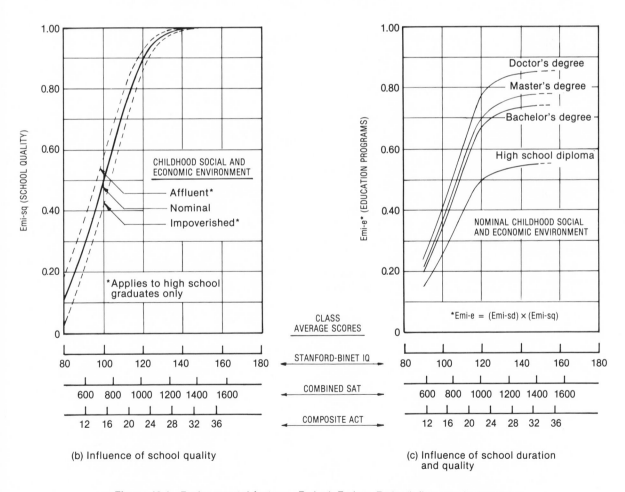

(b) Influence of school quality

(c) Influence of school duration and quality

Figure 10.4 Environmental factors—Emi-sd, Emi-sq, Emi-e (influence of education)

class environment in which the class-average IQ score approaches 180. Indeed, as far as the average student is concerned, there is probably no discernible difference in obtainable information between two classes whose IQ scores are 180 and 150. In both classes, so much more information is available than the average student can absorb that the Emi-sq value of each may be regarded as essentially 1.0. In fact, the percentage of students that can benefit by attending such high-quality schools is extremely small, since less than one person per thousand has an IQ above 150 (see Figure 10.3). Thus, for the highest-quality schools, it is apparent that a difference of 30 points (180 minus 150) in class-average IQ scores has little influence on environmental quality—as quality relates to the entire population.

Yet, at the lower levels of school quality, a 30-point difference in class-average IQ score can have a significant influence on the value of the environmental factor Emi-sq. For example, an average student attending a class whose average IQ score is 130 can be expected to acquire considerably more information than would be possible if the class-average IQ scores were only 100 (average for the population). Hence, the Emi-sq value that represents a class with an average IQ score of 130 is estimated to be much greater than the value for a class whose average IQ score is 100 (Emi-sq = 0.5).

These observations are obviously inadequate for defining precise relationships, but they are useful. One identifies two points on the curve of relationships; the other indicates the general shape of the curve. The curve noted as nominal in Figure 10.4b satisfies these conditions. It has the same characteristics as does the IQ (or PSQ or BSQ) distribution curve shown in Figure 10.3. The difference is that Figure 10.4b is the complement of Figure 10.3. That is, Emi-sq is numerically equal to 1 minus the IQ distribution, where distribution is identified in terms of the upper percentage of the population. Table 10.1 presents some of the most pertinent points in the approximated relationship.

As defined here, Emi-sq refers to the quality of a school a particular student has attended, but it includes no consideration for the quality of the environment the student experienced in earlier childhood. These experiences, like formal schooling, also provide a source of knowledge. Indeed, they

Table 10.1 Class average IQ and school quality

Class average (IQ)	Estimated school quality (Emi-sq)	IQ distribution* (upper percent)
180	1.0 (0.9999 +)	0.00003
148	1.0 (0.9987 +)	0.11
135	0.99	1.0
125	0.95	5.0
115	0.83	17.0
100	0.50	50.0
80	0.11	89.0

*The percentage of the population with an IQ equal to or above the class IQ average indicated (see Figure 10.3).

may be regarded as an informal form of education. It is convenient, therefore, to view the influence of early-life experiences on environmental quality as an increment (Δ Emi-sq) to the environmental factor Emi-sq.

There is, of course, no precise method for determining the value of the increment Δ Emi-sq. But it is related to the social and economic environment to which a child is exposed. The most favorable social and economic environment (highly affluent) affords a child with the best possible opportunity to acquire knowledge and is, therefore, represented by the largest possible environmental factor increment (Δ Emi-sq).

The existence of the increment Δ Emi-sq is most clearly manifested by the knowledge a child possesses when he or she begins formal schooling. And present observations indicate that the difference in the knowledge possessed by children exposed to the most favorable environment and those exposed to an average environment can be equated to as much as 2 years of formal education. By the same reasoning, the influence of the most unfavorable social and economic environment (impoverished) can be expected to produce the opposite effect. The magnitude of such an influence can be estimated from Figure 10.4a, where 2 years of schooling corresponds to a change in the environmental factor Emi-sq of about 0.08 and, therefore, an equivalent change in Emi-sq.

The practical usefulness of this observation depends upon the ability of the evaluator to identify a person's childhood environment—affluent, impoverished, or somewhere in between—and assess its influence in terms of Δ Emi-sq. Figure 10.5 identifies the relationships needed for such an assessment. It is based on the following assumptions:

• A highly affluent family is one whose income is in the upper 5 percent of the population.

• An impoverished family is one whose income is in the lower 12 to 22 percent of the population (22 percent before 1960, 12 percent after 1960).

• A highly affluent family provides the most favorable environment for acquiring knowledge; and, in terms of Emi-sq, it is represented by a value 0.08 greater than the nominal or average.

• An impoverished family affords the least favorable childhood environment for acquiring knowledge; and, in terms of Emi-sq, it is represented by a value 0.08 below the average.

• The relationship between family income and changes in Emi-sq from the nominal value is represented by a continuous function, as shown in Figure 10.5, Chart A.

The influence of a child's early family-life environment on his or her knowledge tends to remain throughout life. The extent of this influence ostensibly depends upon the quality and duration of subsequent environmental exposures. Formal education programs are particularly influential. For example, if the environment provided by formal education programs is only average, the influence of childhood environment can be expected to persist for a lifetime. Yet, if education programs are the most favorable possible, the early influence of childhood environment may be all but negated. The dashed curves in Figure 10.4b (identified as highly affluent and impoverished) illustrate how school quality is postulated to influence the environmental factor Emi-sq. Figure 10.5 Chart B, shows the relationships established for estimating the influence of school quality on Emi-sq for any type of childhood environment.

SCHOOL DURATION AND QUALITY

The combined influence of school duration and quality (Emi-e), defined as the product of the environmental factors Emi-sd and Emi-sq, is shown in Figure 10.4c. This figure includes estimates for four levels of education, but is directly applicable only to the situation where early-life environments are defined as nominal.

Another procedure is used for a childhood en-

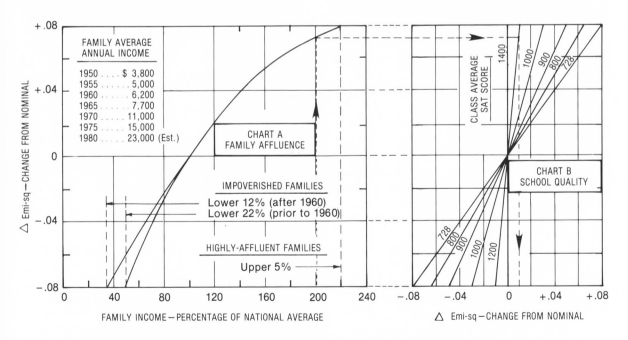

Note: Average family income, income distribution, and percentage of families living in poverty taken from U. S. Department of Commerce, Bureau of the Census, *Statistical Abstract of the United States: National Data Book and Guide to Sources,* 100th Edition, 1979, tables 741 and 758.

Figure 10.5 Estimated influence of family affluence and school quality on the environmental factor Emi-sq

vironment other than nominal. In this case Emi-e is estimated by using Figure 10.4a to determine Emi-sd, Figure 10.4b to determine the nominal value of Emi-sq, and Figure 10.5 to adjust the nominal Emi-sq value for the influence of early-life environment. The following example illustrates the procedure:

Information
• College work completed by individual: master's degree
• College class average SAT score: 1200
• Family income during childhood: 200 percent of the national average (determined from salary information or estimated from occupation)

Estimate
• From Figure 10.4a, a master's degree corresponds to an Emi-sd of 0.76.
• From Figure 10.4b, a college class-average SAT score of 1200 corresponds to a nominal Emi-sq of 0.97.

• From Figure 10.5, Charts A and B, a family income during childhood of 200 percent and a college class-average SAT score of 1200 results in a Emi-sq from the nominal of +0.01 (see path indicated by arrows).
• From Figure 10.4b and Figure 10.5, the total environmental factor Emi-sq is 0.98 (0.97 + 0.01).
• From the product of Emi-sd (0.76) and Emi-sq (0.98), Emi-e = 0.74.

The information required for these estimating procedures normally exists and can be obtained. The level of schoolwork completed is, of course, easily established, the family income during the child's early life can be either determined or estimated, and class average SAT or ACT scores can be obtained directly from colleges. High school class average SAT or ACT scores, however, are not normally available. These scores exist only for college-bound seniors. Thus, class averages can only be estimated. Figure 10.6 pro-

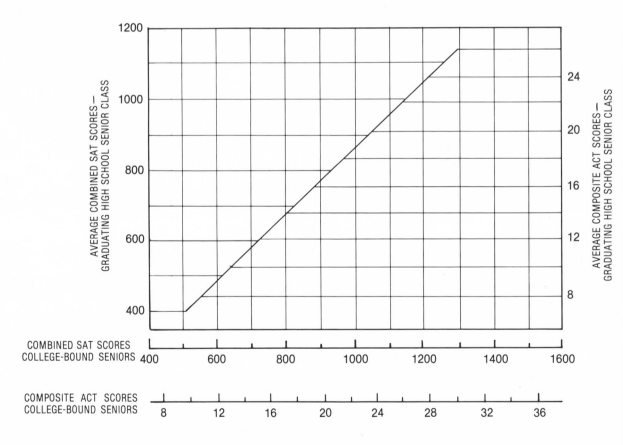

Figure 10.6 Average SAT and ACT scores for high school graduating classes and college-bound seniors

vides the relationship necessary to estimate class averages when only college-bound senior SAT and ACT scores are known. This curve was analytically derived from the following assumptions: The average SAT score of college-bound seniors is approximately 890, and SAT scores (and IQ scores) of seniors in most high school classes are normally distributed.

Work Experiences

The work environment that requires analytical effort provides the most favorable conditions for acquiring professional knowledge. And like education, the influence of the environment depends upon its quality and duration.

For assessment purposes, the quality of the working environment is best indicated by the effective mental capability of those working in that particular environment. In terms of job categories, the most favorable environmental quality (and therefore the reference base) is the one where members are performing basic study and research work. The environments associated with other job categories identified in Figure 9.2 are correspondingly less favorable.

The period of time over which an individual acquires knowledge extends throughout life, with rare exceptions. With respect to a particular profession, however, the knowledge an individual can acquire from education and work experiences may approach a maximum level in a reasonably short life-span. But in each case, the number of years of work experience required to provide the most favorable level of environmental exposure relative to a particular specialty depends primarily upon the school and work environments.

From the relationships postulated and summarized in Figure 10.4c, the most favorable environment possible for knowledge acquisition—through formal schooling—constitutes 85 percent of the most favorable environment possible during a career. This condition (Emi-e = 0.85) is attained by the completion of a doctor's degree at a school where the average SAT or ACT scores of the classes are approximately 1400 or 33, respectively. Just how long it takes under these circumstances to acquire the additional exposure required to reach the most favorable level in a particular specialty area is not at all obvious. However, experience indicates that when an in-

dividual who has completed a doctoral program at a high-quality school is exposed to a high-quality environment (basic study and research) for 10 years or so, the knowledge that can be acquired in that particular technical specialty approaches a maximum.

From this conclusion, other reasonable relationships can be developed. If it is assumed that the quality of a working environment relates to the average IQ of a group (job category) in the same way school quality relates to class average IQ, the relationships in Table 10.2 can be stated.

Table 10.2   Job category and quality of the work environment (Emi-w)

Job category	Effective mental capability	Mean IQ	Estimated Emi-w*
Basic study and research	135	135	0.99
Applied research and development	125	125	0.95
Professional service	120	120	0.89
Semiprofessional service	115	115	0.83
Skilled work	110	110	0.74
Semiskilled work	100	100	0.50
Routine work	85	85	0.18

* Emi-w: environmental factor related to work environment

With these observations, plus the assumption that the relationships among the different variables are linear, one can write the equations

$$YRS = \frac{1 - Emi\text{-}e}{1 - 0.85} \times \frac{0.99}{Emi\text{-}w} \times 10$$

$$= (1 - Emi\text{-}e) \times \frac{66}{Emi\text{-}w} \qquad (10.1)$$

$$Emi = Emi\text{-}e + \frac{Emi\text{-}w}{66} \times years \qquad (10.2)$$

where the terms are as defined below:

YRS represents the number of years of work experience necessary to approach the most favorable environmental exposure for acquiring knowledge (Emi = 1.0).

Emi-e is the environmental factor resulting from exposure to education programs.

Emi is the environmental factor which represents the level of favorable exposure resulting from education programs plus any number of years of work experiences (cannot exceed a value of 1.0).

1 − Emi-e represents the change in the environmental factor through work experiences needed to approach the most favorable level of 1.0.

1 − 0.85 is the change in environmental factor from the most favorable level possible from school exposure to the most favorable level possible from work experience.

0.99 is the environmental factor assigned to the most favorable possible environment (job category designated as basic study and research—see Table 10.2).

Emi-w is the environmental factor associated with the environment of any particular job category (see Table 10.2).

Years is the number of years an individual has worked in the subject work group (job category).

Emps (INFLUENCE OF THE ENVIRONMENT ON PROBLEM-SOLVING CAPABILITY

The information most useful in estimating a person's problem-solving capability is provided by the following three information sources: extracurricular activities, education programs, and work experiences. All are helpful in assessing the environmental factor Emps, but in each case the information provided is highly qualitative.

Extracurricular Activities

Many extracurricular activities help develop problem-solving skills. Individual activities and hobbies which require defining and resolving unique problems provide favorable problem-solving experiences. Extracurricular writing is also beneficial. Since it involves creating something new, writing is a very fundamental form of problem-solving. Hence, writing of any nature provides experiences that are favorable to developing problem-solving skills.

Whether an extracurricular activity is favorable or unfavorable for developing problem-solving skills is most clearly manifested in the creative contributions made by the participants. When these contributions are recognized and widely acclaimed, a favorable environment along with a correspondingly favorable environmental factor (Emps) is indicated; when recognition is lacking, an unfavorable environment and Emps result.

Clearly, the extent to which creative activity groups contribute to developing a person's problem-solving skills is best indicated by the recognition accorded their members. The significance of recognition in terms of environmental factors (Emps), however, depends to a large degree upon the number of persons represented by the recognizing body. That is, what divisions of society does the body encompass? Does it represent the world, nation, state, county, city, school, or other division of society? In this context, an extracurricular activity group whose members receive worldwide acclaim is regarded as representing the most favorable environment possible, with a corresponding environmental factor (Emps) of 1.0. The Emps values associated with other divisions of society are not so easily established. For one thing, the acclaim awarded a person by one city does not necessarily represent the same level of recognition as does the same acclaim awarded by another city. There are, of course, many reasons for this difference, but population is the most apparent. In other words, acclaim awarded by larger cities usually represents greater recognition, simply because the competition for recognition is generally greater.

There is, however, no precise relationship between the Emps value representing a level of recognition and the population of the recognizing body. Certainly the relationship is not linear. For example, the Emps values associated with worldwide recognition and recognition by New York City do not differ by the ratio of their population (approximately 250). In fact, the ratio between the most favorable environmental factor value (Emps = 1.0) and the average value (Emps = 0.5) is only 2.0. Thus, the relationship

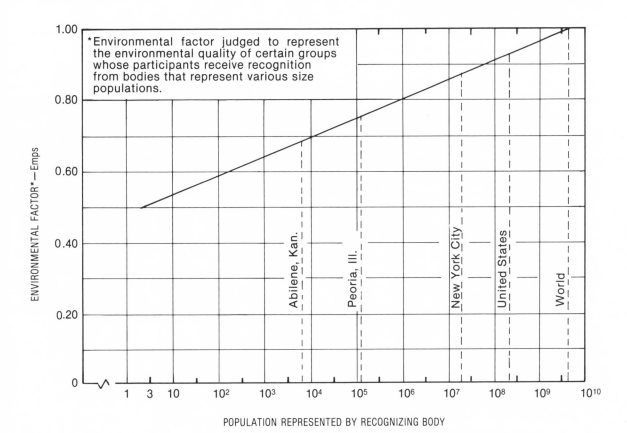

Figure 10.7 Enviromental factor—Emps

between Emps and the population of a recognizing body is complex and highly nonlinear. Even so, a reasonable approximation of the relationship can be made from the information available. The following assumptions and considerations provide the basis for such an approximation:

○ Creative activity groups whose members regularly receive worldwide recognition from a body representing about 4.7 billion persons provide the best possible environments for developing problem-solving skills and are, therefore, accorded an environmental factor (Emps) value of 1.0.

○ Creative activity groups whose members receive recognition by a body representing two persons‡ are presumed to provide average en-

vironments for developing problem-solving skills and a corresponding environmental factor (Emps) of 0.50.

○ Creative activity groups whose members receive recognition from bodies representing other levels of population can be represented by environmental factor (Emps) values that vary exponentially (between 0.50 and 1.0) with the population encompassed by the recognizing body.

Based on the above, the postulated relationships between Emps and the size of the population represented by the recognizing body are presented in Figure 10.7.

Education Programs

Generally speaking, formal education programs are directed toward supplying knowledge, and they contribute little toward developing

‡As can be seen from Figure 10.7 it makes little difference in the relationship whether the Emps value of 0.50 is associated with 2 or 10 persons.

problem-solving capability. One exception is the work associated with the research effort and thesis preparation usually required for advanced college degrees. When the research is original and involves creative problem-solving, the environment is favorable for developing problem-solving skills. Just how favorable such an environment is, however, cannot be directly assessed. But again, as with extracurricular activity groups, it is convenient to relate environmental quality (and the associated Emps value) of a college research organization to the level of recognition its members receive from others. Accordingly, Figure 10.7 may be used for estimating the environmental factor (Emps) value representing the research group of any particular college.

Work Experiences

The most favorable work environment is provided by organizations that are engaged in basic study and research. The effective mental capability of successful participants in this type of organization is 135, and the mean or average PSQ (as well as IQ and BSQ) is the same value, 135 (see Chapter 9). In other words, the most favorable work environment for developing problem-solving skills is an environment in which the average PSQ of the members is 135.

A group whose IQ average is 135 was earlier established as being represented by an environ-

mental factor (Emi) of 0.99. Because of the inherent similarities between IQ and PSQ, the same relationships are presumed to exist between Emps and the average PSQ of group members. Hence, the Emps value associated with the different work organizations or job categories difined in Chapter 9 can be stated as listed in Table 10.3.

Note that the duration of exposure to the different work organizations has not been considered in establishing the environmental factor Emps. This is not entirely valid. However, the time needed for an individual to acquire those problem-solving skills used by members of the organization is relatively short, unlike that required to acquire professional knowledge. Generally, 5 years or so is completely adequate. The quality of the exposure is much more important than duration when the duration exceeds 5 years.

Ebx (INFLUENCE OF THE ENVIRONMENT ON BEHAVIORAL CHARACTERISTICS)

The environmental exposures associated with early-life experiences exert an extremely strong influence on an individual's behavioral characteristics. Indeed, these experiences dominate the environmental factors Ebmo (motivation) and Ebip (interpersonal relationships) that determine Ebx.

Ebmo (Influence of the Environment on Motivation)

Two of the experiences identified in the selected information sources are useful in estimating the environmental factor Ebmo: economic and social status of the family, and the discipline and work imposed by the child's parents.

Exposure in early life to a low-level social and economic environment is known to exert a favorable influence on human motivation. The most favorable environment for motivation is, therefore, the one referred to as poverty. Accordingly, the environmental factor (Ebmo) associated with other childhood exposures are related inversely to the social and economic conditions experienced. The Ebmo values suggested as representative of three different levels of social and economic experiences are listed in Table 10.4.

A childhood environment in which work and discipline are emphasized represents a favorable

Table 10.3 Job category and quality of the work environment (Emps)

Job category*	Effective mental capability	Mean PSQ	Estimated Emps
Basic study and research	135	135	0.99
Applied research and development	125	125	0.95
Professional service	120	120	0.89
Semiprofessional service	115	115	0.83
Skilled work	110	110	0.74
Semiskilled work	100	100	0.50
Routine work	85	85	0.18

*See Figure 9.2

Table 10.4 Influence of early-life social and economic environment on motivation (Ebmo)

Relative social and economic status	Income levels	Suggested Ebmo values
Low	Poverty	1.0
Nominal	Average of population	0.50
High	Upper 5 percent of population	0.30

environment for developing a person's motivation. Although difficult to define, the care and firmness that parents relate to the child are indications of discipline. The part-time work and home chores a child is required to perform also imply discipline. The highest levels of motivation are instilled by a home environment in which both work and discipline are emphasized. Lower levels of emphasis, or course, represent correspondingly less favorable influences.

Three levels of Ebmo values, suggested as representative of three levels of parent-imposed discipline and work, are presented in Table 10.5.

Table 10.5 Influence of childhood work and discipline on motivation (Ebmo)

Level of parents' imposed work and discipline	Nature of work and discipline imposed	Suggested Ebmo values
High	Regular chores, part-time work, mature discipline	1.0
Nominal	Some chores, nominal discipline	0.50
Low	No chores or part-time work, little discipline	0.30

Ebip (Influence of the Environment on Interpersonal Relationships)

Environmental exposures that exert the greatest influence on interpersonal relationships are those early-life experiences associated with family stability and religion.

Stability as used here refers to the relationships existing between members of the family unit. Like

other early-life experiences, these remain with the individual throughout life, and they exert a dominating influence on the individual's actions toward others. The character of these actions determines whether the interpersonal relationships a person develops are favorable or unfavorable. When early-life relationships between family members reflect cordiality, tolerance, and respect, their influence on interpersonal relationships is the most favorable. On the other hand, constant controversy, verbal or physical abuse, and other disruptions like divorce tend to create unfavorable environments for developing desirable interpersonal relationships. The Ebip values suggested as representative of these two extreme environments plus a nominal environment are listed in Table 10.6.

Table 10.6 Influence of childhood experiences on interpersonal relationships (Ebip)

Level of family stability during childhood	Nature of family experiences	Suggested Ebip values
High	Cordiality, tolerance, and respect among family members	1.0
Nominal	Average relationships	0.5
Low	Controversy and mutual abuse within family, often accompanied by divorce	0.3

Participation in religious activities at an early age provides an environment that is conducive to developing favorable interpersonal relationships. Exposure during early life to teachings emphasizing concern and respect for others leaves a lasting impression which enhances interpersonal relationships. Thus, an environment in which there is a high level of stable religious activity represents a highly desirable situation and a corresponding high environmental factor (Ebip) value. Environments void of religious activities, on the other hand, tend to exert unfavorable influences on the development of interpersonal relationships. The Ebip values—high, nominal, and low— suggested as representing different levels of exposure to and participation in religious activities are presented in Table 10.7.

Table 10.7 Influence of early-life religious activities on interpersonal relationships (Ebip)

Level of exposure to religious activities	Religious participation	Suggested Ebip values
High	Regular attendance of religious services and participation by all family members	1.0
Nominal	Occasional attendance by family members	0.5
Low	No church attendance	0.3

COMPOSITE FACTORS

Composite factors (IQ × Emi, PSQ × Emps, and BSQ × Ebx), like most of their constituents (brain capacity factors and environmental factors), cannot be precisely measured. However, since each represents an observable mental quality (knowledge, problem-solving capability, and behavioral characteristics), its relative magnitude can frequently be estimated from a person's actions and accomplishments.

The information sources (Figure 10.1) selected for use in evaluating composite factors identify human actions and accomplishments in many diverse forms. For example, a student's accomplishments in school are usually stated in terms of earned grades (or class standing); and a person's accomplishments in a work environment are often indicated by salary progression and promotions received. These are important and useful observations, but their value in estimating composite factor values is limited: The accomplishments defined by one source are not related directly to those of the other, nor are they directly related to the population as a whole—the reference base for all composite factors.

Thus, to effect a meaningful estimate of the three composite factors, a person's actions and accomplishments (determined from the various information sources) must be properly and systematically related. This has been done by identifying the specific conditions for each information source and applicable composite factor that represent the most favorable possible actions or accomplishments by any person. For these conditions, the value of each composite factor can be derived from information sources identified in Figure 10.1.

The procedure for estimating the composite factor values is simply one of comparison. It involves assessing a person's actions and accomplishments as compared to the most favorable possible (composite factor = 180 and environmental factor = 1.0). Where numerical information is available, such as IQ, it is used. But judgment must be exercised, of course, when a person's observed actions and/or accomplishments provide only qualitative results. In concept, the procedure established is completely general. Yet it differs in detail for each composite factor and applicable information source.

The specific steps and considerations involved in estimating values for each of the composite factors are identified and discussed in the following paragraphs.

IQ × Emi (KNOWLEDGE)

Human knowledge, represented by the composite factor IQ × Emi, can be easily recognized from a person's actions and accomplishments. It manifests itself in many ways and is evidenced by achievements in education programs, is indicated by success in work experiences, and is discernible from observed personal qualities.

Education Programs

A significant part of an individual's knowledge is usually acquired through formal education programs. School records are therefore very useful information sources for assessing the composite factor representing knowledge. Records from high school, college, and advanced study programs are particularly important.

The most useful information from these programs consists of class standing, psychological test scores (IQ, SAT, or ACT), and the quality of the school and duration of attendance. Fortunately for evaluation purposes, each of these qualities can be defined in numerical terms and referred systematically to the population as a whole.

With information from the different education programs, a student's knowledge (as represented by the composite factor IQ × Emi-e) may be estimated by either of two different procedures. One uses *measured* IQ established by psychological testing and the other an *apparent* IQ established from a student's accomplishments in school course work. In both procedures, Emi-e is estimated using information available from specific education programs completed, as described in the preceding section.

MEASURED IQ × Emi-e

At some point in almost every student's education program he or she must take a psychological test. At least three such tests provide a useful measure of IQ. Results from the Stanford-Binet intelligence test—IQ score—can be used directly in the evaluation procedure. Results from college entrance tests—specifically SAT and ACT scores—can also be used when converted to an IQ score by use of Figure 10.2.

As shown in Figure 10.4, Emi-e at the end of any education program depends on the quality of the school attended (Emi-sq) and the duration of the program (Emi-sd). The product of IQ × Emi-e provides an estimate of a student's knowledge at any specific point in his or her education program. The procedure for arriving at this estimate is well defined; but the process is often tedious, because many variables are involved. Figure 10.8 eliminates this problem. It identifies the important variables and their relationships and presents them in a format from which IQ × Emi-e can be easily and rapidly determined.

The use of Figure 10.8 can be explained best by an example. Assume the following information is available from a student's education program:

- SAT score of student: 1100
- Average SAT score of college graduating class: 1000
- Education program completed: master's degree

To determine *measured* IQ × Emi-e from these data, the evaluator has only to enter Chart *A* (Figure 10.8) at the SAT score of 1100 and follow the path indicated by the arrows. The SAT score identifies *measured* IQ in Chart *A*. Charts *B* and *C* simply multiply IQ, Emi-sq, and Emi-sd and define the product of *measured* IQ and Emi-e. In this example, *measured* IQ is 126 and *measured* IQ × Emi-e is 86.

APPARENT IQ × Emi-e

The concept of IQ testing was developed by the psychologist Alfred Binet for one specific purpose: to predict how well any particular child could perform in the French public schools. American colleges still make extensive use of the IQ measuring concept—SAT and ACT scores—in selecting their freshman students.

If it is assumed that IQ (or SAT and ACT scores) is indeed an adequate indicator of a person's ability to succeed in school, there is an obvious corollary: a student's success or accomplishments in school, as indicated by class standing (based on grades earned), is an indicator of that individual's IQ.

Even with this assumption, however, class standing alone is not an adequate measure of a student's IQ, because it depends upon the ability of the competing students (or the quality of the school). Hence, class standing has little meaning unless the quality of the school is known.

School quality was quantitatively defined in the preceding section in terms of the average SAT and ACT scores of the students attending. If, in addition, the distribution of SAT and ACT scores of the students in a school class is assumed to be normal about the average (mean), the SAT and ACT scores (as well as the IQ) of any student in a specific class can be estimated. All that is needed is the student's class standing and the average SAT or ACT score of the class members. How these data can be used to estimated a student's *apparent* IQ is shown in Figure 10.9. (Chart *A*).

When a person's *apparent* IQ is determined in the manner just described, there is of course no assurance the estimated value will agree with the *measured* IQ value. The reason is manifest: *measured* IQ represents a student's potential for accomplishments; *apparent* IQ is a direct measurement of a student's accomplishments. As will be discussed later, there are several reasons why these two IQ values may differ. There are also reasons why the product of *apparent* IQ and Emi-e represent a better estimate of the knowledge acquired by a student than does the product of *measured* IQ and Emi-e.

The procedure for estimating a student's knowledge from *apparent* IQ is best shown by an example. For this illustration, assume the following:

- Student's class standing: upper 20 percent
- Average SAT score of college graduating class: 1000
- Education program completed: master's degree

To determine *apparent* IQ × Emi-e from these data, the evaluator has only to enter Chart *A* in Figure 10.9 at a class standing corresponding to the upper 20 percent and follow the path indicated by the arrows. Chart *A,* at the point where the

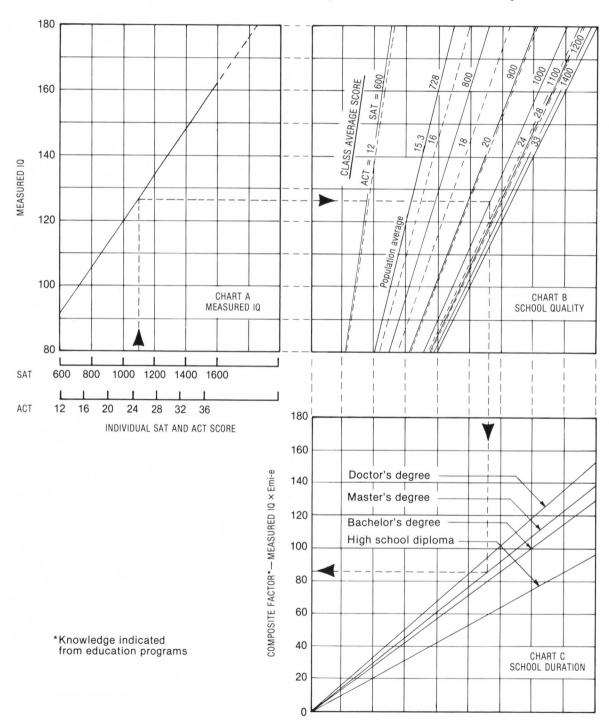

Figure 10.8 Composite factor—measured IQ × Emi-e, knowledge (as indicated from education programs)

dashed line intersects the average SAT score curve of 1000, identifies *apparent* IQ. Charts *B* and *C* simply multiply *apparent* IQ, Emi-sq, and Emi-sd and define the product of *apparent* IQ and Emi-e. In this example, *apparent* IQ is 134 and *apparent* IQ × Emi-e is 91.

MEASURED IQ VERSUS APPARENT IQ

The above procedures for estimating the knowledge a student has acquired from an education program differ only in the IQ value used. One makes use of *measured* IQ and the other *apparent* IQ.

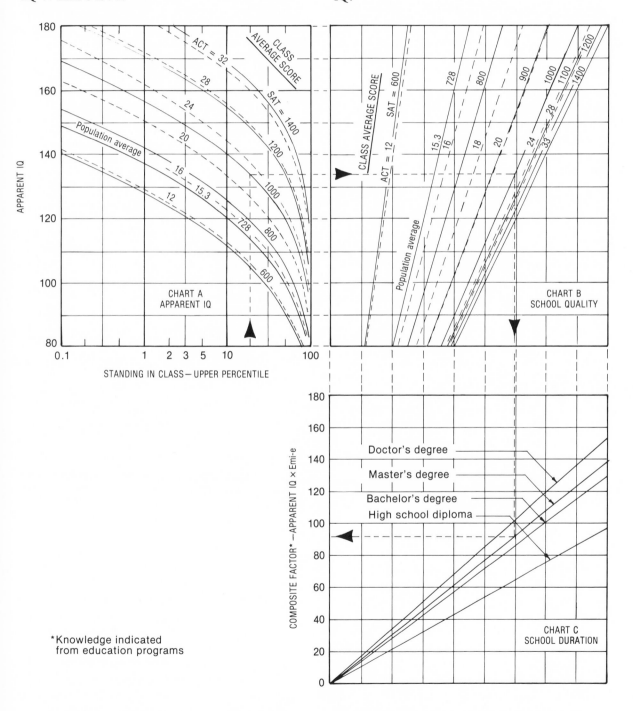

Figure 10.9 Composite factor—apparent IQ × Emi-e, knowledge (as indicated from education programs)

Measured IQ is by definition the only accurate value for IQ. Its primary purpose is to determine *apriori* how well a student will perform in a particular class or education program. Frequently, however, students with the same *measured* IQ scores do not perform equally well. In fact, their performances as indicated by class standing often differ greatly. Under these circumstances the students appear to have different, not the same, IQs.

There are many possible reasons for the difference between a student's *measured* and *apparent* IQs. They usually stem not from inaccurate IQ measurements, but rather from other qualities that influence the knowledge a student possesses at any particular point in an education program. Generally, these differences result from certain early-life experiences and personal attributes not accounted for by IQ.

A student whose early life was spent in a highly affluent family begins school with more knowledge in many subjects than does the student from a less-affluent family. This knowledge difference may be reflected in grades earned and class standing even if the students' IQ scores and school environments are identical.

A number of personal attributes other than IQ contribute to the knowledge a student acquires from a particular school environment. For example, a student with a high level of problem-solving capability is more able to discriminate between the trivial and significant aspects of the environment. Then, by concentrating on the latter, the student can be expected to acquire more pertinent knowledge of a subject and earn higher grades. Also, a highly motivated student will seek to expand the class environment and extend his or her exposure to additional related subject matter, thus enhancing the environment. In addition, although it may be denied by most professors, a student who has favorable interpersonal relationships often receives higher grades than would be indicated by performance in class. Hence, each of the qualities identified as early-life family affluence, problem-solving capability, motivation, and interpersonal relationships may exert a favorable or unfavorable influence on a student's class standing.

That there is frequently a difference between a student's *measured* and *apparent* IQ is well recognized by educators. It is, in fact, this difference that identifies those students referred to by educators as *overachievers* and *underachievers*. In this context, a student is referred to as an overachiever when his *apparent* IQ exceeds the *measured* IQ and as an underachiever when the *apparent* falls short of the *measured*.

Whether a student is an over- or an underachiever is important in the evaluation process, because it shows the influence of one or more of the following: early-family life affluence, problem-solving capability, motivation, or interpersonal relationships. A quantitative indication of this influence can be estimated from Figure 10.9. To illustrate, consider the following conditions:

- Student's class standing: upper 20 percent
- Class SAT score average: 1000

For these conditions, the corresponding *apparent* IQ from Figure 10.9 is 134. In this example, if the student's *measured* IQ is 120, he or she is a significant overachiever, as indicated by the 14-point difference. If the student's *measured* IQ were 154, on the other hand, a comparable degree of underachievement would be indicated.

The degree of a student's over- or underachievement is important, and the magnitude in terms of IQ difference can be useful in assessing the student's problem-solving capability and behavioral characteristics (motivation and interpersonal relationships).

Work Experiences

Although less adaptable to quantitative evaluation than education programs, work experiences are often better indicators of an individual's capability. And when the work involved is that of an analyst, accomplishments become an indicator of his or her knowledge.

The functions of an analyst are to dissect, examine, and evaluate the elements of a problem and define a useful result or conclusion. The design of a bridge and the solution to a fluid-flow problem represent tasks typically performed by the analyst. In each case, success in performing such tasks depends upon the individual's knowledge, including related technical matters as well as applicable analytical procedures. In this type of environment the most important indicators of a person's knowledge are measurable achievements, promotions received, and the rate of salary increase. Accordingly, the level of one member's knowledge relative to others (standing) in any specific organization is rather easy to establish. Where this standing places an individual relative to the population as a whole depends, of course, upon the knowledge possessed by members of the organization and, therefore, the average IQ of its members.

The average (mean) IQ of persons within the different types of organizations was established in Chapter 9 as numerically equal to the effective mental capability of members in the group. Thus, from the standing within a specific organization (see section "Job Categories" in Chapter 9), a member's knowledge relative to the entire population can be determined by the same procedures used in conjunction with the education programs. Figure 10.10 provides the relationships needed for estimating a member's knowledge. This figure is fundamentally the same as Figure 10.9, but with two detailed differences: One, the environment is defined in terms of organization types, or job categories, instead of average SAT and ACT scores of members; and two, there is no allowance for the duration of work within the organization. Such an allowance is not necessary, since the influence of duration is inherently accounted for by the person's standing in the organization. This is so because standing in the organization reflects the relative influence of duration (experience).

The use of Figure 10.10 is best explained by an example. Assume an individual's work experiences are in the professional service job category. Further assume, from work experiences as an analyst, that the individual's accomplishments and salary increases relative to peers are within the upper 20 percent of the organization.

To estimate a person's knowledge ($IQ \times Emi$) from this information, the evaluator has only to enter Chart A in Figure 10.10§ at the upper 20 percent standing and follow the arrows. The ordinate on Chart A identifies *apparent* IQ. Charts B and C simply multiply *apparent* IQ and the appropriate environmental factor (Emi). In this example, the *apparent* IQ is 133 and $IQ \times Emi$ is 120.

§The relationships in this figure also apply to a member's standings in an organization when the individual is working as a synthesist or a supervisor. That is, the ordinate of Chart A represents *apparent* IQ, PSQ, and BSQ; and, the ordinate of Chart C represents the corresponding composite factors $IQ \times Emi$, $PSQ \times Emps$, or $BSQ \times Ebip$.

Observed Personal Qualities

Probably the most accurate way to measure a person's knowledge is by administering a properly constructed comprehensive test covering the field of interest. There are many reasons why such tests are not used, including the lack of suitable tests, the time required to administer them, and individuals' objections to being tested.

In the absence of such tests, a properly conducted personal interview can provide much of the information needed for estimating a person's knowledge of a particular subject. The essentials of such an interview are obvious: properly phrased questions and a competent interviewer.

The number of questions that can be used in a personal interview is, of course, limited. Each question, therefore, must be carefully selected before the interview. And, to cover a broad field, the questions must be phrased to elicit fundamental understanding of the subject. Thus, it is essential for the interviewer to have sufficient knowledge of the vocation to formulate appropriate questions and assess the accuracy of responses. In addition, the interviewer must be able to assess results and exercise the judgment necessary for a valid comparison between the interviewee's knowledge and that of others working in a particular type of organization (job category). Once completed, this comparison (or relative standing) makes it possible to estimate the individual's knowledge from Figure 10.10. The procedure is the same as discussed in the preceding paragraphs.

It should be noted that it makes no difference which job category the evaluator chooses for the comparison as long as it is the one in which he or she is most knowledgeable.

PSQ × Emps (PROBLEM-SOLVING CAPABILITY)

A person's problem-solving capability is most clearly shown by his or her creative contributions in the form of useful concepts and/or inventions. The presence of this important human capability is most evident in a person's accomplishments in extracurricular activities, education programs, work experiences, and observed personal qualities. Unfortunately, the pertinent information from these sources is highly qualitative. Its use in estimating problem-solving capability, therefore,

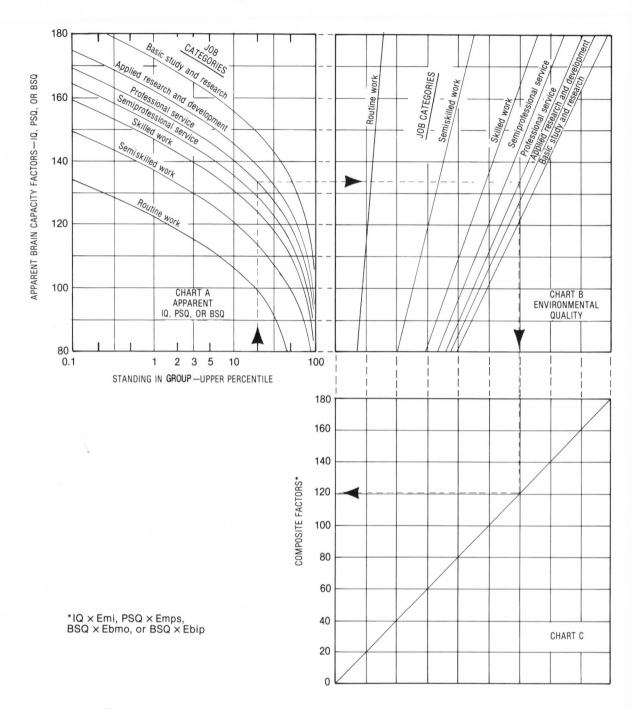

Figure 10.10 Composite factors—IQ × Emi, PSQ × Emps, BSQ × Ebmo, and BSQ × Ebip

requires careful analysis and interpretation.

Those creative accomplishments noted from a person's extracurricular activities and education programs are the most difficult to interpret in terms of problem-solving capability. Although there are obvious relationships between creative accomplishments and the ability to solve problems, no fundamental relationships have been established. Many useful facts are available, however. As has already been noted, the maximum possible value for a composite factor, including problem-solving capability, is about 180. It is also possible to define for each information source those accomplishments—the most favorable possible—associated with the highest level of problem-solving capability. Less favorable accomplishments, of course, represent lower levels of problem-solving capability. Thus, the procedure for estimating problem-solving capability—with information from extracurricular activities and education programs—becomes one of comparing a person's accomplishments with the most favorable possible.

The procedure for using actions and accomplishments to estimate problem-solving capability (PSQ × Emps) from a person's work experiences and observed personal qualities is the same as that used to estimate knowledge (IQ × Emi). It only requires establishing the individual's creative capability standing relative to others working in similar organizations. With this standing defined, the procedure is the same as that illustrated in Figure 10.10.

Extracurricular Activities

Although somewhat subtle, participation in extracurricular activities provides considerable insight into an individual's problem-solving capability. Creative accomplishments in individual activities and hobbies, as well as in written communications, are particularly useful in this respect.

INDIVIDUAL ACTIVITIES AND HOBBIES

Accomplishments in individual activities and hobbies depend to a great degree upon how well the individual is able to define and resolve difficulties that inevitably arise in such activities. For example, creative hobbies such as developing and flying radio-controlled model airplanes are obviously laden with problems to be solved. Therefore, winning in competitive events is generally a good indicator of the participant's problem-solving capability.

Winning a competition is, of course, a measure of real accomplishments only when the quality of the competitors is known. One measure of this quality is the scope of the event. That is, does it involve the world, nation, state, city, school, or other division of society?

When the event is international in scope and the contestants are the world's best, a victory represents the ultimate in success. Such a victory associates the winner's problem-solving capability (PSQ × Emps) with the highest possible level (180), for which the environmental factor (Emps) is 1.0 and the contestant's PSQ is 180.

The composite factors (PSQ × Emps) associated with less-competitive victories are not so easily established. But they can be approximated from the number of persons (population) represented by the recognizing body.

According to Figure 10.7, a unique environmental factor (Emps) is associated with each creative activity. The value of this factor depends upon the level of recognition awarded to the group's foremost members, as indicated by the total population of the recognizing body.

In addition, a unique and definable PSQ characteristic is associated with the population of any recognizing body. For example, if the creative group members are also assumed to be members of the recognizing body (e.g. the same state or city) for which the population is known, the highest most probable PSQ of a group member can be determined from Figure 10.3. The product of this factor (PSQ) and Emps (from Figure 10.7) then provides an estimate of the composite factor (PSQ × Emps), which represents a winning contestant's problem-solving capability.

To illustrate the evaluation procedure, consider an award made by a recognizing body of 1000 persons. For this particular situation the winner is one person out of 1000. In the IQ, PSQ, and BSQ distribution curve shown in Figure 10.3, one person in 1000 is projected to possess a PSQ of 149 or above. Assigning a PSQ value of 149 to the winner of such a contest is therefore appropriate. The environmental factor (Emps) associated with a recognizing body representing 1000 persons is 0.64 (from Figure 10.7). Accordingly, the estimated problem-solving capability of the contest winner in terms of a composite factor is 95 (149 × 0.64).

With the above procedure, the problem-solving capability of any person who has received recognition for superior accomplishments in creative activities and hobbies can be estimated. All that is needed is the number of persons (population) in the recognizing body. Figure

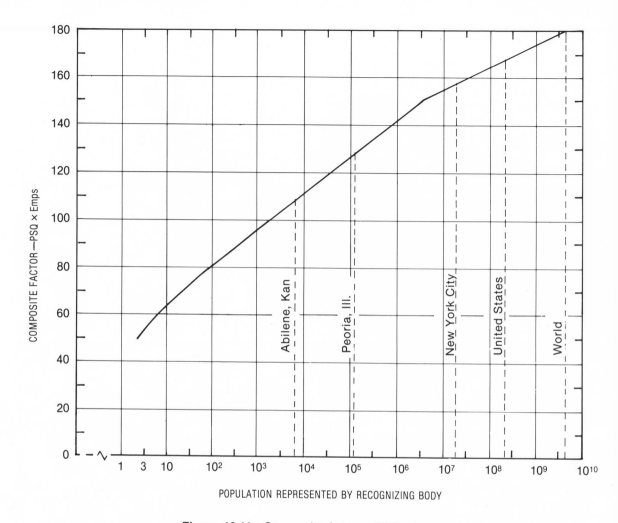

POPULATION REPRESENTED BY RECOGNIZING BODY

Figure 10.11   Composite factor—PSQ × Emps

10.11,¶ which is a general representation of the procedure reviewed above, greatly simplifies the estimating process.

WRITTEN COMMUNICATIONS

The ability to write clearly on complex and multifaceted subjects when accuracy is paramount is an excellent indication of problem-solving capability. Such writings often require assessing and integrating large quantities of ambiguous information into concise and understandable form.

The ability to write, as demonstrated by preparing successful reports, periodical articles,

and newspaper articles is therefore a measure of problem-solving capability. Success as a working editor of a respected publication represents a high level of problem-solving capability in this context. Above-average problem-solving capability is generally indicated for an individual who is able to write successfully for any publication.

In more definitive terms, an individual's success or accomplishments as a writer are indicated by the recognition received. Articles on complex subjects that receive worldwide acclaim should be regarded as representing the most favorable accomplishments possible, for which the writer's problem-solving capability corresponds to a composite factor value of 180. Lower levels of accomplishment indicated by recognition by smaller segments of the population (nation, state, etc.) represent   correspondingly   lower   levels   of

---

¶The abrupt change in slope of the composite factor curve in Figure 10.11 is a result of the assumption that the maximum value for PSQ is 180. The consequence of this assumption is a composite factor that is conservatively low for the rare case where an individual's PSQ is over 180.

problem-solving capability.

These are the same considerations involved in estimating the composite factor PSQ × Emps from a person's creative activities or hobbies. Therefore, the same relationship between PSQ × Emps and the segment of the population encompassed by the recognizing body are valid. Hence, Figure 10.11 may be used for estimating PSQ × Emps based on a person's success in written communications.

Education Programs

The primary purpose of education programs is to provide knowledge. School accomplishments are therefore good indicators of a student's knowledge. Yet such accomplishments indicate little about problem-solving capability, except when advanced studies are involved.

Most advanced degrees require research effort and a thesis. The success with which this work is completed is obviously an indication of problem-solving capability. Even so, its quality is often difficult to judge because of complexity. Again it is convenient to turn to the level of recognition received for the work accomplished. Worldwide acclaim may be regarded as representing the highest level of problem-solving capability and an associated composite factor of 180.

When other degrees of acclaim or recognition indicate lower levels of accomplishments and problem-solving capability, the associated composite factors can be estimated from Figure 10.11.

Another important indication of a student's problem-solving capability is the relative time needed to complete the required research and thesis preparation. Every university has a nominal time period for completing this work. When an appreciably longer time is required, it reflects a lack in problem-solving capability in at least one of two ways. First, it may indicate a lack of judgment in selecting a project that could not be completed on schedule. Second, it may indicate the lack of ability to plan the project and integrate complex results. Long delays in the research program should therefore be regarded as an indication of a below nominal problem-solving capability. The situation is even more adverse when the student finishes the necessary course work, but never completes the required research and thesis preparation.

Also, as discussed earlier, over- or under-achievement by a student may indicate the presence or absence of favorable problem-solving capability; and this consideration is often useful in establishing the value of PSQ × Emps.

Work Experiences

The experience of an individual working as a synthesist provides, by far, the best information for evaluating problem-solving capability.

The functions of a synthesist are to evolve new concepts or develop tangible entities through combining and integrating information from many sources. The discovery of buoyancy, calculus, relativity, radio, transistors, and atomic structure are examples of achievements by the synthesist. Another important characteristic of a synthesist is the ability to plan work effort.

The most essential attribute of a synthesist, therefore, may be stated as the ability to logically and simultaneously consider many complex variables and evolve useful results or products. The success with which this function can be done is an indication of problem-solving capability. This quality is most clearly revealed in a working environment by the level of creativity exhibited (such as inventions and useful new concepts developed), promotions received, and the salary increases awarded while working as a synthesist. When such accomplishments are compared with those of others working in the same organization, the resulting standing is a measure of that person's problem-solving capability.

Once relative standing within an organization is established, a person's problem-solving capability, as indicated by the composite factor value, can be readily estimated from Figure 10.10. The procedure is the same as that used in estimating a person's knowledge.

Observed Personal Qualities

A properly conducted interview can provide very important information for assessing problem-solving capability. The interviewee's ability to solve problems is discernible by the logic and creativeness used in responding to general information-seeking questions. Questions with many facets are obviously the most useful. For example, the question "How do you see yourself progressing in this organization?" is broad enough to require considerable logic in the response. The interviewer, of course, must have adequate capability to assess the answer.

The desired result of such an interview is a comparison of the interviewee's logic and creative qualities relative to others working in a particular organization. This comparison, stated as a relative standing, makes it possible to estimate the problem-solving capability in terms of a composite factor, using the relationships identified in Figure 10.10.

Again, as noted previously, it makes no difference which type of organization (job category) the evaluator chooses for the comparison as long as it is the one in which he or she is most knowledgeable.

BSQ × Ebx (BEHAVIORAL CHARACTERISTICS)

Human behavioral characteristics (BSQ × Ebx) are most clearly revealed through those qualities frequently referred to as motivation (BSQ × Ebmo) and interpersonal relationships (BSQ × Ebip), where

$$BSQ \times Ebx = \frac{BSQ \times Ebmo + BSQ \times Ebip}{2}$$

Both motivation and interpersonal relationships are influenced by the brain capacity factor BSQ. But, as indicated by their symbolic representations (BSQ × Ebmo and BSQ × Ebip), each depends upon different environmental qualities. Hence, among individuals, these factors and behavioral characteristics can be expected to differ accordingly.

BSQ × Ebmo (Motivation)

Although it cannot be measured directly, motivation is an easily recognized human quality. It appears in many forms, but that aspect of interest here is most clearly shown by the way an individual uses his or her discretionary time.

Discretionary time is that time left over after all of a person's required duties and personal needs are satisfied. Not everyone has the same amount of discretionary time. While it can be influenced by many factors, the amount of time available often depends upon the individual's age and the life interest being pursued. For example, a high school student may have only 4 or 5 hours a day (say 30 hours per week) free from classwork and homelife responsibilities. In comparison, the college student, whose hours in class and home responsibilities are fewer, may have an average of 8 or 9 hours a day (say 60 hours per week) of discretionary time. A person pursuing a vocation also has discretionary time. Typically such an individual is committed to a 40-hour workweek (8 hours per working day) plus a number of homelife time-consuming responsibilities. Even so, it is reasonable to assume the average salaried professional may enjoy 4 to 5 hours per day (say 30 hours per week) of discretionary time.

Very few individuals commit all their discretionary time to productive activities or programs. When such a commitment does occur, it indicates the highest level of human motivation and is represented by a BSQ × Ebmo factor of 180. But individuals with the highest level of motivation are rare. That is, the motivation of most everyone, in terms of BSQ × Ebmo, falls below the limit value of 180.

With respect to schoolwork, it has been estimated that, on the average, *study* homework by high school and college students amounts to 10 hours and 20 hours a week, respectively. Further, the average salaried professional person is estimated to spend 10 hours a week in extra effort related to his or her job. In each of these cases, it can be noted that the average level of effort (average hours) represents one-third of the discretionary time available. On this basis, it appears reasonable to state that when one-third of a person's discretionary time is spent in a particular activity, an average level of motivation corresponding to BSQ × Ebmo = 90 (0.5 × 180) is indicated.

By themselves, the specific relationships between motivation and discretionary time, discussed above, have limited usefulness. However, if the relationship existing between the two variables is assumed to be linear (ostensibly a logical assumption), more general relationships can be written.

For high school students and salaried professionals whose maximum discretionary time available is 30 hours a week, the resulting relationship is

$$BSQ \times Ebmo = 45 + 4.5 Hd_1 \qquad (10.3)$$

where Hd_1 is the number of hours spent in an activity but is never more than 30 hours.

For a college student, where the maximum discretionary time available is 60 hours per week, the applicable relationship is

$$BSQ \times Ebmo = 45 + 2.25Hd_2 \qquad (10.4)$$

where Hd_2 is the number of hours spent in an activity but is never more than 60 hours.

For the more general case, where the maximum discretionary time available is neither 30 nor 60 hours per week, the following relationship is applicable:

$$BSQ \times Ebmo = 45 + 1.35P_d \qquad (10.5)$$

where P_d is the percentage of a person's discretionary time spent in a particular activity.

The information needed for estimating a person's motivation level from the above equations may be obtained from the amount of time he or she devotes to extracurricular activities, education programs, and work experiences and from observed personal qualities.

EDUCATION PROGRAMS

A student's level of study is an excellent indication of his or her level of motivation. From the hours of study devoted to homework, a student's motivation ($BSQ \times Ebmo$) can be estimated from the following equations: for high school students, Equation 10.3; and for college students, Equation 10.4.

Another possible indicator of motivation characteristics is the individual's academic achievements relative to those expected, based on SAT and ACT scores. As shown previously, when a student's *measured* IQ (from psychological tests) is less than his or her *apparent* IQ, as determined from class standing (Figure 10.9), the student is regarded as an overachiever; and when the *measured* IQ is the higher, the student is considered an underachiever.

Overachievement may be associated with high motivation and underachievement with low motivation. Therefore, the difference between *measured* IQ and *apparent* IQ is often an indicator of a student's motivation.

EXTRACURRICULAR ACTIVITIES

Extracurricular activities reveal much about a person's motivation characteristics. And where the level of participation is known in terms of

hours per week, the corresponding value of $BSQ \times Ebmo$ can be estimated by the applicable equation: for high school students and salaried professionals, Equation 10.3; for college students, Equation 10.4; and for others, Equation 10.5.

WORK EXPERIENCES

Job-related activities are probably the most useful indicators of an individual's motivation characteristics. A highly motivated person is one whose undivided attention is directed to the job to be done and who is willing to work whatever free overtime is necessary to complete important tasks. Since free overtime is in reality discretionary time, this quantity when known can be used in Equation 10.3 for estimating a person's motivation characteristics in terms of $BSQ \times Ebmo$.

OBSERVED PERSONAL QUALITIES

An individual's motivation characteristics are frequently evident in a personal interview. Enthusiasm and aggressiveness, both manifestations of motivation, are easily detected. Often the experienced evaluator can interpret these qualities in percentages of discretionary time the interviewee will commit to the job. When this can be done, the applicable motivation factor $BSQ \times Ebmo$ can be estimated from Equation 10.3.

BSQ × Ebip (Interpersonal Relationships)

Every interaction between human beings reveals something about each participant's interpersonal relationships. Although these revelations never appear in quantitative form, certain information sources provide results that can be used to estimate values that represent, in relative terms, those qualities defined as interpersonal relationships. For estimating purposes the most useful information sources are work experiences and observed personal qualities.

WORK EXPERIENCES

In the work environment, the interpersonal relationship characteristics an individual possesses are best indicated by the success achieved as a supervisor. The function of a supervisor is to achieve goals or objectives by directing the activities of others. It involves establishing an environment that encourages high performance and minimizes controversy between workers. The success of a supervisor in meeting objectives, along with salary increases earned, is a good indicator of his or her interpersonal relationships. When these results are defined in relation to the successes of other supervisors working in an organization, the composite factor (BSQ × Ebip) representing interpersonal relationships can be estimated from Figure 10.10.

OBSERVED PERSONAL QUALITIES

The personal interview is a very favorable environment for assessing interpersonal relationships. The attitude, friendliness, and consideration the interviewee expresses toward those participating in the interview are all manifestations of interpersonal relationships.

An experienced evaluator can compare these observed qualities with those of others working as supervisors in a specific organization. The resulting relative standing can then be used in conjunction with Figure 10.10 to estimate a value for the related composite factor (BSQ × Ebip).

EFFECTIVE MENTAL CAPABILITY

Once values for the three composite factors—IQ × Emi, PSQ × Emps, and BSQ × Ebx#—are established, a person's effective mental capability can be estimated simply by applying Equation 8.3. The procedures described above provide means for estimating the values of these factors. In most instances, however, each factor can be estimated by more than one procedure, each of which often uses information from different sources. Moreover, some procedures produce relatively precise estimates; some give reasonable approximations; and still others supply only useful approximations. Thus, an adequate estimate of the three composite factors (and a person's effective mental capability) requires special emphasis on information collection and effective implementaion of the estimating procedures.

The preceding sections describe each of the estimating techniques in detail. The following chapter defines the information collection techniques considered to be the most useful in acquiring the data needed for the estimating process.

To aid the evaluator in effectively implementing the estimating procedure, each step in the estimating process is illustrated in Appendix C. Information typical of that available about an applicant is presented; step-by-step procedures for estimating the various factors are illustrated; and the considerations involved in determining the factor values that best represent a person's mental qualities are reviewed and discussed.

$$\#\text{Where BSQ} \times \text{Ebx} = \frac{\text{BSQ} \times \text{Ebmo} + \text{BSQ} \times \text{Ebip}}{2}$$

11

Information Collection

To comprehend a man's life it is necessary to know not merely what he does but what he purposely leaves undone.

GLADSTONE

Every environmental exposure, action, utterance, and accomplishment of an individual reveals information about one or more of his or her mental qualities: knowledge, problem-solving capability, behavioral characteristics, and effective mental capability. There is, therefore, an almost limitless number of information sources that are potentially useful in estimating values for these human mental qualities. Yet only a few of these sources are of practical value for evaluation purposes. Their usefulness depends upon three criteria:

• The clarity with which the source identifies pertinent environmental exposures and individual actions and accomplishments

• The ease with which information can be acquired from the source

• The ease with which information from that source can be interpreted

The information sources that most nearly meet these criteria are those presented in Figure 10.1. According to their relative importance in the estimating process, these sources are

Work experiences
Education programs

Observed personal qualities
Extracurricular activities
Early family-life experiences

Whenever the candidate or applicant has work experiences, information collection should concentrate on this source. If acquired with accuracy and completeness, this information alone may be adequate to assure a reasonable selection. Yet, additional information from other sources will almost always enhance confidence in the final selection.

Under circumstances where the individual has no appreciable work experiences, an adequate estimate of human mental qualities may require information from all the other sources listed above. For example, the education programs, which rank just below work experiences as an information source, may provide little information about problem-solving capability and personal motivation. These programs may provide nothing regarding interpersonal relationships. Hence, for this particular situation, information from each of the other sources will be necessary to assure an acceptable selection.

The importance of complete and accurate information from all sources places special emphasis

135

EMPLOYMENT APPLICATION

Name _____ Phone _____ Date _____

Address _____

Marital Status _____ Number of Children _____ Ages _____

Children's Vocation (when applicable) _____

<u>WORK EXPERIENCE</u> (including part-time)

(Most recent position first)

Company	Position and Duties	From Mo/Yr	To Mo/Yr	Reason For Change	Salary
1.	*a.				
	b.				
	c.				
	d.				
2.					

* Specify <u>all</u> significant positions and duties for last 10 years

Most significant accomplishments, awards, recognitions, publications (and position at time)

1. _____

2. _____

3. _____

4. _____

_____

_____

<u>EXTRACURRICULAR ACTIVITIES</u>

	Activities	Awards/Recognitions	Leadership Roles
Hobbies			
Sports			
Social or School Organizations			

Figure 11.1(a) Employment application form (Part 1 of 2)

EMPLOYMENT APPLICATION—CONTINUED

	Name of School and Location	Course of Study	Degree Awarded	Year Begin	End
High School					
College					

Class standing (Upper percent):   High School _____College _____

SAT or ACT Score: Individual _____;   Class average—High School *_____College _____Graduate _____

Level of Study Effort (High, medium, low):   High School _____College _____

Advanced Degree (if applicable):   Thesis subject _____

_____ Type (analytical or experimental)   _____

Time spent in preparation? _____Years   Early or late completion? _____

EARLY LIFE AND FAMILY HISTORY (through age 17)

Mother's Occupation _____Father's Occupation_____

Parents' Marital Status: together _____ separated _____ divorced _____others _____

Relationships: with parents—Good____Average____Poor_____; between parents—Good____Average____Poor_____

Family Activities (clubs, organizations, etc.):

Home Duties and Chores:

REFERENCES

Name	Address	Phone
1.		
2.		
3.		

*Average of college-bound students

Applicant's Signature

Figure 11.1(b)   Employment application form (Part 2 of 2)

on information collection. Only that information necessary for estimating human mental qualities should be sought. Other interesting but useless information should be avoided out of consideration for both applicant and evaluator.

The employment application, personal interview, and personal reference checks all are useful information-collecting techniques. For most effective use, however, each must be directed toward acquiring the information for which it is best suited. Accordingly, formats and procedures which allow effective utilization of each technique have been established. The important aspects of each are discussed in the following sections.

EMPLOYMENT APPLICATION

A properly conceived employment application is the single most important mechanism for acquiring useful evaluation information. Despite its importance, the application form often fails to serve this valuable function. The forms used by many organizations require more information than can actually be used, and some still use forms that request information forbidden by law. For example, federal laws prohibit preemployment inquiries concerning color, race, religion, national origin, age, and sex. Some states go even further and prohibit inquiries about marital status, type of military discharge, home ownership, birthplace, citizenship, ancestry, and medical history.

When unnecessary information requests are removed from the typical application form and illegal inquiries are eliminated, the form reduces to a reasonable and useful information-gathering device. Figure 11.1 is an example of such an application form. With two exceptions the information requested in this form should be readily available and willingly supplied by the applicant. These exceptions relate to SAT or ACT scores and early family-life experiences.

SAT AND ACT SCORES

Most applicants who have taken the SAT or ACT tests will know their scores. If not, the scores can be obtained from their high school, college, or administering testing service.

In general, however, applicants will not know the SAT or ACT score averages of college-bound seniors from their high school class, nor the aver-

age scores of their college's graduating class. These will have to be obtained from the respective high schools and colleges. When this is not possible, these average scores—which indicate the quality of the school—must be estimated by the evaluator.

For a high school, this is a difficult if not impossible task. Too many of the high schools may be unknown to the evaluator. And there is no common source of data.

The large number of colleges presents a similar problem for the evaluator. But there is a source of information that can be useful in estimating the SAT and ACT score averages of college classes. This is the *Peterson's Annual Guide to Undergraduate Study*. It presents the SAT and ACT score-distribution for the freshman classes entering most American colleges each year. From these scores, freshman class averages can be determined. But even this information must be used judiciously. The college freshman class score averages are not the averages of the graduating class.

This is particularly true in universities that accept large numbers of transfer students, whose SAT and ACT scores vary appreciably from those of students entering as freshmen. Also, in those universities whose curriculums cover a wide range of study, the SAT and ACT scores of students in the highly technical courses of study are usually higher than those in less challenging studies. Under these circumstances, the average SAT or ACT scores of the freshman class (for the entire university) may not adequately represent the quality of the graduating classes in all university departments.

Nevertheless, the freshman class averages can serve a useful purpose in the evaluation when applicable class average scores are not available. Accordingly, the SAT and ACT scores for freshmen entering many American colleges have been evaluated, categorized into groups, and summarized in Table 11.1. The colleges included were selected as those typical of their group. In some instances, however, well-known colleges were not included because their scores were not published in *Peterson's Guide*.

EARLY FAMILY-LIFE EXPERIENCES

The evaluation information needed about early family-life is often regarded as private and

Table 11.1   College freshman class SAT and ACT score averages *

GROUP DESIGNATION	COLLEGES AND UNIVERSITIES	
Group I SAT: 1280 and above or ACT: 29 and above	California Inst. of Technology Dartmouth College Johns Hopkins University Massachusetts Inst. of Technology	Princeton University Rice University Stanford University Yale University
Group II SAT: 1160-1280 or ACT: 26-29	Colgate University Cornell University Duke University Lehigh University Northwestern University Tufts University	United States Military Academy University of Chicago University of Notre Dame University of Virginia Washington University Wesleyan University
Group III SAT: 1060-1160 or ACT: 23-26	Boston College Bradley University Furman University Iowa State University Rutgers University Tulane University	University of Colorado University of Denver University of So. California University of Michigan University of Wisconsin Wake Forest University
Group IV SAT: 960-1060 or ACT: 20-23	Arizona State University Auburn University Brigham Young University Fordham University Kansas State University North Carolina State University Purdue University St. Louis University Texas A & M University University of Arizona	University of California, L. A. University of Kansas University of Massachusetts University of Minnesota University of Missouri University of Oklahoma University of Oregon University of South Dakota University of Tulsa University of Wyoming
Group V SAT: 870-960 or ACT: 17-20	So. Illinois University, Edwardsville University of Arkansas University of Texas, San Antonio University of Nevada University of New Mexico	University of Maryland University of Utah Tennessee Technological U. Wright State University Drury College
Group VI SAT: 870-and below or ACT: 17 and below	Ball State University Bethune-Cookman College Black Hill State College Clark College	Glassboro State College Southeastern Louisiana U. Sul Ross State University Tennessee State University

*Averages computed from information in *Peterson's Annual Guide to Undergraduate Study 1979,* Peterson's Guide, Princeton, New Jersey.

sensitive. In fact, some states prohibit the type of questions included in the suggested application form. Elimination of this information presents no particular problem where significant work experiences are involved. However, lack of this information can compromise the evaluation process when such is not the case.

PERSONAL INTERVIEW

The personal interview serves important purposes for both the applicant and the potential employer. For the applicant, the interview presents an opportunity to learn about the company and meet potential coworkers and management personnel. For the interviewer, it affords an opportunity to convey the company attributes to the applicant and to acquire any additional information needed to complete the evaluation process. These needed facts generally include information necessary to assure a complete and accurate application and observation of personal qualities to aid in assessing the applicant's knowledge, problem-solving capability, and behavioral characteristics.

Much has been written about effective techniques and procedures for conducting an evaluation interview. The interviewer would be wise to study these. Many are useful and some essential for a successful interview.

For example, an interview should involve only two persons: applicant and interviewer. It should be conducted in isolated privacy and without outside disturbances. The applicant should be interviewed, separately, by more than one competent interviewer. As a minimum, the interviewers should include the person who might be the applicant's immediate supervisor and the supervisor at the next higher level. In addition, when highly specialized requirements are involved, it is often desirable to use specialists with particular competence in interviewing.

Under no circumstances should an interview begin until the interviewer has carefully studied the completed application form and knows exactly what information is needed to complete the evaluation, as indicated by the Capability Evaluation Form shown in Figure 12.2. A set of specific questions should be prepared for use during the interview to make sure all the necessary information is acquired. Also, whenever possible, the interviewer should pursue information in the order discussed below.

APPLICATION COMPLETION

If the applicant provided improper information or failed to complete certain sections of the application form, his or her reasons should be ascertained. And, of course, arrangements should be made to obtain the necessary information.

OBSERVED PERSONAL QUALITIES

The responses of an individual to specific questions and environmental exposures during a personal interview can be very useful in assessing each of the three factors which determine effective mental capability: knowledge, problem-solving capability, and behavioral characteristics.

Knowledge

The knowledge an applicant has in any specialty area can be fairly accurately ascertained by the response he or she gives to well-chosen questions. The questions should be fundamental in nature and cover different aspects of the specialty area, and the interviewer must be sufficiently competent in the field to recognize the level of knowledge exhibited by the applicant.

Problem-solving Capability

The logic the applicant exhibits through actions and statements is a good indication of problem-solving capability. His or her ability to think logically will be reflected throughout the interview, and the results should be observed and recorded. The applicant's responses to general questions, which have many facets, are even more useful. Typical questions might be the following:

• In your application you listed _____ as one of your most significant accomplishments. Why do you think so?

• How do you see yourself progressing in an organization like this one?

• Are you interested in becoming an analyst? a synthesist? a supervisor or a manager? Why? Why not?

The specific answers are not necessarily important. The indicated ability to think logically with the limited information at hand, however, is very important.

To gain useful information from this part of the interview, it is obviously essential that the interviewer be able to recognize logical thought processes. This ability requires a person that thinks logically—one with a high degree of problem-solving capability. An interviewer whose strongest attribute is, for example, the knowledge possessed (analyst) is likely to mistake knowledge for logic and thus to misinterpret interview results.

Behavioral Characteristics

The actions of an applicant during an interview are excellent indicators of behavioral characteristics. Accordingly, the enthusiasm, confidence, courtesy, self-respect, and respect for others displayed should be carefully observed and documented as completely as possible for use in the assessment process.

PERSONAL REFERENCE CHECKS

The completed employment application form and the personal interview should provide all the information needed for evaluating the applicant's capabilities. Even so, the assessment process which requires converting qualitative information to quantitative results can often be enhanced by interviewing former employers or other references, usually via telephone. While a face-to-face interview is preferred, this method is seldom feasible or practical.

Like interviews with applicants, discussions with an applicant's references should be directed toward the particular information needed to complete the evaluation. If other information is volunteered, however, it should be recorded for possible support of already acquired material. Unfortunately, the quality of the information obtained from references is often more difficult to evaluate than that received from the applicant.

In making reference checks, interviewers often face one or more of the following situations:

• Company policy restrains the reference, who refers the interviewer to the personnel department, which usually only confirms the applicant's last salary and employment dates.

• The reference likes the applicant and wants to help, so all comments and recommendations are favorable.

• The reference dislikes the applicant and gives a very negative assessment.

• The reference is incompetent in personnel matters and provides information that is either incorrect or not pertinent to the evaluation.

Personal reference checks can obviously supply valuable information for assessing human capabilities, but they must be used with care and considerable judgment. Under no circumstances should the interviewer depend on information from a single reference interview. To be most useful, several such checks must be made and the results cross-checked.

12

The Personnel Selection Process

The question "who ought to be the boss?" is like asking "who ought to be the tenor in a quartet?" Obviously the man who can sing tenor.

HENRY FORD

The preceding three chapters establish the framework for a new approach to personnel selection. This chapter explains and illustrates how the approach is implemented. It enumerates and reviews the procedures and considerations utilized in each step of the selection process:

1. Definition of job requirements
2. Estimation of human mental qualities
3. Consideration of qualitative factors
4. Selection of the most suitable personnel

DEFINITION OF JOB REQUIREMENTS

In this new approach to personnel selection, job requirements—as defined in Chapter 9—are stated in terms of a vocation, job category, and functional specialist.

VOCATION

Defining the vocation of needed personnel is the first and an essential step in the selection process. It is also relatively simple, because managers will always be able to state their needs in terms of a vocation. For example:

Aerodynamicist (performance)
Nuclear physicist (reactor design)
Lawyer (corporate tax)
Nurse (surgical)

JOB CATEGORY

Defining personnel needs in terms of a job category requires an assessment of job complexity. Chapter 9 provides the information necessary for this assessment. It shows how job complexity is related to job category and provides the basis for defining personnel requirements in terms of job category and, therefore, effective mental capability. The levels of effective mental capability associated with each job category are presented in Figure 9.2 and restated below:

Basic study and research --------------------- 135
Applied research and development --------- 125
Professional service ---------------------------- 120
Semiprofessional service ---------------------- 115
Skilled work ------------------------------------- 110
Semiskilled work ------------------------------- 100
Routine work ------------------------------------- 85

In defining personnel requirements in terms of a job category, it is essential for managers to remember that this requirement depends only upon the complexity of the job. It has nothing to do with vocation. Vocation establishes the character of the work to be done; job category determines the effective mental capability required to do it.

FUNCTIONAL SPECIALISTS

The specific functions to be performed in a particular job category determine which functional specialist is required. The human mental qualities (or quality) associated with each functional specialist are identified in Table 9.2

In some instances, the manager responsible for determining personnel requirements will know which functional specialist is needed. Often, however, the requirement may not be at all clear. In this case, the most useful information is conveyed by the nature of the organization involved. More specifically, these needs depend upon the organization's size and whether it is stable or growing.

Figure 12.1 illustrates the typical needs of various types of organizations. This figure and the following comments are provided to aid in establishing this requirement.

Small Organizations (5 to 25 persons)

Figure 12.1a shows a desirable personnel arrangement for a small stable organization—one in which no significant future change in size is expected. The absence of change allows this organization to place emphasis on functional specialists; that is, individuals with the highest possible human mental quality in each specialty area can be selected. The only constraint is that the other two mental qualities be adequate to provide the required effective mental capability. This arrangement assures the highest overall performance capability for the organization because the level is limited only by the integrating capability of the manager. For such a system to work successfully, however, each individual must possess an *actual* (not potential) effective mental capability required

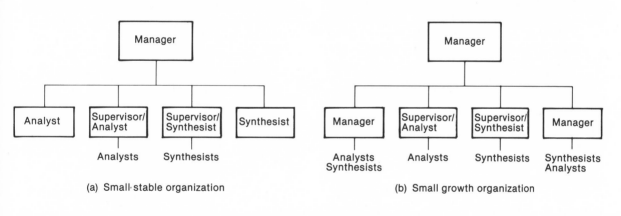

(a) Small stable organization   (b) Small growth organization

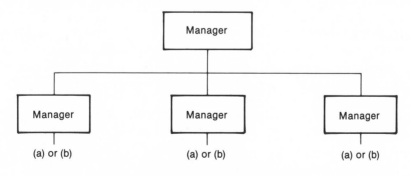

(c) Large stable or growth organization

Figure 12.1 Organization arrangements—small and large organizations

by the organization. There is therefore little flexibility for developing those who have only *potential* capability.

The personnel needed for a small growth organization differ from those of the small stable organization in one important respect. Figures 12.1*a* and 12.1*b* show this difference. Organizational growth implies the need for additional managers. Thus, emphasis must be placed on selecting employees with a balance of human mental qualities—those suited for management. Unfortunately, when managers are placed in other specialist roles awaiting a management assignment, the overall capability of the specialty group is lowered. But this is often a necessary step in organizations preparing for and responding to the needs for growth. This organization shares with the stable small organization the lack of flexibility for developing its own personnel.

Large Organizations (100 or more persons)

From the standpoint of personnel selection, the large organization actually consists of several small organizations, as indicated in Figure 12.1*c*. And appropriate personnel selection depends upon whether the organization is stable or oriented toward growth, as in a small organization.

There is, however, one major advantage associated with the large organization. It is more adaptable to hiring persons whose *potential* capability in a particular speciality area has not been reached. This characteristic adds considerable flexibility to the organization, provides a much larger source of applicants, and allows for planned development of personnel in a way best calculated to serve an organization.

Medium-size Organizations (25 to 100 persons)

In between the small and large organization, the medium-size organization shares some of the characteristics of both. Accordingly, personnel selection can be treated in a manner consistent with the organization's similarities.

STATEMENT OF JOB REQUIREMENTS

Once identified, job requirements can be simply stated in the terms just discussed: vocation, job category, and functional specialist. In some instances, however, it may be desirable to state the functional specialist requirement in different ways. The following examples illustrate:

Example A

Vocation: Aerodynamicist (performance)
Job category: Applied research and development (effective mental capability = 125)
Functional specialist: Synthesist
or optionally

Knowledge (IQ × Emi)	= 110 to 120
Problem-solving capability (PSQ × Emps)	= 130 to 140
Behavioral characteristics (BSQ × Ebx)	= 110 to 120

Example B

Vocation: Neurosurgeon (brain)
Job category: Basic study and research (effective mental capability = 135)
Functional specialist: Analyst/synthesist
or optionally

Knowledge (IQ × Emi)	= 150 to 160
Problem-solving capability (PSQ × Emps)	= 140 to 150
Behavioral characteristics (BSQ × Ebx)	= 100 to 110

ESTIMATION OF HUMAN MENTAL QUALITIES

Estimating a person's human mental qualities simply means estimating values for each of the composite factors in Equation 8.3, restated as follows:

Effective mental capability

$$= \sqrt[3]{(IQ \times Emi)(PSQ \times Emps)(BSQ \times Ebx)}$$

The information and the procedures necessary for estimating these factors are identified in Chapter 10. Chapter 11 describes the devices and techniques deemed to be most effective in collecting the information needed for each procedure.

With the procedures identified in Chapter 10, one can estimate the value of the various factors in

SELECTED INFORMATION SOURCES	BRAIN CAPACITY FACTORS			ENVIRONMENTAL FACTORS				COMPOSITE FACTORS			
						Ebx				BSQ × Ebx	
	IQ	PSQ	BSQ	Emi or Emi-e	Emps	Ebmo	Ebip	IQ × Emi	PSQ × Emps	BSQ × Ebmo	BSQ × Ebip
Early Family-Life Experiences							e				
Stability				a		c					
Social and economic status							f				
Religion						d					
Discipline and work											
Extracurricular Activities										p	
Organization and group activities						i			m	p	
Individual activities and hobbies						i			m		
Written communications						i					
Education Programs	j										
Psychological tests	k			g,h				k		p	
High school	k			g,h				k		q	
College	k			g,h		i		k	m		
Advanced study											
Work Experiences				o				l		p	
Analyst					b				l	p	
Synthesist										p	l
Supervisor											
Observed Personal Qualities								l			
Knowledge									l		
Problem-solving capability										l	l
Behavioral characteristics											
						a				a	
"Best-estimate" of factor values											

Effective mental capability

$$= \sqrt[3]{(IQ \times Emi)(PSQ \times Emps)(BSQ \times Ebx)} = \sqrt[3]{(\quad)(\quad)(\quad)} = (\quad)^n$$

a See text, Chapter 10, under heading of applicable factor
b Estimate from Table 10.3
c Estimate from Table 10.4
d Estimate from Table 10.5
e Estimate from Table 10.6

f Estimate from Table 10.7
g Estimate from Figure 10.4
h Estimate from Figure 10.5
i Estimate from Figure 10.7
j Estimate from Figure 10.8
k Estimate from Figure 10.9

l Estimate from Figure 10.10
m Estimate from Figure 10.11
n Estimate from Equation 8.3
o Estimate from Equation 10.2
p Estimate from Equation 10.3
q Estimate from Equation 10.4

Figure 12.2 Capability evaluation form

SELECTED INFORMATION SOURCES	BRAIN CAPACITY FACTORS			ENVIRONMENTAL FACTORS				COMPOSITE FACTORS			
						Ebx				BSQ × Ebx	
	IQ	PSQ	BSQ	Emi or Emi-e	Emps	Ebmo	Ebip	IQ × Emi	PSQ × Emps	BSQ × Ebmo	BSQ × Ebip
Early Family-Life Experiences											
Stability							e .90				
Social and economic status				a ⊠		c .40					
Religion							f .80				
Discipline and work						d .90					
Extracurricular Activities										p 117	
Organization and group activities									m 125	p 117	
Individual activities and hobbies				i .74					m 142		
Written communications				i .80							
Education Programs	j 126										
Psychological tests	k 134			g,h .50				k 65		p 90	
High school	k 142			g,h .71				k 95		q 124	
College	k 133			g,h .75	i .93			k 100	m 168		
Advanced study											
Work Experiences				o .85				l 122		p 117	
Analyst					b .95				l 135	p 117	
Synthesist										p 117	l 123
Supervisor											
Observed Personal Qualities								l 120			
Knowledge									l 125		
Problem-solving capability										l 120	l 120
Behavioral characteristics											
						a .80 + .85 2				a 117 + 123 2	
"Best-estimate" of factor values	126			.85	.95	.83		122	135	120	

Effective mental capability

$$= \sqrt[3]{(IQ \times Emi)(PSQ \times Emps)(BSQ \times Ebx)} = \sqrt[3]{(122)(135)(120)} = (125)[n]$$

a See text, Chapter 10, under heading of applicable factor	f Estimate from Table 10.7	l Estimate from Figure 10.10
	g Estimate from Figure 10.4	m Estimate from Figure 10.11
b Estimate from Table 10.3	h Estimate from Figure 10.5	n Estimate from Equation 8.3
c Estimate from Table 10.4	i Estimate from Figure 10.7	o Estimate from Equation 10.2
d Estimate from Table 10.5	j Estimate from Figure 10.8	p Estimate from Equation 10.3
e Estimate from Table 10.6	k Estimate from Figure 10.9	q Estimate from Equation 10.4

Figure 12.3 Capability evaluation form (illustration)

several ways. Altogether, 37 different estimating procedures have been defined. Figure 12.2 delineates these procedures and identifies the information sources required for each. Ostensibly, the accuracy with which each factor can be estimated differs considerably. It depends upon the quality of the information available and the adequacy of the applicable procedures. Some estimates produce results that are relatively precise; some provide reasonable approximations; and still others supply only useful postulations. The evaluator, of course, is responsible for determining which procedure provides the "best-estimate" value in each case.

Because of the large quantities of information required and the numerous procedures involved, the estimating process must be done carefully and systematically. An example which illustrates this process is presented in Appendix C. First, it enumerates the information typically available about an applicant from his application form, personal interviews, and personal reference checks; second, it illustrates how this information is used in conjunction with the 37 estimating procedures in establishing values for the various factors; and, third, it reviews the considerations involved in establishing the "best-estimate" value for each factor.

The results from Appendix C are summarized in Figure 12.3, which shows the applicant, an aerodynamicist (performance), was estimated to have the following human mental qualities:

Effective mental capability	= 125
Knowledge	
(IQ × Emi)	= 122
Problem-solving capability	
(PSQ × Emps)	= 135
Behavioral characteristics	
(BSQ × Ebx)	= 120

Thus, according to these estimates, the applicant is qualified to be a synthesist in an applied research and development organization.

CONSIDERATION OF QUALITATIVE FACTORS

The preceding sections (and Appendix C) illustrate procedures for establishing, in quantitative terms, specific job requirements and the human mental qualities of job candidates. These quantitative factors are essential elements of the personnel selection process. Alone, however, they are seldom adequate to assure the most suitable selection for two reasons: first, candidates with precisely the required human mental qualities are not usually available; and second, errors in defining job requirements and estimating human mental qualities are always possible because of the numerous variables involved. Currently, there are no systematic procedures for dealing with these problems in quantitative terms. But such problems can usually be dealt with effectively in qualitative terms by managers who understand the following:

1. The nature of the population from which personnel are selected
2. The consequences of an unsuitable selection
3. The basic nature of organizations

THE NATURE OF THE POPULATION

Every human being has a unique set of mental qualities. That is, each person has a specific level of knowledge, problem-solving capability, and behavioral characteristics. The levels of these basic human mental qualities determine a person's effective mental capability and, therefore, the job category for which he or she is qualified. The distribution of these mental qualities determine which functional specialist job an individual is capable of doing. The level and distribution of these human mental qualities among individuals establish the nature of the population.

Job Category

Just how many persons there are in the population who have the effective mental capability to perform successfully in each job category cannot be determined precisely. However, an order-of-magnitude approximation has been made for each job category based on the statistical relationships that exist among the different human mental qualities:

Job category	Approximate number of persons per million population
Basic study and research	Less than 70
Applied research and development	Less than 3,000

Professional service	Less than 15,000
Semiprofessional service	Less than 50,000
Skilled work	Less than 140,000
Semiskilled work	Less than 500,000
Routine work	Less than 950,000

Functional Specialists

The number of persons who can serve as a particular functional specialist in each job category is only a fraction of that population. Figure 12.4, based on Equation 8.3, indicates why this is so. This figure, applicable to persons in the basic study and research job category, shows there are almost unlimited combinations of knowledge, problem-solving capability, and behavioral characteristics that can provide the effective mental

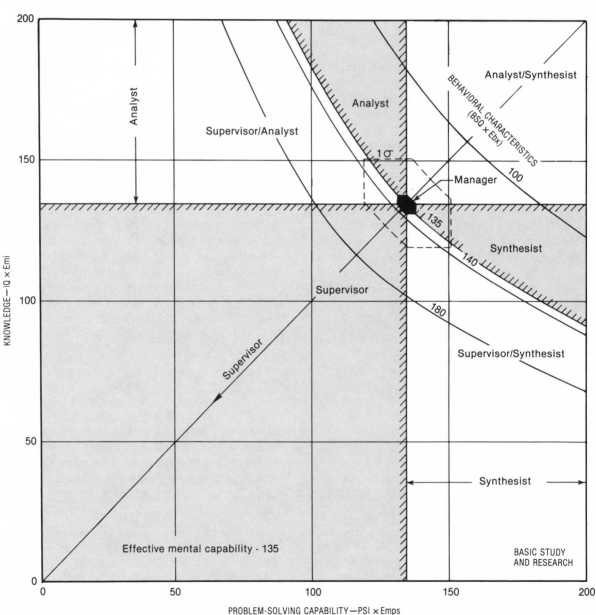

Figure 12.4 Possible distribution of human mental qualities within a job category

capability necessary for successful performance. But it also shows that only a fraction of these possible combinations satisfy the requirements of the different functional specialists: analysts, synthesists, supervisors, supervisor/analyst, supervisor/synthesists, analyst/synthesists, and managers. How the various functional specialists are distributed within the job category is not readily apparent from Figure 12.4. Statistical considerations suggest that those individuals capable of performing successfully as analysts, synthesists, and supervisors are equally divided, however, with each representing one-third of the population. There are, of course, fewer individuals who can perform two or three functions. The manager, for whom nearly equal values of knowledge, problem-solving capability, and behavioral characteristics are necessary, is the one of greatest importance in this latter group. Fortunately, from the standpoint of the number of managers potentially available in a job category, there is a high concentration of persons with basic human mental qualities near the nominal levels (in this case 135). Figure 12.4 illustrates the character of this concentration. This figure, based on the assumption of normal distribution, shows that 68 percent of the group's population (that is, plus or minus 1 sigma) possesses basic human mental qualities that fall between the values of 119 and 151. It also shows that about 16 percent of the population (that is, plus or minus $1/5$ sigma) has basic human mental qualities whose variations are constrained between 132 and 138. The range over which these mental qualities can vary without precluding acceptable management capability is, of course, unknown. However, the above variation—plus or minus 3 points from the nominal—appears to be a reasonable expectation. If this is so, and if the distribution of basic human mental qualities is indeed normal about the mean value, it follows, statistically, that 16 percent or so of the group's population can successfully perform as managers.

The above example reveals the nature of the population as it is reflected by one job category: basic study and research. Figure 12.5 provides essentially the same information for this and three other job categories: applied research and development, professional service, and semiprofessional service. This figure defines the nature of the population from which managers must make personnel selection, and it provides the basis for several important conclusions and useful implications.

Conclusions and Implications

o Within a job category, every individual is a specialist. Depending upon which human mental quality dominates, individuals are divided into three basic groups: analysts, synthesists, and supervisors. And, within these groups, there are four important subgroups: supervisor/analysts, supervisor/synthesists, analyst/synthesists, and managers. Each represents a unique functional specialist.

o Individuals with one highly dominating human mental quality in any specialty area are rare. This conclusion is clear from the 1-sigma and 3-sigma boundaries superimposed on the illustration in Figure 12.5. For instance, in a basic study and research organization, only 16 percent of that population (1-sigma limit) has a single mental quality of 151 or more (compared to an average value for the groups of 135.) And only 0.01 percent of that population (3-sigma limit) has a single human mental quality of 183 or above.

o An individual with a human mental quality (for example, knowledge—IQ × Emi) significantly above 135 cannot successfully serve as a manager in a basic study and research organization. This situation results because the other two mental qualities (in this case, problem-solving capability and behavioral characteristics) are too low to allow the balanced performance required of a manager. Such a person could likely perform as a manager in a lower-level job category. But, under these circumstances, that individual's capability would not be fully utilized.

o No single human mental quality is adequate to determine how well a person can and will perform in any job category. This conclusion, derived from relationships defined in Figure 12.5, is consistent with the well-recognized fact that IQ and knowledge (IQ × Emi) are inadequate indicators of what a person can accomplish in life. To illustrate this consider a person whose level of knowledge in terms of IQ × Emi is 160. According to Figure 12.5, this level is well above that necessary for performing in any of four job categories: basic study and research, applied research and development, professional service, and semi-

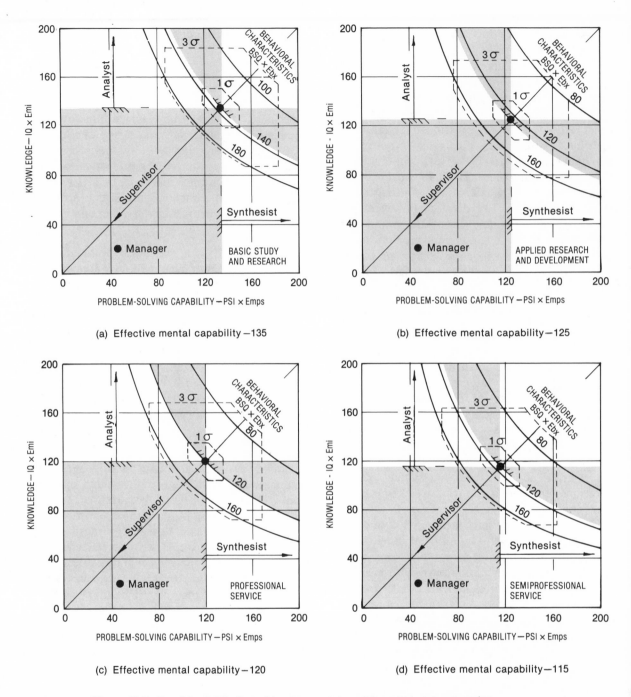

(a) Effective mental capability—135

(b) Effective mental capability—125

(c) Effective mental capability—120

(d) Effective mental capability—115

Figure 12.5 Possible distribution of human mental qualities within job categories

professional service. But knowledge alone is not sufficient. It must be accompanied with appropriate levels of problem-solving capability (PSQ × Emps) and behavioral characteristics (BSQ × Ebx). For example, the person with a knowledge level of 160 can do basic study and research work only if his or her problem-solving capability

and behavioral characteristics combine to produce an average level of approximately 125 (see Figure 12.5a). If each of the latter factors is equal only to the mean value for the population (100), however, the individual will be able to serve only as an analyst and then at a level no higher than semiprofessional service.

o The importance of knowledge to the success of a particular individual is often overemphasized in our society. Contrary to common belief, it is not necessary for a person to possess large quantities of knowledge, or have a high IQ, to reach the highest level of success. Indeed, as is shown in Figure 12.5a, a person with a knowledge level of 100 or less can successfully perform basic study and research work. The estimated IQ scores of eminent geniuses, discussed in Chapter 8, support this conclusion. For this superior performance, of course, a knowledge level of 100 must be accompanied by adequate levels of problem-solving capability and behavioral characteristics. According to Figure 12.5a, the value of these latter two factors, if equal, must be about 157 (when IQ × Emi = 100).

o The relative importance of knowledge to society is greatly overemphasized by the institutions of higher education. Their programs are directed primarily at supplying knowledge and graduating students with high levels of knowledge. This is a commendable objective, of course, but it falls short when compared to an objective of aiding our citizens and country to achieve the greatest possible success. The implications are clear: ways should be found for aiding students to develop improved problem-solving capability and behavioral characteristics. The fundamentals and concepts in this chapter provide the framework for achieving this goal, but time will be required.

There is, however, a more immediate and perhaps even more serious problem that can be addressed today. The problem stems from the mechanisms used for selecting college students: the SAT and ACT programs. The average IQ scores of students attending some of the higher-quality, more prestigious, schools approach 150 (SAT scores of 1400+). Thus, according to Figure 12.5 (and contrary to what many educators believe) these colleges are not producing managers or leaders—nor are they producing synthesists and supervisors. They are graduating analysts. And, as is evident from Figure 12.5, some of the highly qualified analysts may not be able to perform successfully even at a semiprofessional level—a fact for which there are adequate supporting data. Certainly no one can condemn colleges for turning out graduates with high levels of knowledge. This is not the problem. The problem is with the student selection procedure, which emphasizes IQ

(and therefore potential knowledge) to the detriment of the other two human mental qualities. This procedure statistically excludes many students with high-potential problem-solving capability and behavioral characteristics. As a result, many students with the great overall potential capability (effective mental capability) are denied the opportunity to study at high-quality colleges, or sometimes at any college at all. This indeed is a disturbing revelation when it is considered that current college selection procedures would likely exclude such eminent problem-solvers (synthesists) as Nicholas Copernicus (IQ, 105*), Sir Francis Drake (IQ, 105*), Michael Faraday (IQ, 105*), and Thomas Edison (IQ unknown).

o The population is about equally divided among three basic groups, or functional specialists: analysts, synthesists, and supervisors. Approximately 16 percent of each group falls into a subgroup designated as managers. Within the framework of these subdivisions, the character of the population can be described as follows:

Twenty-eight percent of the population consists of analysts. Relative to others in each job category, their strongest attribute is their knowledge, or information possessed. Their weaker attributes are problem-solving capability and behavioral characteristics. Weakness in problem-solving capability manifests itself in the relative inability of analysts to plan, foresee problems, produce creative problem solutions, and exercise good judgment. Weakness in behavioral characteristics is reflected in their relative inability to relate to and influence others.

Twenty-eight percent of the population consists of synthesists. Relative to others in each job category, their strongest attribute is problem-solving capability: the ability to plan, foresee problems, produce creative problem solutions, and exercise judgment. Their weaker attributes are knowledge and behavioral characteristics. Weakness in knowledge simply means that synthesists have relatively less knowledge than others in the category. Weakness in behavioral characteristics is reflected in their relative inability to relate to and influence others.

Twenty-eight percent of the population consists of supervisors. Relative to others in each job category, their strongest attribute is their ability to

---

*Estimated IQ; see Chapter 8.

relate to and influence others. Their weaker attributes are knowledge and problem-solving capability. Weakness in knowledge means that supervisors have relatively less knowledge than others in the job category. Weakness in problem-solving capability manifests itself in their relative inability to plan, foresee problems, produce creative problem solutions, and exercise good judgment.

Sixteen percent of the population consists of managers—a special subgroup of analysts, synthesists, and supervisors—who have neither strong nor weak attributes relatively. Their levels of knowledge, problem-solving capability, and behavioral characteristics are about equal.

○ Because their mental attributes differ greatly, each functional specialist will respond differently when exposed to a particular environment or problem. Each will act to increase pleasure or decrease displeasure in accordance with the unified concept of brain function and processes.

Analysts approach a problem by using the knowledge available. Their inability to plan and foresee consequences may cause them to accept an undesirable solution because they are unable to consider certain important factors. Moreover, because of their deficiency in behavioral characteristics, they are likely to overlook the effects of their decisions on others. Thus, their actions tend to be directed toward their own immediate welfare because of their inability to consider other important factors and probable adverse consequences.

Synthesists approach a problem with emphasis on new combinations of available information. Their ability to plan and foresee consequences results in their seeking the information necessary to assure an adequate solution. They often require extra time to find the information needed because of their comparatively low levels of knowledge and behavioral characteristics. But when completed, the problem solutions are generally comprehensive and valid far into the future.

Supervisors approach a problem with emphasis on how it affects others. Their relatively low levels of knowledge and inability to plan and foresee new problems essentially preclude a successful result. Their solutions and resulting decisions tend to please those involved at the time. However, the future consequences are often adverse to all concerned.

Managers approach a problem with emphasis on all its aspects. They carefully weigh each consideration, and the result is a solution that will not necessarily please everyone at the time; but in the long run its merits will be demonstrated to the satisfaction of all.

○ The social and political views held by members of society are consistent with the character of the population as described above.

Analysts tend to act for immediate pleasure without adequate considerations of pitfalls in the future, primarily because of their inability to foresee and assess potential problems. Thus, their views on social and political issues are regarded as liberal.

Synthesists seek out and consider all facets of the problem, in order to treat every problem with forethought and creativeness. Although their approach is comprehensive and the results are usually accurate, they produce results later than other functional specialists. Synthesists are therefore viewed as conservatives.

Supervisors are relatively weak in ability to foresee and solve problems creatively. But they are very sensitive to human wants and needs. Hence, their views on social and political issues are regarded as highly liberal.

Managers, because of their ability to approach a problem with equal emphasis on each aspect, have views on social and political issues that are regarded as independent.

According to these observations, the population—in terms of social and political views—consists of 56 percent liberals, 28 percent conservatives, and 16 percent independents. Just what these percentages are for the population have not been precisely determined. However, it is generally agreed that liberals outnumber conservatives by 2 to 1, a ratio that is in agreement with the percentages given above.

THE CONSEQUENCES OF AN UNSUITABLE SELECTION

Despite the comprehensiveness of the personnel selection procedures outlined above, errors and unsuitable selections are always possible. Certain errors pose greater problems than others. Understanding the consequences of various selection errors allows managers some tolerance in matching job requirements with the candidates' human mental qualities and minimizes the risk to their organizations. Indeed, because of the large number of variables involved and the human judgment required in the selection process, some errors are almost inevitable.

To many managers it may seem that the best way to avoid an error in personnel selection is to select individuals whose human mental qualities are greater than required for the job at hand. Certainly, it would appear that a person with the ability to perform successfully in the basic study and research category could also perform successfully in the applied research and development category. Additionally, a functional specialist in a high-level job category may be able to do the jobs of one or more functional specialists in lower job categories. For example, an analyst in the basic study and research job category could conceivably do any or all of the other specialist functions in the applied research and development, or less-complex-job, categories. Unfortunately, selecting personnel with excess qualifications is not a satisfactory approach, because an employee with excess capability presents as much of a problem as one with inadequate capability. Obviously some difference between job requirements and capability is tolerable. But when the difference becomes appreciable, severe personnel problems generally arise.

Errors in personnel selection may, of course, occur in estimating either effective mental capability or the distribution of human mental qualities. However, an error in effective mental capability may be the more difficult to remedy.

Difficulties usually arise when there is appreciable mismatch between an employee's effective mental capability and that required for the job. When effective mental capability exceeds job requirements, there are few if any challenging tasks for the employee. Thus—as indicated by the unified concept—there is little opportunity for that individual to experience pleasure or satisfaction with the job. Even though his or her performance may be acceptable, the usual consequence is employee-initiated termination. The end result is, accordingly, a period of reduced group performance and added cost for finding a replacement. An employee with inadequate effective mental capability presents an even more difficult situation. When an employee is unable to resolve problems or complete tasks successfully, periods of unpleasantness develop and frustration prevails—as indicated by the unified concept. The resulting

lack of performance also frustrates the supervisor, and the most likely result is termination—initiated by either the employee or the employer. Again, the penalty includes a period of reduced group performance and the cost of recruiting a replacement.

When a selection error involves only the distribution of human mental qualities—that is, improper assignment of a functional specialist—the results are also serious. Again, performance is unsatisfactory and frustration develops, since the employee is confronted with problems he or she cannot resolve. However, a satisfactory remedy for this situation can usually be effected by simply reassigning the employee to another specialty area. Not only are such moves desirable, but they also are absolutely essential for an organization to operate successfully. The problem is particularly acute when specialists other than managers are assigned to a manager's functions.

Perhaps the worst possible situation—and unfortunately the most common one—is created when a highly competent analyst is placed in a manager's position. Under these circumstances, the analyst's deficiency in problem-solving capability is manifested in the lack of ability to foresee problems, plan programs, synthesize ideas, and judge complex situations. In addition, the analyst lacks the behavioral characteristics necessary for effectively directing subordinates. The results are readily predictable from the unified concept. With inadequate problem-solving capability and behavioral characteristics, the analyst is unable to cope with the problems facing a manager, and frustration appears. Decisions become more emotional than logical. And the analyst (acting as a manager) often attempts to direct subordinates by intimidation, using the great quantities of knowledge at his or her disposal. The usual result is an "intellectual" organization with low morale that produces little. When other specialists are assigned manager roles, the problems that arise are somewhat different but the consequences are much the same: few useful results.

THE BASIC NATURE OF ORGANIZATIONS

History shows that every meaningful organization passes through the same basic phases: formation, rise, decay, and fall. Although the life-span may vary from a very short time to hundreds of years, the phases are persistent. Why the different phases occur as they do can be explained by the nature of the population. Understanding these phases and the reasons for their occurrence can help the manager to develop and retain a productive organization.

Typical Organizations

Each phase of a typical organization's life is related to the roles and performance of its functional specialists. The following scenario illustrates:

In the formation phase, the manager, aided by the synthesist, plays the primary role. The synthesist provides the ideas or concepts and identifies the objectives the organization is to pursue. The manager provides the ability to select personnel and direct their efforts toward the organization's objectives. In this phase, ideas, objectives, and management are all essential.

The rise phase of an organization begins as soon as the manager is able to select and assign analysts, synthesists, supervisors, and other managers as required to achieve the organization's objectives. The rise, or progress, will continue as long as a manager is in control.

With time, however, changes in personnel are inevitable. And this is where problems often begin. Unlike the conditions that prevailed when the organization was formed, a strong organization is in place. And it will survive, at least for a short period, even if a functional specialist other than a manager is assigned to the manager's role. Moreover, such an assignment is highly likely in the absence of a systematic method for selecting personnel, because in any organization there are usually fewer managers than other functional specialists. Also, by this time in the life of a typical organization, analysts, supervisors, and synthesists are all playing major roles and each is recognized as an important and essential contributor. Analysts, because of their great knowledge and "intelligence," often stand out. Supervisors, because of their sensitivity to human wants and needs, have many followers. The synthesist—whose role involves creating ideas, identifying goals, solving problems, and keeping matters in logical order—seldom makes a unique impression on members of an organization. Hence, when someone is selected for the manager's role and the choice, as it generally does, reflects a consensus of the organization members, the assignment usually goes to an analyst or supervisor. When this happens, the consequences are predestined. Neither the analyst nor the supervisor has the foresight and creativeness to set meaningful operating objectives. Both are also lacking in problem-solving capability and in the ability to understand and integrate the contributions of other functional specialists. As a result, objectives, if they are ever set, necessarily reflect the character of the analyst or supervisor in charge. These specialists place emphasis on the value of knowledge or on meeting personal wants and needs. In the absence of foresight, they set objectives that address only the immediate problems (at the expense of the future and overall performance of the organization). Their lack of problem-solving capability precludes any significant success in pursuing even immediate objectives. The result is a drop in performance of the organization, and decay begins.

There is little chance that a true manager—once removed—will ever be returned to the manager's role, since in most organizations (as in the population as a whole) analysts and supervisors together constitute a majority. As a result, decay in performance continues and final failure of the organization is inevitable.

Actual Organizations
BUSINESS ORGANIZATIONS

Every experienced manager has witnessed the scenario outlined above at some organizational level: section, department, division, or company. Management consultants have witnessed the ultimate consequences of this senario in terms of the performance of organizations. They, for example, have estimated that organizations typically make effective use of only 10 percent of their personnel.

But to many observers, the phases of an organization's life are even more vivid when viewed in terms of the history of real business organizations. The life history of many organizations in this country illustrates the reality of this phenomenon. Two aerospace companies provide classic examples: the Glenn L. Martin Company and Douglas Aircraft Company. These companies, founded by two great managers—Glenn L. Martin and Donald W. Douglas, respectively—became and remained successful while these men were in control. Decay began when they relinquished control. Today neither of these organizations exists as an entity.

CIVILIZATIONS

The reality of the four phases of an organization's life is all too clear to historians and political scientists.

A study of the ancient Greek and Roman civilizations indicates each experienced the same four phases of life as do the typical business organizations, and for the same reasons: formation—strong leadership (managers) with comprehensive long-range objectives; rise—continued strong leadership with ability to utilize human qualities to achieve objectives; decay—weak leadership (analysts or supervisors) with short-term objectives that place emphasis on knowledge (for its own sake) and immediate human wants and needs, at the expense of the overall and long-range well-being of the citizens; fall—weak leadership without objectives and inability to harness the abilities of the population.

A study of more modern civilizations indicates that the same four phases are still applicable. For example, the British Empire has evidently passed the first two phases and appears to be well into the third. Unfortunately, the United States apparently is not far behind.

SELECTION OF THE MOST SUITABLE PERSONNEL

All the information needed for selecting suitable personnel can be acquired through the procedures and techniques outlined and discussed in the three preceding sections. Thus, identifying and selecting the most suitable job candidate simply requires examining and interpreting the information derived. Figure 12.6 shows a convenient way to summarize the more quantitative information. The job requirements included are those identified as Example A in the first section of this chapter. The human mental qualities shown for candidate A are those estimated for the individual identified and used in the illustrative example discussed in the second section. Candidates B to F, in Figure 12.6, represent individuals whose human mental qualities are typical of those found in the selection process.

FACTORS	JOB REQUIREMENT	ESTIMATED HUMAN MENTAL QUALITIES					
		Candidates					
		A	B	C	D	E	F
Effective mental capability	125	125	120	133	127	125	127
Knowledge (IQ x Emi)	120-130	122	110	125	130	105	130
Problem-solving capability (PSQ x Emps)	130-140	135	140	145	140	140	130
Behavioral characteristics (BSQ x Ebs)	120-130	120	110	130	110	130	125
Vocation	Aerodynamicist (performance)						
Job category	Applied research and development						
Functional specialty	Synthesist						

Figure 12.6 Summary of typical job requirements and estimated human mental qualities of job candidates

If one assumes that the job requirements in Figure 12.6 adequately define the personnel needs of an organization and that the estimated human mental qualities of the candidates are supported with sufficient data, the most suitable selection is clearly candidate A. Often, however, neither of these assumptions is valid. Moreover, such close agreement between the job requirements and a candidate's human mental qualities seldom occurs. Yet, despite these limitations, managers who use quantitative data in the selection process like that summarized in Figure 12.6 can be assured of considerable success. Even greater success can be realized by managers who are also able to use the qualitative factors discussed in the preceding section ("Consideration of Qualitative Factors"). Indeed, it is through these considerations that the manager is able to effect the most suitable selection when, for whatever reason, the match between the quantitative values stated for job requirements and the estimated human mental qualities of the candidates are at variance. How some of the more important qualitative considerations are used in the selection process are reviewed below.

If it is assumed that each of the quantitative values in Figure 12.6 is equally valid, the most suitable choice—as already stated—is candidate A. The match is almost perfect. No prudent manager would seriously consider either candidate B or C. Each is clearly a synthesist with superior problem-solving capability. It would be too risky to select candidate B, even when estimating errors are considered. The estimated effective mental capability of 120, if only approximately correct, would manifest itself in inferior performance, as well as in frustration for both manager and the new employee. Candidate C, on the other hand, has more than adequate effective mental capability to satisfy the stated job requirements. For this reason, the selection of candidate C would likely create serious personnel problems and frustration for all concerned. However, candidate $D, E,$ or F may, under certain circumstances, offer a better choice than even candidate A. For example, if the manager's organization is relatively weak in analytical capability (knowledge), it might be wise to select candidate D. In this case, if an error were made in assessing the candidate's problem-solving capability, this candidate could probably be later reassigned as an analyst and the effects of the selection error negated. The same logic applies to the selection of candidate E if the organization is relatively weak in supervisory capability (behavioral characteristics). Also, if the organization is for some reason top-heavy with analysts and supervisors, candidate F might well be the most suitable choice. If this particular individual's human mental qualities turn out to be more equally distributed than indicated (which is entirely possible), he could be successfully reassigned to a manager's role. Moreover, the availability of such a person would allow the organization to name a qualified manager to any new manager's position that might become available, thus avoiding an almost certain catastrophe if it became necessary to assign either an analyst or a supervisor to a manager's position.

To managers using this new approach to personnel selection for the first time, it may seem complex and tedious. And to some degree it is. In fact, it can hardly be otherwise, considering the many variables involved. With reasonable study and practice, however, any potentially competent manager can learn to apply this approach effectively and achieve results superior to those feasible with any other known selection process. Such results are possible because the new approach is fundamental and comprehensive; and it includes systematic procedures which assure proper consideration of every factor known to have an appreciable influence on the ultimate performance of human beings. This approach has also been proven in practice. In more than 25 years as a manager in the aerospace industry, the author has used this basic approach to build and help build a number of highly successful organizations—organizations whose superior performance have been recognized throughout the aerospace industry.

APPENDIXES

Fundamentals of the Electronic Digital Computer

Very few computer users have any idea of how the computer hardware performs its many functions. Indeed, it is not necessary for them to do so. However, for one seeking to use the similarity between the brain and computer to reach a better understanding of how the brain operates, an understanding of the fundamentals of computer hardware is obviously essential. The fundamentals needed to pursue such an understanding are summarized in the following sections: "The Binary Number System," "Control and Processing Functions," "Memory Functions," and "Input and Output Functions."

THE BINARY NUMBER SYSTEM

The binary number system is the key to the digital computer system. It differs from the conventional decimal system only in the number of symbols employed. While 10 symbols (0 to 9) are used in the decimal system, only two (0 to 1) are used in the binary system. Figure A.1 illustrates the differences and similarities in the two number systems.

Number values are represented in both systems by placing digits in the appropriate position in a sequence. In such a number sequence, the position or column at the extreme right represents the value of the digit placed there. Digits placed to its left must be multiplied by multiples of the base to produce a decimal quantity. In the decimal system the multiple is 10. In the binary system the multiple is 2. Figure A.1a shows the multiplier and column position relationships.

One disadvantage of the binary system is clear from Figure A.1b. More positions, or columns of digits, are required to represent a decimal number greater than 1. For example, five columns are required to represent the decimal number 31 in the binary system, while only two columns are needed in the decimal system. Despite this advantage, the binary system is the overwhelming choice for digital computers, since it can be implemented with simpler components, namely, on-off (1 and 0) devices.

Arithmetic operations in the binary system are quite simple, involving procedural rules paralleling those of the decimal system. Figure A.2 shows the procedural rules for adding and gives an example of addition. Other arithmetic operations (subtraction, multiplication, and division) are likewise easily done in the binary number system.

CONTROL AND PROCESSING FUNCTIONS

As a system, the electronic computer is an extremely sophisticated and complex machine. Yet, the basic circuits used are few and relatively simple, since it operates with binary numbers. These circuits are, of course, used in many different combinations to produce the necessary arithmetic, logic, and control circuits. In computer terminology, these circuits are referred to as *logic circuits* or *gates*. The most basic of these are designated AND, OR, and NOT gates. All required computer control and processing functions can be done with selected combinations of these basic gates. Figure

POSITION FROM LEFT (OR COLUMN NUMBER)	5	4	3	2	1	POSSIBLE DIGITS IN ANY COLUMN
Decimal multiplier	10,000	1,000	100	10	1	0 through 9
Binary multiplier	16	8	4	2	1	0 and 1

(a) Decimal and binary multipliers

DECIMAL NUMBER	BINARY NUMBER		DECIMAL NUMBER	BINARY NUMBER
0	00000		15	01111
1	00001		16	10000
2	00010		20	10100
3	00011		27	11011
4	00100		31	11111

(b) Examples of equivalent decimal and binary numbers

Figure A.1   Decimal and binary number illustrations

0 + 0 = 0	0 + 1 = 1	1 + 0 = 1	1 + 1 = 0 + (1 carry)

(a) Binary addition rules

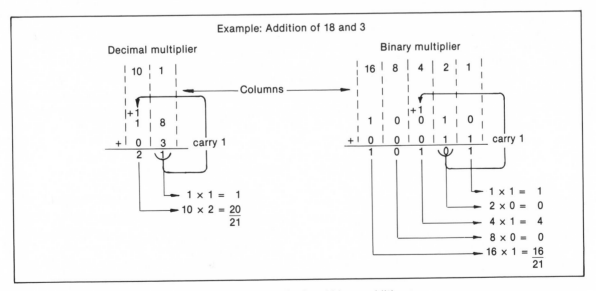

(b) Example of decimal and binary addition

Figure A.2   Binary addition rules and examples

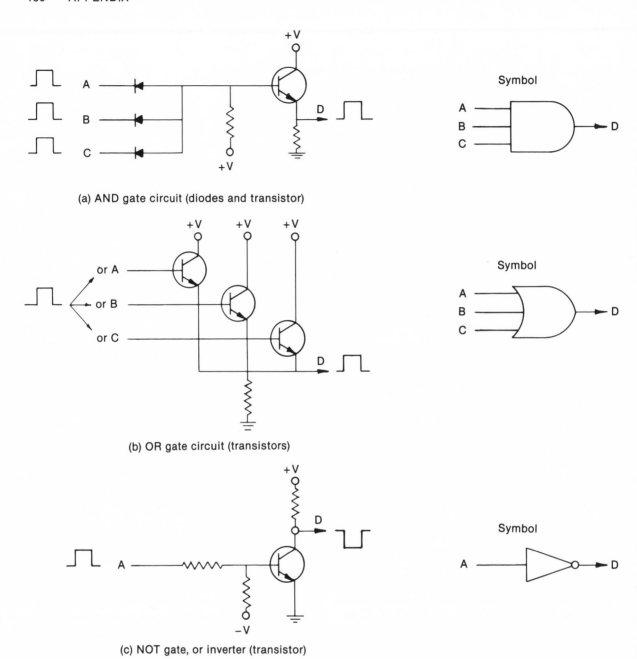

(a) AND gate circuit (diodes and transistor)

Symbol

(b) OR gate circuit (transistors)

Symbol

(c) NOT gate, or inverter (transistor)

Symbol

Figure A.3   Basic computer-control circuits

A.3 shows typical AND, OR, and NOT circuit designs. For simplicity of illustration, these designs include the most basic semiconductor devices: conventional transistors and diodes. More advanced logic-circuit designs use more compact and economical semiconductors—metal oxide semiconductors (MOS)—integrated into a unit called a *microprocessor*.

The AND gate is a circuit that has two or more inputs, all of which must be activated to produce an output. Figure A.3*a* shows such a gate. It has three input points and uses three diodes and a transistor. In the quiescent state, when all inputs (*A, B,* and *C*) are zero, all diodes conduct and the output voltage (point *D*) is near zero. A voltage increase above a certain level at any input point

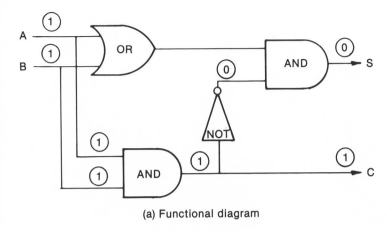

(a) Functional diagram

Input		Output	
A	B	S	C
0	0	0	0
0	1	1	0
1	0	1	0
1	1	0	1

(b) Truth table

Figure A.4   Adder circuit (half-adder)

will cut off that diode, but the others will conduct more, and the output will remain at zero. If, however, the voltage at all input points is increased above a certain value, none of the diodes will conduct and the output voltage will increase to a positive value. Thus A and B and C must be activated to produce a positive output.

The OR gate circuit has two or more inputs, any one of which will produce a positive output signal when activated. A typical design which uses three transistors is illustrated in Figure A.3b. Here input voltages at points A, B, and C are zero and none of the transistors conduct. The output at point D is then near zero. A positive voltage above a certain level at any one or all terminals will allow conduction and produce a positive output at point D. Thus a positive input at A or B or C will result in a positive output.

The NOT gate, shown in Figure A.3c, has only one transistor unit. Its primary function is to invert any incoming signal. When the voltage input is negative, the output is positive, and vice versa.

These three basic gate units are used in various combinations to make up the computer's control and processing circuits. Typical functional circuits are adders, multipliers, subtractors, decoders, encoders, counters, registers, and basic YES and NO logic circuits. Some examples serve to show how these components are formed from the basic circuits.

THE ADDER CIRCUIT

A circuit which can accomplish binary addition using a combination of AND, OR, and NOT gates is shown in Figure A.4. It is the simplest form of an adder and is referred to as a half-adder. This is because it has only two input points and cannot accommodate carryover digits from another adder.

The digital inputs and outputs during the process of adding 1 and 1 are circled in Figure A.4a. A so-called truth table, Figure A.4b, shows the output of a half-adder resulting from the various possible inputs. Half-adders can be combined to provide the addition of any number of digits desired.

THE DECODER AND ENCODER CIRCUITS

Decoding and encoding functions, required to convert from decimal to binary numbers and vice versa, are crucial to the digital computer. Typical circuits are shown in Figure A.5. Figure A.5a shows how combinations of AND and NOT gate circuits may be used to decode binary numbers in terms of decimal numbers. Figure A.5b shows how simple OR gate circuits can be used to convert decimal to binary numbers. Both operations are extremely simple. Examples illustrate the conversions. The digits encircled are inputs and resulting outputs. The binary digit 011 input to the decoder circuit results in a decimal 3 output; while a decimal 3 input to the encoder yields the proper binary digits 011.

COUNTER AND REGISTER CIRCUITS

The counter and register circuits have similar characteristics. The counter circuit is an essential element of the arithmetic and logic circuits. The register circuit is used primarily to hold information during complex computations and information transfer between the various computer units.

The basic component in each of these devices is the so-called flip-flop circuit. It can be implemented either with gates derived from conventional transistors and diodes, as shown in Figure A.3, or with gates derived from metal oxide semiconductors (MOS). Figure A.6 shows a typical flip-flop circuit design.

The flip-flop operates as a bistable system. In one stable state the output at Q is 1 and $\overline{Q}$ is 0. In the other stable state Q is 0 and $\overline{Q}$ is 1. A positive signal applied at T causes the output to reverse regardless of the state condition at application.

When activated, the flip-flop will always assume one of the bistable states, but which one is indeterminate. In applications where it is necessary to set a particular state condition, this is achieved by applying a signal to one of the inputs identified as S_D and C_D. A positive input to S_D results in a 1 output at Q and a 0 at $\overline{Q}$. A positive input to C_D produces the opposite result.

How this device functions in one of many types of counters used in computer systems is shown in Figure A.7. The counter illustrated utilizes three flip-flop devices connected to provide an output digit and its complement to another flip-flop unit. When a positive pulse is applied to FF1, the output changes to 1 and $\overline{Q}1$ becomes 0 if Q1 is initially 0 (refer to Figure A.6). When the se-

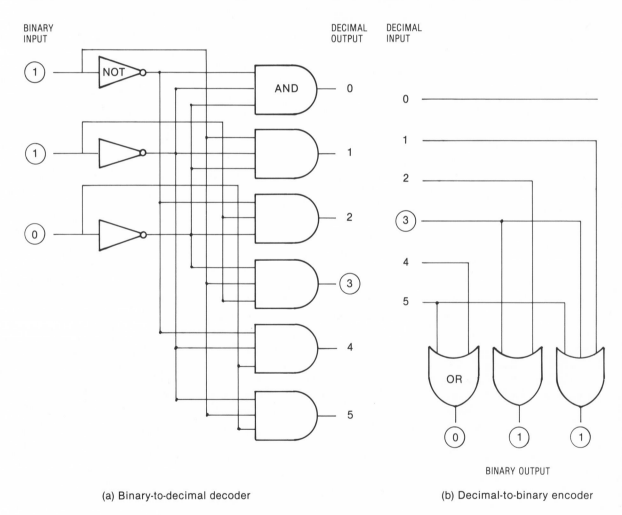

(a) Binary-to-decimal decoder

(b) Decimal-to-binary encoder

Figure A.5   Decoder and encoder circuits

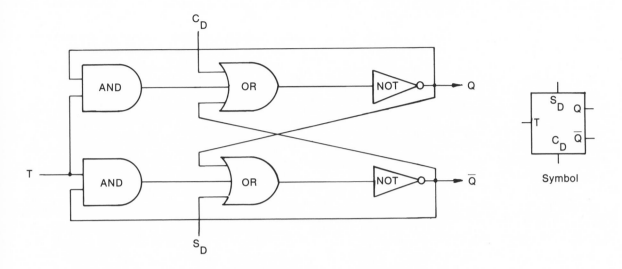

Figure A.6   Flip-flop circuit

cond pulse enters FF1, Q1 returns to 0, $\overline{Q}1$ becomes 1, and then the Q2 output changes to 1. As pulses continue, the Q and $\overline{Q}$ outputs change as indicated in Figure A.7*b*. After each pulse, the values of Q1, Q2, and Q3 can be determined by reading the flip-flop outputs. In the example shown, the binary output after one pulse is 001, or one decimal unit. After seven pulses the output is 111, or 7 in decimal units.

The binary counter is easily converted to a register suitable for holding and transferring information. Figure A.8 illustrates such an adaptation. AND gates are connected to the output of each flip-flop unit and provisions for a READ command are added. Information (binary digits) transfer is then effected by applying a positive impulse to the AND gate. When the READ command is activated by a positive impulse, information (binary digits) is transferred. If the output (Q) of any flip-flop unit is 1, the output of the AND gate becomes 1. If the output of a flip-flop unit is 0, the output of the AND gate is also 0.

THE LOGIC CIRCUIT

The logic processes performed by the computer may be its most important function. The circuits required for these functions use the same basic gate designs discussed above. The only difference is that the binary digits 1 and 0 are used to represent YES and NO. Thus problems which im-

pose various conditions for satisfactory resolution can be accurately and rapidly treated. This logic capability is required for mathematical operations, as well as data organization and data processing. Figure A.9 provides two illustrations.

In solving numerical problems, the digital computer uses an iterative process for converging on the solution. The logic process is therefore crucial to the operation. An oversimplified example of this process is illustrated in Figure A.9*a*, where the problem is to extract the square root of a decimal number, in this case 100. The computer is programmed to start by squaring a random number, compare the results with 100, and systematically converge on the square root. Such an iteration could continue indefinitely, so some logic must be introduced. In the example, limits are set such that if a product yields a value within ±0.01 of 100, or if the iteration is repeated 15 times, a YES signal is transmitted through the OR gate. The YES signal then enters the NOT gate and another part of the computer. The NOT gate inverts the YES signal to NO and stops the iterative operation. The YES signal initiates another operation in the computer.

The use of computer logic by an automobile dealer to locate an automobile with specific features is a typical example of data-processing. Assume the desired features are as follows: red, four-door, full-size, and air-conditioned. The

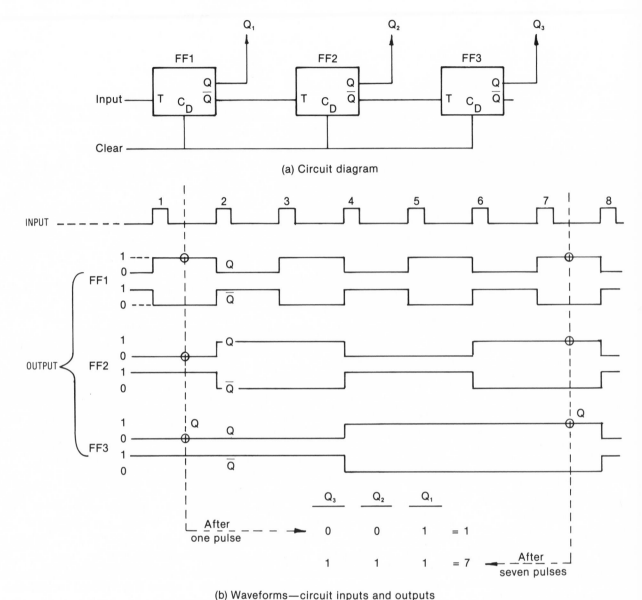

(a) Circuit diagram

(b) Waveforms—circuit inputs and outputs

Figure A.7 Typical counter circuit

AND circuit for this logic process is as shown in Figure A.9b. With these requirements the computer can survey the automobile inventory on record. When an automobile with the specified features is located, all inputs become YES; then the AND circuit signals that an automobile has been located. Suppose another limitation is placed on the requirement, say a vehicle manufactured in France is not acceptable. The added dashed line and symbols show how this restriction can be imposed. Any time a French-made car appears as output, a NO signal results. So the search process continues.

The YES and NO logic processes in a computer are obviously much more complex than these simple examples. A typical high-speed digital computer has millions of gate circuits. Hence their selection and design require careful analyses. This is done by the use of boolean algebra, which is a highly developed method for representing and evaluating logic statements. Among other things, this analytical method permits the circuit-designer to determine explicitly the simplest design to perform a required function.

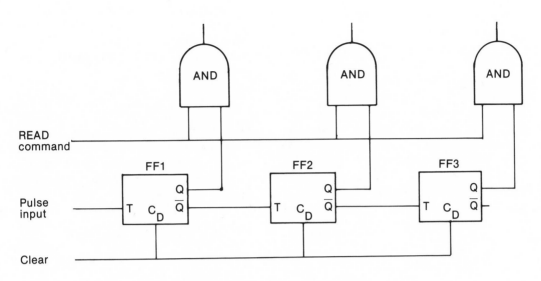

Figure A.8 Typical register circuit

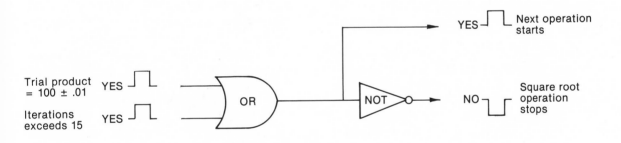

(a) Logic control of computer operation

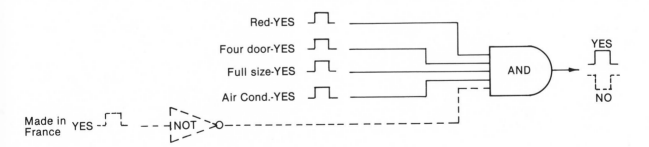

(b) Logic control of data processing

Figure A.9 Examples of logic control circuits

MEMORY FUNCTIONS

The memory storage unit is the heart of a digital computer. It holds and supplies all instructions and basic data required for computer operation.

Depending upon the computer size, the memory capacity may vary between a few thousand and several million binary digits (bits). Independent of size, however, all high-speed computer memories are similar in two important respects: each stores computer-operating instructions and data in coded binary digit form; and each consists of special binary storage devices arranged in a configuration which provides for rapid location, storage, and retrieval of information anywhere within the memory unit.

BINARY DIGIT CODES

Since electronic digital computers operate only with binary digits, all information stored or processed by the computer must be converted into binary form. This conversion is accomplished through special coding techniques, the character of which depends upon the capacity and type of computer involved.

Actually, the coding methods used in computer systems are quite simple and highly standardized. Codes are established simply by assigning a sequence of binary digits to represent alphabetical characters, numbers, and other symbols. For example, in one of the more popular standard codes (ASCII) the following are coded representations:

Symbols	Binary Codes
A	1 0 0 0 0 0 1
B	1 0 0 0 0 1 0
a	1 1 0 0 0 0 1
8	0 1 1 1 0 0 0
9	0 1 1 1 0 0 1
[	1 0 1 1 0 1 1

This particular code, having seven binary digits, or bits, allows for representation of 128 (2^7)

symbols. Figure A.10 shows the entire ASCII code in matrix form. There are both smaller and larger standard computer codes. The selection of a code for any computer depends primarily on its purpose and size, although the designer's preference is frequently the deciding factor.

INFORMATION LOCATION, STORAGE, AND RETRIEVAL

The techniques and associated hardware commonly used for storing binary digital information are numerous and involve mechanical, magnetic, and electronic devices.

Mechanical devices include punched cards and paper tapes. Magnetic devices make use of tapes, cards, drums, disks, and small toroidal magnetic cores. Electronic devices consist primarily of solid-state semiconductors.

The time required for locating, storing, and retrieving information precludes the practical use of most of these devices in high-speed memory units. Locating desired information stored on punched cards, paper tapes, and even magnetic tapes may require several seconds. The time required for the same operation on magnetic disks and drum may be several milliseconds. Only the magnetic core and the semiconductor devices can operate within the micro- and nano-second time regime required for high-speed computers.

The critical difference between acceptable and unacceptable devices is fundamental. The tape, drum, and disk type of storage devices require mechanical motion for locating information, while magnetic core and semiconductor units use high-speed electronic switches in their operation.

Memory Storage Devices

Some of the more significant features of the semiconductor and magnetic-core storage devices are shown in Figures A.11 and A.12.

The semiconductor memory device stores information in the form of the electric voltage, using a flip-flop circuit of the type shown schematically in Figure A.6. As illustrated, each flip-flop unit is inherently capable of storing a binary digit (bit). That is, when active, each output terminal of the flip-flop is either positive (1) or neutral (0). By adding two AND gates to the flip-flop circuit, as shown in Figure A.11, the designer can create the

BITS	b_7 b_6 b_5			0 0 0	0 0 1	0 1 0	0 1 1	1 0 0	1 0 1	1 1 0	1 1 1
b_4	b_3	b_2	b_1								
0	0	0	0	NUL	DLE	SP	0	@	P	\	p
0	0	0	1	SOH	DC1	!	1	A	Q	a	q
0	0	1	0	STX	DC2	"	2	B	R	b	s
0	0	1	1	ETX	DC3	#	3	C	S	c	r
0	1	0	0	EOT	DC4	$	4	D	T	d	t
0	1	0	1	ENQ	NAK	%	5	E	U	e	u
0	1	1	0	ACK	SYN	&	6	F	V	f	v
0	1	1	1	BEL	ETB	'	7	G	W	g	w
1	0	0	0	BS	CAN	(	8	H	X	h	x
1	0	0	1	HT	EM	)	9	I	Y	i	y
1	0	1	0	LF	SUB	*	:	J	Z	j	z
1	0	1	1	VT	ESC	+	;	K	[	k	{
1	1	0	0	FF	FS	,	<	L	\	l	/ ;
1	1	0	1	CR	GS	-	=	M	]	m	}
1	1	1	0	SO	RS	.	>	N	∧	n	~
1	1	1	1	SI	US	/	?	O	_	o	DEL

Figure A.10   ASCII code

circuitry needed for storing and retrieving a single bit of coded information.

One of the AND gates serves to identify the storage device within an X-Y coordinate system. It permits selective storage. The other AND gate is used for data retrieval (READ). The desired storage cell or device is identified or located simply by activating the appropriate X and Y terminals. Storage or retrieval is then accomplished through the WRITE or READ terminals, respectively.

The magnetic core performs the same basic function as the semiconductor flip-flop circuit, but in a different manner. Storage is effected by magnetic means. Figure A.12 illustrates some of the pertinent characteristics and features of the magnetic core. It consists of a small ring of ferromagnetic material, slightly over 1 millimeter in diameter. When a certain level of current passes through its center, it becomes magnetized in one direction; when current flows in the other direction, the magnetic state is reversed. When current flow is reduced to 0, the core retains its most re-

cent magnetic state. The different states are shown in A.12a. Once magnetized, the core never returns to neutral. It is always magnetized in one direction or the other. Hence, the magnetic core is a reliable bistable device applicable to binary storage in which one magnetic state represents 1 and the other represents 0.

The magnetic core is inherently well suited for bit storage where identification and location of the core inside the memory unit are essential. To accomplish this selection, two wires are threaded through the core (see Figure A.12b). Half the current required to magnetize the core is passed through each of the two wires, designated X and Y. This permits storage in any core selected. Current flow in one direction stores a 1 in the core; flow in the opposite direction places a 0 in the core.

For retrieving or reading digits stored in the magnetic core, a third sense wire is threaded through the core. The principle is simple. To retrieve or identify digits stored in the magnetic

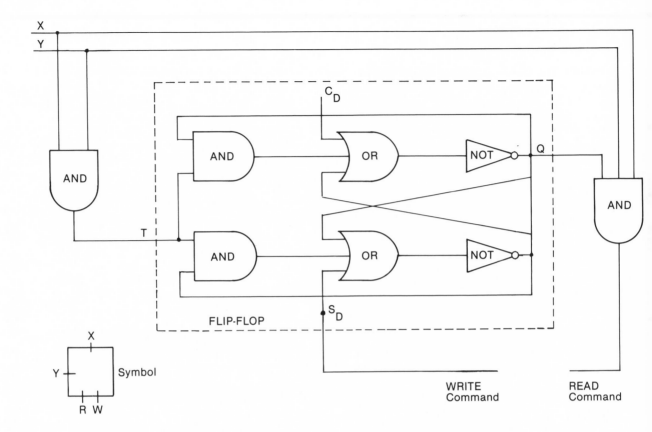

Figure A.11   Flip-flop circuit for storing and retrieving one bit

core, it is necessary only to pass a current through the core, as if to effect storage. If the magnetic state of the core corresponds to direction of current flow, nothing happens to the sense wire. On the other hand, if the magnetic state is set opposite to the current flow, the state changes. This changes the magnetic field and induces a pulse in the sense line. The pulse or the absence of one indicates the storage of 1 or 0.

The storage and retrieval circuit necessary for using the magnetic core as a memory unit is somewhat more complex than that needed for the semiconductor flip-flop. In a functional sense, however, their operations are identical, and, in a memory system design, the two units can be used interchangeably.

The Memory System

The storage capacity of computer memory units varies between a few thousand and several million bits. Each bit requires a separate storage cell, such as the semiconductor or magnetic-core circuit discussed above. Hence, the design and arrangement of the storage cells for efficient operation are major considerations. Typically, the storage cells are arranged in a three-dimensional matrix, with the specific geometry depending upon the total capacity required and the binary code used.

Figure A.13 illustrates how the storage cells are arranged in a typical memory unit. Essentially, all high-speed electronic digital computers utilize this type of arrangement. Capacity or size requirements are met by the number of memory planes and the number of storage cells used per plane. A typical basic memory plane is 64 cells wide and 64 cells long, a total of 4096 cells.

This basic memory plane is used in different combinations to achieve the desired storage capability. For example, the memory unit of one relatively large computer uses four basic memory planes to form a single memory plane with 16,384 bits. Seventy-two of these planes are stacked to form the complete memory unit, yielding a total capacity of 1,179,648 bits.

The three-dimensional matrix arrangement, illustrated in Figure A.13a, offers a number of advantages in locating, storing, and retrieving information within the memory unit. It permits simple selection of cells in X and Y coordinates and provides for storing and retrieving bits in desirable groupings.

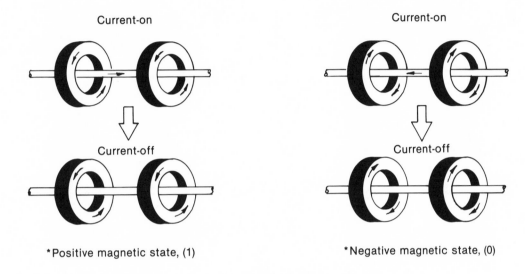

(a) Two possible states of a magnetic core with and without current flow

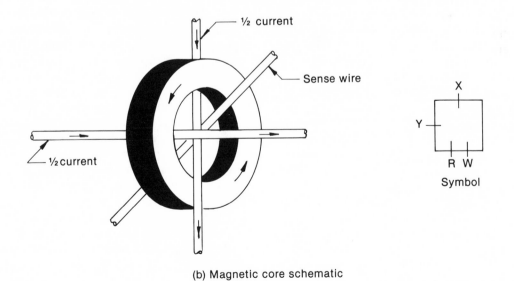

(b) Magnetic core schematic

Figure A.12   Magnetic core features and characteristics

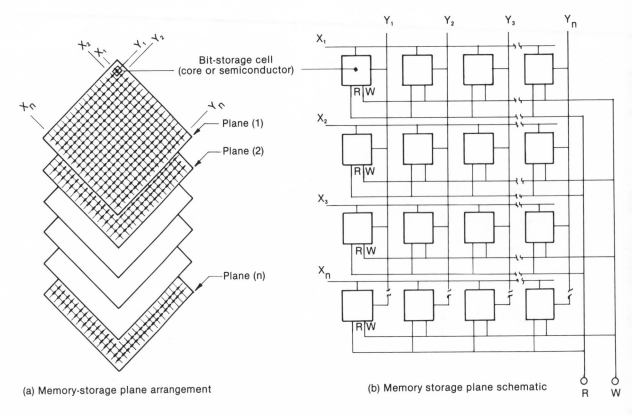

(a) Memory-storage plane arrangement

(b) Memory storage plane schematic

Figure A.13   Memory storage system

Figure A.13b illustrates the arrangement of storage cells (either semiconductor or magnetic core) within a memory plane. In this structure, cell selection or identification is made by activating the appropriate X and Y input terminals. Once selected, either storage or retrieval can be effected at the WRITE or READ terminals, respectively. In this arrangement all storage cells within each memory plane are served by one READ command and one WRITE command. This type of operation is possible because only the cell at the selected X and Y coordinate (in any single plane) can respond to storage or retrieval command.

In a complete memory unit (see Figure A.14) binary bits representing characters, symbols, or numbers are stored in separate memory planes. Hence, the number of planes required to represent a symbol or number depends upon the binary coding system used. Figure A.14a shows how the letter A, represented by 1000001 in the seven-bit ASCII code, is stored in a memory unit.

This grouping of cells greatly simplifies the storage and retrieving operations. Figure A.14b indicates why this is so. The memory planes are so connected that when activated, the affected X and Y coordinates form perpendicular planes which intersect the memory planes in a straight line. Thus, by activating X_2 and Y_3, storage cells at the intersection in each plane are readied for operation. When the system is activated, a WRITE command to any one plane results in a single-bit storage, or a READ command retrieves a stored bit.

The number of planes and the binary code used determine the number of characters, symbols, or numbers that can be stored in a single string. With the seven-bit ASCII code, a 72-plane memory unit can store 10 characters, symbols, or numbers in a single line. The information which can be stored in one X and Y combination is illustrated in Figure A.15.

The basic memory unit which provides for high-speed storage and retrieval of information is an essential part of any high-speed computer. However, for most operation of large computers it is often necessary to provide supplemental memory capacity.

Magnetic drums and disks are widely used to supplement a computer's basic memory capacity.

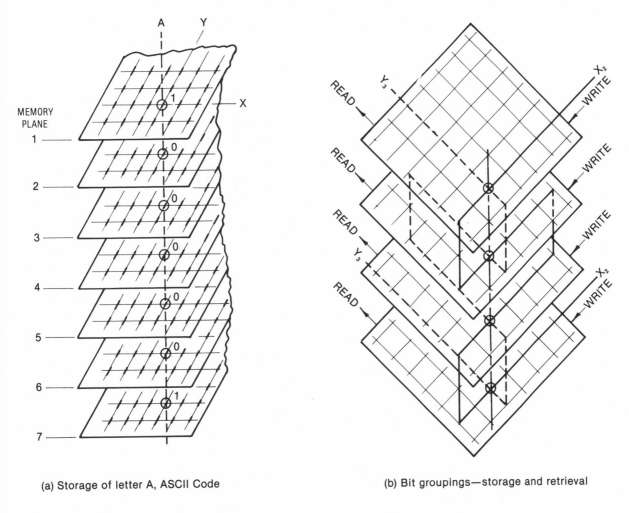

(a) Storage of letter A, ASCII Code

(b) Bit groupings—storage and retrieval

Figure A.14   Memory storage and retrieval

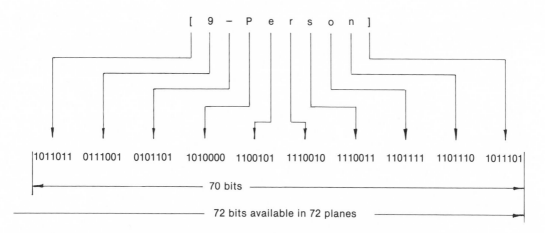

[9 – P e r s o n]

| 1011011 | 0111001 | 0101101 | 1010000 | 1100101 | 1110010 | 1110011 | 1101111 | 1101110 | 1011101 |

— 70 bits —

— 72 bits available in 72 planes —

Figure A.15   Example of storage—one string through 72 planes

Either can provide greatly increased capacity for storing and retrieving information. The major problem with each is the slow storage and retrieval times associated with the mechanical movement necessary for locating a selected storage area. But when large quantities of data are involved, mechanical systems can sometimes be efficiently used. This is done by scheduling drum and disk units only when large quantities of information are required in a sequence. In this way, the time required for mechanical motion to locate desired storage areas becomes acceptably small.

So far, only that part of the computer memory which can accept rapid storage has been discussed. There is, however, another type memory unit, used frequently in large computers, which cannot be changed or reprogrammed. It is referred to as *read-only memory (ROM)*. The ROM is widely used to store instructions for certain mathematical procedures and important data used frequently in a computer. This permanent-type storage unit greatly reduces the user's preparation time when special complex problems are involved.

The ROM also has wide applications in computer control and other control systems. Figure A.16 shows an example of a ROM control circuit and its characteristics. Figure A.16a illustrates a simple ROM unit in a schematic form. The open diodes shown in the schematic result in the input and output relationship shown in Figure A.16b. In this type of circuit the storage cells are usually solid-state diodes. In some designs all diodes are initially connected. To store the desired information to be read, it is necessary to destroy selected diodes (usually by excessive voltage). In this manner any desired input-output relationship can be achieved. This unique-type ROM is referred to as a *programmable read-only memory (PROM)*, and it is in wide use in control system development.

In the above discussion the term *memory* applies to the hardware in which information is stored for use in the computer system. This is a convenient definition. However, to fully appreciate the digital computer system, one should realize that "real" memory exists throughout the computer network. For example, memory registers surround the basic memory unit, temporarily storing instructions and data as necessary to control and regulate operation. Also, when activated,

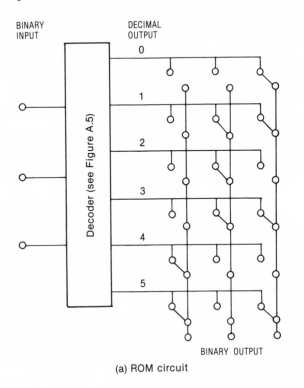

(a) ROM circuit

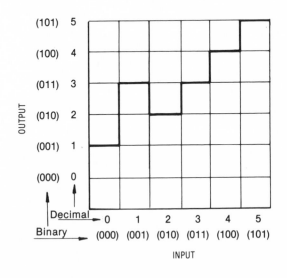

(b) Typical ROM circuit characteristics

Figure A.16   Read-only memory (ROM) circuit and characteristics

the encoder remembers to convert decimal digits to binary digits and the OR gate remembers to produce a positive output with any single positive input. These operations are indeed the result of memory.

INPUT AND OUTPUT FUNCTIONS

Input and output units provide the interfaces required for communication between the user and the computer. Their primary functions are to translate input data and computer instructions into computer language and convert computer language into usable output results.

Communications with the computer may be conducted in different languages, depending on the type of computer, the equipment available, and the desires of the user. Figure A.17 schematically illustrates the input and output elements involved.

INPUT

A hierarchy of languages may be used on the input side. These have been designated as *machine language, symbolic language, and high-level language.*

Machine language is the most basic and is the only language directly usable by the computer control, memory, and processing units. From the user's viewpoint, however, it is usually the least desirable, because it requires the user to input all information in binary form. This process is laborious and time consuming and is highly subject to human error because of the large number of digits involved.

Symbolic language greatly reduces the time and effort required for input communications, and its usage significantly decreases the potential for human errors. This language makes use of special codes which define how the computer is to operate. The codes consist of alphabetical characters (usually three) which, when written together, provide reminders (mnemonics) of the operation to be performed. Computer information put in this form by the user is then converted to machine language by a device called an *assembler*. The user avoids any interaction with binary digits.

High-level languages add another degree of

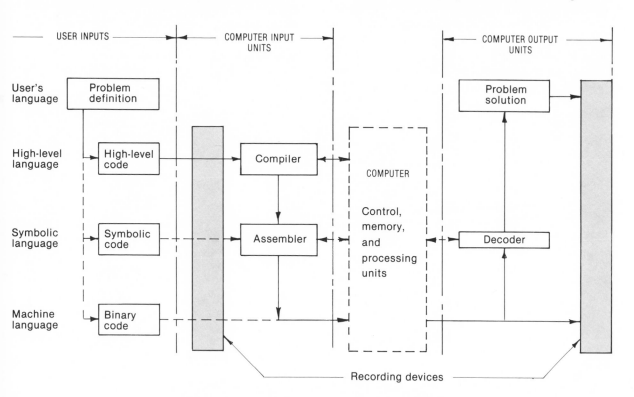

Figure A.17 Computer input and output schematic

simplification to communication with the computer. They are easier to use than symbolic languages, because they allow the user to input information in terms of equations and logic statements that are very similar to the language spoken by the user. They employ extensive codes, which, of course, must ultimately be converted to binary machine language for use in the computer. This translation is effected by a device called a *compiler*. Working with the computer control, memory, and processing units, the compiler converts inputs to the binary code required by the machine. Well-known high-level languages are FORTRAN (Formula Translation), a mathematical language; COBOL (Common Business Oriented Language), a business language; and PL/1 (Programming Language 1), a combination of mathematical and business languages.

The user's options in submitting input information are illustrated in Figure A.17. The process begins with a problem definition in the user's language, which must then be translated into one of the coded languages. From here, if machine language is chosen, no further conversion is required for computer operation. The symbolic language requires use of the assembler which, in conjunction with the computer control, memory, and processing units, translates the coded input to binary form. The translation from high-level language to machine language requires use of the compiler along with the computer control, memory, and processing units.

OUTPUT

The basic output from the computer is in machine language which can be recorded and stored or used as input to another computer operation. Of primary interest, however, are results in terms of the user's language. The necessary conversion from machine language to the user's language is done with a decoder, which operates in conjunction with the computer control, memory, and processing units.

RECORDING AND STORAGE

The computer processing system operates much faster than information can be coded by the user and compiled or assembled by the input equipment. The information must therefore be recorded or stored before it is submitted to the computer for processing. Storing the output information for use in the future is equally important. Commonly used input and recording methods include punched cards, typewriters, paper tapes, magnetic tapes, magnetic disks, and magnetic drums. Output and recording methods include all the above plus such other devices as high-speed printers and visual readers.

B

Bases for the Conceptual Model

The conceptual model of the brain, described in Chapter 4, was synthesized to account for all major operations known to be performed by the brain. Where the information was not available to define explicitly all functional areas and their related functions and processes, they were postulated based on observations and related experimental data. The new concepts and those which may be considered controversial, along with the information on which the concepts are based, are discussed in this appendix.

A. HYPOTHALAMUS

The hypothalamus is primarily a sensory and control center, but it is often referred to as the center of emotions and human well-being. Intense interest in the hypothalamus has resulted in extensive research and experimentation involving cats, dogs, monkeys, cows, and even human beings.

The sensory and control functions of the hypothalamus are numerous. However, only those functions involving certain sensors are important to the unified concept and the associated conceptual model. These are the sensors referred to as internal sensors and designated as internal physiology sensors and emotion sensors.

INTERNAL PHYSIOLOGY SENSORS

Numerous experiments show conclusively that hunger, thirst, and sexual desire can be induced in both animals and human beings by electrical stimulation of specific areas in the hypothalamus. From these findings, it is concluded that such sensors do, in fact, exist within the hypothalamus. And it is further concluded that various human desires are normally induced through excitations created by brain processes.

Hunger

Experimental evidence indicates clearly that hunger sensors are present within the hypothalamus. Furthermore, the sources of input to the sensors, both internal and external, are identifiable.

Internal hunger sensors are responsive to blood chemistry and certain external sensory inputs. That internal sensors are sensitive to blood chemistry has been shown in animals that evidenced increased hunger when insulin was injected into the blood stream, reducing sugar concentration. Also, injecting blood from a hungry animal into a hunger-satiated animal has been shown to induce hunger. External sensory inputs which pass through the consciousness area to the hunger sensors of the hypothalamus may be induced by sight, smell, and taste. Everyone has observed how these sensory inputs can intensify hunger.

Thirst

The existence of thirst sensors within the hypothalamus has been well established by various experiments. Internally, the source of sensory input is the salt concentration in body fluids. Externally, sight is perhaps the most significant input to the thirst sensors.

In experiments involving several types of animals, salt water injected into certain regions of the hypothalamus was found to cause the same desire for water as normal thirst or electrical stimulation. On the other hand, fresh water injected into the same location produced the opposite effect. The recognized fact that the sight of water magnifies human thirst indicates that inputs from the external sensors do, indeed, reach the hypothalamus sensory areas.

Sexual Desire

Sexual desire comparable to, or perhaps even greater than, that occurring normally has been created by electrical stimulation within the hypothalamus. The sensor involved is sensitive to both body hormone concentrations and external sensory inputs.

Extensive information is available to show how sexual desire can be increased through the use of hormones to which the hypothalamus sensors are responsive. The same sensors are also obviously responsive to sensations of sight and feeling, and their effect on sexual desire is well known.

EMOTION SENSORS

The emotional responses which can be produced by electrical stimulation of the hypothalamus have been extensively studied in both animals and human beings. The results of several experiments are summarized in Chapter 2. The wide range of responses which have been reported as a result of electrical stimulation include aggression, rage, anger, fear, docility, pleasure, and euphoria. Regardless of type of emotion, one thing is clear: there are sensors within the hypothalamus that produce a wide range of emotional effects. All these effects are considered to fall into two groups. One group is concerned with aggression, where stimulations create feelings varying from overt aggression to indifference. The other group involves pleasantness, where stimulations produce feelings ranging from pleasure to displeasure. How stimulations influence these areas of the hypothalamus is clear from Figure 4.3.

B. CONSCIOUSNESS AREA

The existence of human consciousness is, of course, well recognized and accepted. However, how and from where it originates remain a mystery.

The unified concept, which treats the brain as a complete system, places the consciousness area in the thalamus. This is because essentially every impulse or bit of information entering or leaving the brain passes through the thalamus. Located atop the brain stem, the thalamus projects to and receives reciprocal neuron fibers from every area of the brain. It is, therefore, the logical area for consciousness. In fact, it is the only known place within the brain that has adequate direct nerve fiber connections to effect human consciousness.

C. MEMORY AREA

Memory is one of the least understood and perhaps the most controversial of the brain functions. Not even its location is known; nor is the mechanism by which information is stored and retrieved understood.

MEMORY LOCATION

In the unified concept, memory storage is postulated to be widely spread throughout the brain. Because of the symmetrical hemispheres of the brain and the connecting neuronal fibers, it is logical to presume that each hemisphere is exposed to and retains similar or at least related sets of information. Hence, there are at least two possible locations for storing each bit of information received. Clinical observations and experimental results involving both humans and animals indicate that similar bits of information may be even more widely dispersed within the brain.

In a number of instances involving removal of large portions of the human brain both accidentally and surgically, there was little or no loss of memory. In one experiment involving rats, those trained to run a maze continued to run the maze as increasingly larger parts of the brain were removed. In fact, the rats in this experiment were able to run the maze as long as any part of the brain remained, though with decreasing proficiency.

Somewhat at odds with the above postulate is the fact that the functions of certain regions of the brain have been rather specifically assigned and do not appear to involve memory. These include the sensory reception areas, the motor cortex, and the association cortex. Even if these are correctly designated, however, there are large areas of the brain for which functions have not been defined. Furthermore, there are six layers of neurons throughout the cerebral cortex; thus, it is entirely possible that various layers are associated with different functions, and memory storage may indeed be distributed throughout the entire brain.

MEMORY SYSTEM

The memory system postulated herein is a key element in the unified concept. It accounts for all the memory storage and recall associated with every brain function. It involves two major postulates: one, all information reaching consciousness is passed to the memory area and permanently stored in coded binary form by billions of neurons and associated synapses located therein; and two, recall of stored information to consciousness requires stimulating the appropriate neurons by pulse-coded frequencies at or near the value at which storage was effected.

Memory Storage

The storage of information in the memory system, as postulated here, is analogous to storage in

the core memory of a digital computer. It is accomplished in computerlike binary digit form, much as illustrated in Appendix A, Figures A.13 and A.14.

The memory system consists of an extensive network of neurons and associated synapses in which each synapse stores a single bit of information. In such a system the various bits are stored in proper relationship with each other to represent information in terms of words, symbols, figures, etc. Related bits of information stored in this manner are referred to as an *engram*. A typical engram extends in pathlike fashion over a wide region of the memory area and involves numerous neurons. The solid black symbols in Figure B.1 exemplify an engram path. This grouping of information bits is the same as that used in a digital computer (see Appendix A, Figure A.14).

The specific mechanism by which bits of information and, hence, engrams are stored in memory synapses is not fully established. Some specialists believe storage is accomplished by processes that induce changes in the anatomical structure of the neurons. Others believe the changes are induced by chemical processes. Whether it is effected by anatomical, chemical, or other means, some changes obviously occur within the synapses when storage is implemented.

The unified concept postulates that all information entering the consciousness area is passed to the memory area, where it is immediately stored in the most readily available unoccupied set of

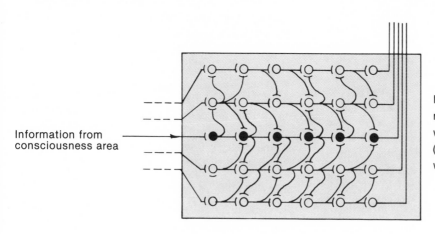

Information from consciousness area

NOTE: Solid black symbols represent a string of synapses with bits of information (engram) stored to represent words, letters, numbers, etc.

Figure B.1   Illustration of a memory engram path

synapses. Once storage occurs, the resulting en-gram becomes permanent. Its availability for fu-ture use, however, is limited by the ability for recall, which is discussed later.

The fact that information is stored in brain neurons is well substantiated. There is also con-siderable evidence which indicates that not all in-formation stored in the memory area is readily recallable. Numerous experiences and observa-tions support these conclusions. For example, dur-ing brain surgery for epilepsy, electrical stimula-tion has been used to find the area of the brain associated with the epileptic condition. Such stimulation, administered during wakefulness, often evoked memories which could be related in detail, but the patients could not recall the memories when stimulation ceased. Other signifi-cant experiences involve hypnotism. Myriads of incidents are recorded in which witnessess have recalled happenings under hypnosis that were foreign to any conscious recall. In one recent inci-dent, a kidnap victim was able to recall the kid-napper's automobile tag number while under hyp-nosis. Prior to hypnosis he could not recall even seeing the automobile tag. Another such incident was reported in the June 27, 1978 issue of *The Wall Street Journal.* Part of the article by Ronald Alsop follows:

> The 1976 slaying of Hollywood publicist Robert Yeager had the Los Angeles police stumped.
> Their only hope was John Sheehan, age 18, who lived near Mr. Yeager. He had seen a suspicious-looking pickup truck roaming the area on the night of the shooting. Unfortu-nately, Mr. Sheehan couldn't remember much about the mystery vehicle.
> Enter Lt. William Gaida, a Los Angeles policeman also trained in hypnosis. He hypno-tized the skeptical Mr. Sheehan, who amazed himself by recalling, in the mesmerized state, the truck's license number and by describing it down to the mud flaps and bumper sticker. Those details, says Lt. Gaida, led to the arrest of three juveniles, one of whom was convicted of the killing.

---

*Reprinted by permission of *The Wall Street Journal,* © Dow Jones & Company, Inc., 1978. All Rights Reserved.

"I said things under hypnosis that I hadn't realized I'd even seen," says Mr. Sheehan. "I guess it was all just buried somewhere in my mind."*

The capacity of the brain to accommodate the postulated memory storage system is well estab-lished. According to most authorities the brain contains over 10 billion neurons, with an average of 50,000 synapses each. This amounts to over 500 trillion synapses, with the storage capacity of 500 trillion information bits. Since, according to one observation, the brain stores an average of 100 trillion bits of information during a lifetime, the capacity of a brain that can store 500 trillion bits of information may be considered essentially lim-itless. Moreover, some recent findings indicate that the currently accepted estimates of 10 billion neurons in the brain is possibly too low by several orders of magnitude. As a further reference point for this tremendous storage capacity, current large high-speed digital computers operate with fewer than 1 billion bits of storage capacity.

Memory Recall

According to the unified concept, recalling in-formation stored in the memory area requires ex-citing the neuron synapses by coded impulses with frequencies at or near those corresponding to the information stored. As indicated in Figure 4.3, ex-citing impulses enter the memory area only from the consciousness area. But the consciousness area receives information from the various sensors, the memory area, and the concept and logic center. Thus, any one of these sources can supply the related information (coded impulses) necessary to effect memory recall.

The ease with which information, or engrams, can be recalled from memory depends upon the conditions under which storage occurs. The stor-age conditions which enhance memory recall are multisensory inputs of information and repetitive submission of information to the memory area.

MULTISENSORY INPUTS

How different sensory inputs influence mem-ory recall can best be explained by referring to Figure B.2. Initially, consider the storage of infor-mation in a memory area with no previous stor-age. Further, consider an observation in which

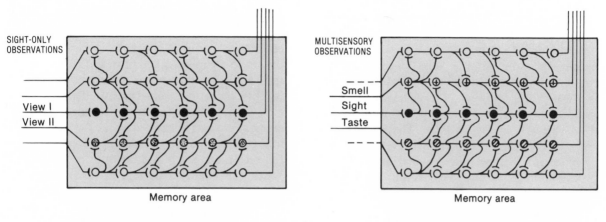

(a) Illustration of sight-only engram   (b) Illustration of multisensory engrams

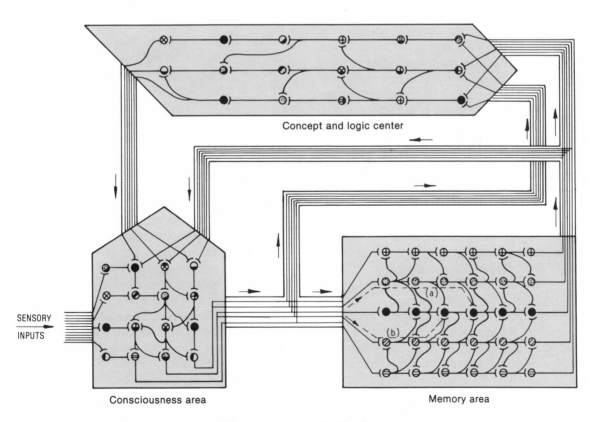

(c) Memory storage and retrieval process

Figure B.2   Illustration of memory storage and retrieval

sight is the only input to the consciousness area. Under these circumstances, the frequency-coded information or message in the consciousness area is passed to the memory area. Since no related engrams are present, there is no recall to the consciousness area. However, the message is stored in coded form, as indicated by the solid black symbols (View I) in Figure B.2a. The message, or engram, remains there indefinitely even if the view is removed. Reappearance of the identical view will result in the excitation of neurons in the memory area, and the view will be recalled (evoked) and recognized. A change to a different view produces another information input to consciousness, and it will likewise be projected to and stored as an engram in the memory area. If the new engram, represented by the symbols with small dots (View II) in Figure B.2a, is significantly different from that previously stored, the frequencies carrying the message will not excite the corresponding neurons. Indeed, recall of View I is unlikely, except by exposure to the identical view.

To further clarify the concept, consider the same initial memory conditions discussed above, but assume that information is supplied through smell and taste, as well as sight. In this case, memory storage is effected in the same manner discussed previously. But there is a difference. The frequencies corresponding to the stored information are much more extensive, representing the information available from three sensors instead of one. Figure B.2b illustrates the characteristics of engrams formed under these conditions—multisensory inputs. The significant point here is this: when extensive information is stored about a subject, the range of excitation frequencies which can initiate recall is greatly increased. As an example, if the subject under discussion were a delicious prize-winning cake, information collected through sight, smell, and taste sensors would be recorded in memory. Some time after completion of storage, recall of the experience might be initiated by frequencies representing any one of the sensory inputs. But even multisensory inputs do not ensure ready recall of stored information. The information may be too isolated from related information or engrams. Under these circumstances, the concept and logic center plays a key role in effecting memory recall.

As an example of this latter case, consider the situation where exposure to the prize-winning cake

has been experienced, and extensive sensory information is stored as indicated by several different coded symbols in Figure B.2c. A subsequent exposure to a similar cake but of a different shape, size, and color may not evoke adequate recall to identify the object as a cake. If detected, smell alone would excite certain neurons within the memory area, as illustrated by the dash-line path a in Figure B.2c. This may fail, however, to initiate full recall, and the object may not be recognized. When this situation occurs, as discussed earlier and illustrated in Figure 4.3, a signal indicating a difference between the memory engram recalled and information in the consciousness area activates the concept and logic center. The engram retrieved from memory passes to the concept and logic center, and processing directed toward resolution of the difference is initiated. The results then pass to the consciousness area and return to the memory area. If this new information evokes additional memory recall, the cycle will continue (thinking process). Continued processing may not, however, result in complete recall. When this happens, additional sensory information may be required. Perhaps a taste of the cake will activate the neurons along the dash-line path b and be adequate to support complete recall.

REPETITIVE SUBMISSION OF INFORMATION TO MEMORY AREA

The fact that memory recall is enhanced by repeated exposure to information is generally accepted. This observation is consistent with and can be explained by the unified concept.

According to the concept, any engram stored in the memory area exists there along with millions of others. Once stored, a single engram has a low probability of being stimulated during normal brain processes. Under certain conditions, this probability may be essentially nonexistent. By repetition of information, however, the resulting engram becomes associated with other engrams. As repetition continues, associations increase and the probability of recall is likewise increased. Engram associations that enhance memory recall may be formed either by repeated exposure of the consciousness and memory areas to information from sensory sources or by repetitive processing of information through the concept and logic center, the consciousness area, and the memory area. These two repetitive processes are similar, but not identical. They both influence memory recall and, in combination, account for all recallable memory engrams.

Memory engram storage begins early in a person's life and continues until death. Exactly when memory storage begins is not clear. It probably begins even before birth. Certainly those sensors that detect such conditions as hunger, thirst, and pain are well developed in a newborn child. This being the case, it must be assumed that the associated sensors also function before birth. The child's environment is inherently passive during this prenatal period. It is fed and protected by the mother's body, so its sensors are exposed to conditions in which hunger, thirst, and pain are absent. Thus, sensory signals representing these passive conditions are transmitted, not repetitively but continuously, to the memory area of the brain. This process results in the formation of related memory engrams that are readily recallable.

At birth, other sensory inputs such as sight, smell, and taste begin entering the memory area. But in the new environment, sensory information inputs exhibit a completely different character. The environment is in a continuous state of change, so that exact repetition of sensory inputs is infrequent. As a result, the probability of recalling engrams stored under these conditions is very low. However, with time, some of the sensory information inputs (or very similar inputs) are inevitably repeated, and recallable engrams are eventually formed. Obviously, the number of recallable engrams that can be formed in this manner is small, but their influence is far-reaching. Once a recallable engram is stored, it can be evoked by related incoming information. When this happens, the concept and logic center is activated. The resulting processes subject the memory area to repeated bits of related information, and recallable engrams are stored at an accelerated rate. Thus, it is this process that is responsible for the storage of most readily recallable engrams.

Concept-supporting Observations

The validity and soundness of the memory and recall process discussed above are supported by many general and specific observations. These observations span such diverse subjects as learning rates, emotional experiences, and memory loss occurrence.

LEARNING RATES

The memory storage and recall process established by the unified concept is in complete harmony with the observed learning (storing of recallable information) rates of people in general. The low learning rate experienced during early life is what would be expected from the nonrepetitive sensory information inputs experienced by a person during that period of life. And the accelerated learning rate experienced in the years that follow is consistent with the information repetition processes attributed to the concept and logic center.

EMOTIONAL EXPERIENCES

Experiences which produce human emotions are well recognized as being the ones most readily recalled. For example, few individuals will fail to remember something about their first day in school, their first day on a job, and the birth of their first child. Certain historical events are equally well remembered. The Japanese attack on Pearl Harbor, the assassination of President Kennedy, and the lunar landing of Armstrong and Aldrin are excellent examples.

The memory recall associated with such incidents is fully consistent with and supports the unified concept. Happenings of this kind evoke related memory engrams that differ from those being experienced. As the concept and logic center operates to resolve these differences, related information from many sources is circulated. As a result, many related recallable engrams are stored and memory recall is enhanced.

MEMORY LOSS

Individuals who have experienced some degree of memory loss are not uncommon in our society, but attempts to explain these losses have heretofore met with little success. However, there is considerable evidence indicating that such memory losses are associated with damage to the limbic system of the brain. Moreover, it has been observed that memory losses usually result from exposure to one or more of the following: neurosurgery, head injury, brain disease, and mental stress.

Each of the above observations is consistent with and can be explained by the unified concept and the associated conceptual model presented in Figure 4.3.

Neurosurgery

Certain brain surgery procedures sometimes result in damage to the hippocampus area. If the damage involves both hemispheres, the patient's memory is adversely affected.

For example, in one case, a brain operation performed to relieve epilepsy resulted in severe damage to the hippocampus area. Many of the individual's actions and capabilities appeared normal after the operation, and he recalled experiences that occurred before the operation. But his ability to recall information from experiences following the operation was essentially destroyed. On occasion, however, he surprised everyone by recalling information from a recent experience. One such surprise involved President John F. Kennedy. Although the operation occurred before Kennedy's election, he recognized the President's head on the half-dollar coin several years after Kennedy's death and recalled the assassination.

All these observations are consistent with the unified concept and could have been predicted from the conceptual model of the brain as follows:

The hippocampus area, where the nerve damage was sustained, is a complex network of fibers that extends to the frontal lobe (concept and logic center). These fibers, located in the region designated as A in Figure 4.3, supply activating signals to the concept and logic center. Thus, when these fibers are severed the concept and logic center loses its influence on storage of recallable information. However, as discussed previously, a low level of memory storage and recall can be effected by repeated exposure to sensory information. The individual's ability in this instance to recognize the President's head on a coin and remember his assassination can be attributed to the latter storage process.

Head Injury

Severe brain concussions frequently result in some form of memory loss. Lacerations or damage to the brain surface, on the other hand, seldom affect a person's memory. These observations are consistent with the unified concept.

According to this concept, brain memory storage is distributed widely throughout the cerebral cortex. Local surface damage to the brain, therefore, usually has no observable effect on memory.

The limbic system, which controls memory storage and recall, is located well inside the brain and is well protected against surface damage. However, since the major components of this system consist of hard and dense nuclei, their interfacing tissue and nerve fibers can be easily damaged by a sudden blow to the head.

Thus, a concussion that inflicts damage to the limbic system at any of the points designated as A, B, and C in Figure 4.3, as discussed earlier, will affect a person's ability to store and recall information subsequent to the damage. Damage inflicted at point B is even more critical. It may prevent any information from entering the memory area and, thereby, negate all storage and recall. When this happens, the victim loses the ability to recall both new and old experiences. Damage at point C may introduce either or both of the effects caused by damage at points A and B. Of course, as is indicated by the conceptual model of the brain, memory is restored if the damaged areas heal.

Brain Disease

A number of brain diseases are known to cause memory loss. Korsakoff's syndrome and Alzheimer's disease are examples. In both cases, loss of memory results from the damage these diseases inflict on elements of the limbic system. Thus, the fact that these diseases have an adverse effect on memory is consistent with the unified concept.

Mental Stress

Excessive mental stress which often culminates in depression is known to be one cause of memory loss. This observation is consistent with the brain functions and processes identified by the unified concept.

According to this concept, high levels of displeasure develop when a person is subjected to monumental problems which he or she is unable to resolve. When this situation exists, as has already been discussed, the high-frequency signal output, produced at point T in Figure 4.3, subjects the neuronal network to intensive activity. If this condition persists for an extended period, the displeasure produced may lead to depression. Also, under these conditions it is conceivable that the high level of neuronal activity could cause fatigue or even damage to the control synapses involved.

Thus, as is clear from the conceptual model of the brain, either of these conditions could produce some level of memory loss.

Memory Engrams

So far, memory engrams have been identified as recallable or nonrecallable. This is an over-simplification, because, depending upon the conditions under which the engrams are stored, their ease of recall varies greatly. Many engrams are recallable; some are readily recallable; others are impossible to recall.

Here, according to the ease of recall, these memory engrams have been grouped into four categories designated as *enate, associated, synthesized,* and *isolated.*

Enate engrams are unique in many ways. They stem from sensory sources, and they involve only information associated with physiological conditions of the body such as hunger, thirst, and pain. Enate engram formation is postulated to begin as sensors develop in the body of the unborn child. During this prenatal period, all the child's needs are supplied by the mother's body on a high-priority basis. The child's sensors, therefore, are not generally exposed to conditions that produce sensations of hunger, thirst, pain, or the likes. Under such conditions, the different sensors continuously transmit signals through the consciousness area to the memory area that are neutral relative to these physiological conditions. Thus, the enate engrams stored include information that usually reflects the absence of hunger, thirst, pain, etc. Since these engrams result from repeated, in fact nearly continuous, exposures, they are easily recalled.†

Associated engrams are, perhaps, the most important of the engram types. To a large degree they determine what an individual can and will accomplish in life. Beginning with birth, they are formed throughout life. Their formation results from the combined influence of repeated sensory information from the environment and repeated

processing by the concept and logic center. The type of information involved is that related to general observation and specific training. The characteristics of an associated engram—relative to content and recallability—depend, therefore, upon the specific information received from the environment and the extent to which it is repeatedly passed to the memory area.

Synthesized engrams are formed from the same information as associated engrams. But there is a significant difference. The difference results from logic-processing and information re-arrangement by the concept and logic center. Formed in this manner, these engrams represent new creations in the form of new concepts and ideas for tangible entities. These engrams, once stored, are recallable, although less easily than are enate and associated engrams.

Isolated engrams are those formed in virtual isolation from other related information. They are essentially impossible to recall and are of little value at the present state of understanding. However, these can sometimes be recalled by the aid of hypnosis.

D. CONCEPT AND LOGIC CENTER

Perhaps more than any other faculty, the capability to develop concepts and perform logic operations distinguishes the human being from other animals. In the unified concept, this capability is postulated to originate in the prefrontal lobe of the cerebral cortex. In addition to performing this important logic operation, the concept and logic center also exerts a significant influence on human emotions. As has already been discussed, when the concept and logic center is successful in performing its basic function—that is, problem-solving—it produces a sensation of pleasure (or decrease in displeasure) and reduces aggressiveness. Conversely, when it cannot resolve the problems at hand, the opposite result is produced: displeasure and aggressiveness.

Evidence supporting the postulated role of the concept and logic center (prefrontal lobe of the cerebral cortex) is available from numerous observations and test results, including the following: observations of the neuronal connection with

---

†The formation of enate engrams in the manner described is reasonable and consistent with the unified concept. There is, however, a recognized possibility that some of these engrams are genetic in origin. If such does turn out to be the case, it will not invalidate the basic premise of the unified concept.

other parts of the brain; results of electrical stimulation tests; electroencephalogram records; and results of accidental frontal lobe damage and psychosurgery.

NEURONAL CONNECTIONS

The prefrontal lobe projects to and receives neuronal fibers from the brain stem and most other areas of the cerebral cortex. The neuronal connections with the thalamus, the center of consciousness and control, are particularly extensive. Hence, the fibers necessary for the functions postulated by the conceptual model are in the appropriate places.

ELECTRICAL STIMULATION TESTS

Electrical stimulation when applied to many regions of the brain evokes significant responses such as pain, body movement, and speech impairment. Mild electrical stimulation of the prefrontal lobe has no such dramatic effect. This characteristic is consistent with the unified concept in which the prefrontal lobe functions involve only logic-processing, using numerous neuronal inputs from the consciousness and memory areas.

ELECTROENCEPHALOGRAM RECORDS

Electroencephalogram records show a definite correlation between the frontal lobe activity and brain logic-processing. In one experiment, an electroencephalogram recorded during a period when the subject was sitting quietly revealed only jumbled waves. The waves became synchronous in the frontal lobe area when the individual was given a pair of two-digit numbers to multiply, however, indicating systematic processing of the problem.

ACCIDENTAL DAMAGE AND PSYCHOSURGERY

The observation of individuals with accidentally damaged or surgically removed sections of frontal lobes provides considerable insight into the functions of the prefrontal area. Both industrial-accident and war-casualty victims have been closely observed, and the effects of numerous frontal lobotomies (performed for psychological reasons) have been widely reported. Although observations and tests were not conducted in a uniform manner, certain important conclusions relating to both logic and other psychological processes can be made.

Logic-processing

With respect to logic-processing, individuals with damaged prefrontal lobes were observed to lose their ability to plan, exercise judgment, perform creative tasks, develop concepts, and perform logic operations.

Certain specific tests have further confirmed the effects of frontal lobe damage on logic-processing. The results of formboard tests given to patients with and without frontal lobe damage are quite revealing. (A formboard is a thin, flat board with various-shaped figure cutouts, for which matching insert-pieces are provided.) The tests were conducted with patients blindfolded. Those without frontal lobe damage were able to locate and match all parts to the board, but those with frontal lobe damage could not. These results are consistent with and could have been predicted from the unified concept.

Emotions

Frontal lobotomy was introduced primarily as a remedy for emotional disorders. Its success is a matter of controversy, for results are varied with respect to both the intended objective and the side effects. However, these operations and other incidents of frontal lobe damage show the frontal lobe has a significant influence on certain human emotions. Lobotomies are generally successful in relieving severe anxiety and violent psychotic conditions, but they often introduced undesirable side results. Commonly reported results include loss of ambition, loss of personality, quick changes in mood (short-lived emotional display), carelessness in personal habits, insensitivity to criticism, unconcern about social relationships, and general apathy. It has also been observed that the favorable effects of lobotomy probably resulted from removal of fear and anxiety rather than removal of the basic problem. According to one often-reported incident, a lawyer concerned about his excessive drinking submitted to a lobotomy. As a result of the operation, his desire for and use of alcohol was unchanged but he no longer viewed his drinking as a problem. Also, in one instance in which an individual underwent the operation for pain, the pain remained after the operation but the patient ceased complaining.

These observations may appear random and unrelated; however, each is consistent with and supportive of the role played by the concept and logic center. In more specific terms, if control nerve fibers passing from the concept and logic center to the hippocampus area (Figure 4.3) were severed in a lobotomy, the patient's emotional responses would be greatly modified and appreciably reduced.

E. AMYGDALA

Because of its close association with emotions, the amygdala has been the subject of numerous investigations. Electrical stimulations of the amygdala have been reported to cause essentially every type of emotional response. But these results require interpretation. The neuronal connections between the amygdala and the emotion-sensitive hypothalamus are extensive and complex. Thus, when electrical stimulation is applied to the amygdala, it is difficult to discern whether the amygdala or the hypothalamus is responsible for the resulting response. The preponderance of results, however, indicates that motivation—ranging from aggression to indifference—is the emotion most closely associated with the amygdala. Other functions of the amygdala are less clear, although there are indications that the amygdala may have some influence on pleasure and displeasure. The neuronal connections that permit the amygdala to perform the postulated functions are indicated in Figure 4.3.

The functions of the amygdala as identified here are also consistent with observations made of individuals with damaged or surgically removed prefrontal lobes. These individuals generally lose all concern for problems and often experience highly aggressive moods. As shown in the conceptual model (Figure 4.3), frontal lobotomy could be expected to destroy the neuron fibers carrying signals to the pleasure and displeasure areas. But it

would not disturb the fibers carrying signals to the aggression and indifference areas via the amygdala.

F. HIPPOCAMPUS

Like the amygdala, the hippocampus is closely associated with emotions. It is also involved with memory storage and recall. The mechanism responsible for performing the particular functions ascribed to the hippocampus have not been physiologically defined. In fact, detailed knowledge of its functions is extremely sparse. Hence, in developing the conceptual model for the unified concept the characteristics and functions of the hippocampus were postulated from more general observations.

As part of the limbic system (sometimes called the emotional brain), the hippocampus is situated in a region which is very sensitive to emotions. Its specific role in emotions is vague, although behavioral changes have been noted in individuals who have experienced damage to the hippocampus.

A number of investigative studies have shown the hippocampus has considerable influence on memory storage and recall. Where individuals have experienced severe hippocampus damage, the effects on memory have been dramatic, and the ability to retain new information for more than a few minutes is usually lost. In other words, the individual is unable to store and recall, for future use, new facts or skills. However, such damage does not prevent recall of information previously stored in the memory. These are important observations which support the unified concept and the associated conceptual model, as Figure 4.3 serves to illustrate. The signal which activates the concept and logic center originates within the thalamus, as discussed earlier. It passes through certain elements of the limbic system to the amygdala, then proceeds to the concept and logic center via the hippocampus. Damage to the hippocampus area, therefore, subjects the signal-carrying fiber to potential damage. Damage to these fibers essentially inactivates the concept and logic center. As shown previously, processing by the concept and logic center is crucial to long-term memory and recall. Hence, the conceptual model and the postulated functions and processes are completely consistent with characteristics exhibited by individuals who have experienced hippocampus damage.

G. RETICULAR ACTIVATING SYSTEM

The fact that the reticular activating system plays a primary role in establishing the state of human consciousness is generally accepted. The process by which it accomplishes its functions, however, has never been thoroughly delineated. Even so, much is known about the reticular activating system and how it influences human consciousness.

As a network of reverberating circuits, the reticular activating system is always operating at some level of excitation. This excitation is continuously transmitted to crucial regions of the brain. There it influences the transfer of information, memory storage and recall, logic-processing, and body actions. In this way, the reticular ac-

tivating system controls brain activity and the state of human consciousness.

The relationship between states of consciousness and brain activity is well documented by extensive data from electroencephalograph records. Typical levels of brain activity associated with several states of consciousness are listed below:

Consciousness state	Brain activity* (hertz or cycles per second)
Awake	
Alert	14 to 30
Relaxed	8 to 13
Asleep	
Deep sleep	1 to 3
Intermediate sleep	4 to 14
Dream sleep	14+

*Electroencephalograph measurements

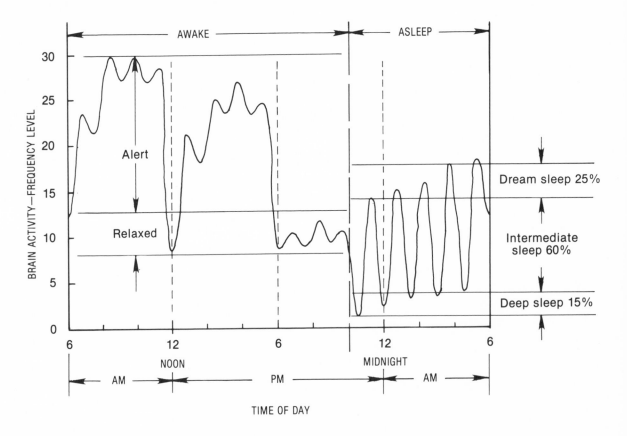

Figure B.3   Illustration of typical daily brain activities as induced by the reticular activating system

Brain activity, as defined above, follows two cyclic periods. One period, the normal wake-and-sleep cycle, is 24 hours in duration. The other, an approximately 90-minute period, is superimposed on the 24-hour cycle. The combined influence of these two cycles on brain activity over a typical 24-hour period is illustrated in Figure B.3.

The cause of cyclic variations in brain activity is generally believed to be associated with some type of biological clock. How it operates is unknown. However, based on current understanding of the brain and its elements, the clock operation seems to depend on the fatigue-and-recovery characteristics of synapses in the reticular activating system. These synapses evidently go through a fatigue-and-recovery cycle every 90 minutes or so, and the resulting variations produce corresponding changes in brain activity.

During the awake period, the reticular activating system is stimulated continuously by external sources (sensors or the consciousness area). This stimulation tends to keep brain activity at a relatively high level. Because of the external stimulation, however, the synapses in the reticular activating system apparently become more fatigued after each fatigue-and-recovery cycle. Consequently, the brain activity produced by the reticular activating system drops after each successive 90-minute cycle. After approximately ten such cycles following a condition in which the synapses are fully rested, brain activity falls to a level that induces sleep.

During the sleep period, synapses in the reticular activating system go through the same fatigue-and-recovery cycles. But there is an important difference: no external stimulations are applied. Under these conditions, fatigue of the synapses is reduced after each 90-minute fatigue-and-recovery cycle. After approximately six such cycles, the synapses approach a condition near full-recovery from fatigue, and a period of wakefulness follows.

The above discussion and observations are in complete harmony with the conceptual model of the brain presented in Figure 4.3. They are also consistent with the different states of consciousness, variously defined as wakefulness, sleep, arousal, insomnia, and hallucinations.

WAKEFULNESS

After a sufficient period of sleep, the synapses

in the reticular activating system become rested, or reach a low state of fatigue. Under these conditions, high levels of stimulation from external sources cause correspondingly high levels of brain activity. This activity, in turn, produces an alert state of wakefulness. On the other hand, when external stimulation is relatively low, brain activity is low and a relaxed state of wakefulness prevails.

During the awake period, brain activity indicated by frequency measurements varies between approximately 8 and 30 cycles per second (hertz). The frequency range of 14 to 30 hertz is associated with the alert state of consciousness, while the frequency range of 8 to 13 hertz identifies the relaxed state. Figure B.3 illustrates typical variations in the alert and relaxed states, during an awake period.

SLEEP

Sleep results when the synapses in the reticular activating system become fatigued (following a period of wakefulness) and external stimulation is low. During this period, brain activity, in terms of frequency, ranges from slightly above 14 to near 1 hertz. There are many stages of sleep within this range.

Deep sleep is the least active stage. It occurs when the frequency of brain activity is between approximately 1 and 3 hertz.

Intermediate sleep covers those stages of sleep that occur when the brain activity frequencies are between approximately 4 and 14 hertz.

Dreaming is the most active and also the most interesting stage of sleep. During dreaming, the frequency level of brain activity reaches values above 14 hertz. This is a unique situation, since 14 hertz is above the frequency level associated with wakefulness. There is, however, a reasonable explanation for this apparent paradox. It involves the different frequency characteristics exhibited by the many reverberating circuits in the reticular activating system.

Since each circuit consists of a unique group of neurons and synapses, each can be expected to reverberate at a different frequency. Furthermore, as discussed earlier, the frequency output of each circuit undergoes cyclic variation every 90 minutes or so.

How frequency variations in the reverberating circuits induce dreaming is best explained by referring to the conceptual model of the brain, shown schematically in Figure 4.3. In this figure, the circuits designated as *a, b,* and *c* represent the many reverberating circuits that make up the reticular activating system. The dash lines, identified by *W, X, Y,* and *Z,* represent the numerous nerve fibers that connect the many reverberating circuits with crucial regions of the brain.

To illustrate how these reverberating circuits operate to produce the different stages of sleep, the following conditions have been chosen as typical: the reverberating circuits represented by *a* and *b* are operating at relatively low frequencies; and the reverberating circuits represented by *c* are operating at a relatively high frequency.

When these conditions prevail, the average excitation applied to the brain is comparatively low. But the excitation is not uniform. The local regions of the brain connected to the reverberating circuits represented by *a* and *b* receive low levels of excitation through nerve fibers identified as *W* and *X*. Even at the peak circuit frequencies reached during the 90-minute cycle, the level of excitation remains relatively low. On the other hand, the local regions of the brain connected to the circuits represented by *c* receive a comparatively high level of excitation every 90 minutes through nerve fibers identified as *Y* and *Z*.

The reverberating circuit characteristics and the brain excitations they produce account for all stages of sleep. Each stage of sleep is associated with a particular level of brain activity, and each is repeated every 90-minute cycle. Dreaming occurs in that part of the sleep cycle where brain activity, as measured by an electroencephalograph, is highest. The dreaming phenomenon and the accompanying high level of brain activity can be explained as follows:

When the reverberating circuits reach their peak frequency levels, those circuits represented by *c* supply relatively high levels of excitation to certain local regions of the brain. In Figure 4.3, these local regions include those parts of the brain identified as the consciousness area, the concept and logic center, and the memory area. The excitation applied to these areas is adequate to induce limited information transfer and logic-processing. The operations, however, are uncoordinated and out of harmony with other brain activities. Under these conditions, the information transferred between areas is necessarily random and possibly ambiguous. Therefore, when this information enters the consciousness area, it can reasonably be expected to produce the seemingly nonsensical visions, ideas, and fantasies that characterize dreams.

During dreaming, both the concept and logic center and the memory area receive relatively high levels of excitation. Since both are located in the cerebral cortex (brain surface), these excitations are readily sensed by an electroencephalograph. Thus the relatively high level of brain activity (over 14 hertz) reported for the dreaming phase of sleep is as would be expected on the basis of the conceptual model.

AROUSAL

Once sleep is induced, it tends to continue until the reticular activating system is excited from an external source. This can and usually does occur as a result of disturbance by external sensors. Noise, touch, or any source of pain may create the disturbance required to cause arousal.

INSOMNIA

The state of wakefulness exists when the reticular activating system transmits sufficient excitation to all areas of the brain. Normally, this condition occurs only when the synapses in the reticular activating system are in a low state of fatigue. However, wakefulness may be induced by strong stimulations from either sensors or the consciousness area, even when the synapses of the reticular activating system are in a highly fatigued state. As an example, when an individual faces severe problems, forces inside the brain tend to keep the concept and logic center, the memory area, and consciousness area active. If stimulation of the reticular activating system resulting from these processes is sufficiently high, sleep may be impossible. Sensory inputs such as pain can also prevent sleep even when the reticular activating system is in a highly fatigued state. These are the conditions which produce insomnia.

HALLUCINATIONS

Hallucinations are related to both insomnia and dreaming. They usually occur when an individual is awake for an extended period of time and the synapses of the reticular activating system are in a highly fatigued state. Under these conditions the wakefulness state is maintained only by external stimulation of the reticular activating system. Eventually, even the effects of external stimulation deteriorate, and the brain functions tend to become uncoordinated. At this time, a dreamlike situation develops and hallucinations occur.

C

Application Of Estimating Procedures: An Example

The techniques and procedures used in estimating a person's mental qualities are identified in Chapter 10. This appendix illustrates how the various techniques and procedures are used in the estimating process.

First, information about a typical applicant is summarized. Then, step-by-step procedures used in estimating the applicant's human mental qualities are delineated.

AVAILABLE INFORMATION

The information normally available for evaluating a person's mental qualities is that which can be acquired through the proper use of a job application, personal interviews, and personal references. It consists of specific and relevant facts about the applicant's past accomplishments, actions, and environmental exposures. For the particular job applicant considered in this example, the pertinent information is summarized as follows:

EARLY FAMILY-LIFE EXPERIENCES

Stability

Relationship between applicant's mother and father was generally good; amiable relationships prevailed among all family members.

Social and Economic Status

Father was a small-business man, with income estimated to be twice that of the national (U.S.) average.

Religion

Family participated frequently in religious activities.

Discipline and Work

Parents exercised rather firm discipline. They required home chores and encouraged part-time work after school and between school terms.

EXTRACURRICULAR ACTIVITIES

Organization and Group Activities

In high school, applicant played 4 years of football. During the football season, about 16 hours a week were spent in supervised and unsupervised practice and workout.

Individual Activities and Hobbies

Applicant attended a high school where students consistently won statewide recognition in science exhibit competitions. He participated each year in statewide science fairs and once won first-place recognition. During the period of exhibit preparation the applicant spent approximately 16 hours per week on the project. (School population represented by competing students: 70,000.)

Written Communications

Applicant was a reporter for a college newspaper whose articles often received statewide recognition (state population: 1 million). He occasionally wrote by-line articles, and some were published in state papers and magazines.

EDUCATION PROGRAMS

Psychological Tests

Applicant's combined SAT (verbal + math) score: 1100.

High School

Average combined SAT score of college-bound students in applicant's high school graduating class: 1150. Class standing: upper 20 percent. Level of homework study effort: about 10 hours a week.

College

Average combined SAT score of applicant's graduating class (bachelor's degree): 1200. Class standing: upper 20 percent. Level of homework study effort: about 35 hours a week.

Advanced Study

Average combined SAT score of graduating class (master's degree): 1200. Standing in class: upper 50 percent. Research and thesis: completed work and thesis within the nominal period established by the college. A paper covering the research work was published in a nationally recognized publication, an accomplishment often achieved by students of the college.

WORK EXPERIENCES

Work experiences span 10 years in an applied research and development organization and included work as an analyst, a synthesist, and a supervisor. The applicant enjoyed most facets of the required work and frequently worked voluntary overtime, which averaged about 16 hours a week.

Analyst

Did analytical work for 7 years, during which time performance as indicated by salary increases was estimated to be in the upper 40 percent of the group.

Synthesist

Prepared and assisted in preparing several reports. Made a number of original contributions in the form of new ideas and concepts. Performance as a synthesist, covering much of the past 6 years, was estimated to be in the upper 10 percent of the group.

Supervisor

Supervised 6 to 10 persons during last 4 years. Performance as a supervisor rated in the upper 30 percent of the group.

OBSERVED PERSONAL QUALITIES

Knowledge

Response to questions during interview indicated substantial knowledge about subjects studied in college, which resulted in the applicant's placement in the upper 20 percent (relative to knowledge) of a professional service organization.

Problem-solving Capability

Discussions with the applicant revealed a full appreciation of what is required to succeed in his selected vocation. There was considerable completeness and logic in discussion of past activities and future plans, which led the evaluator to rate the applicant in the upper 10 percent of a professional service organization.

Behavioral Characteristics

The applicant's actions during the interview reflected considerable enthusiasm, confidence, and ability to interact favorably with others. Relative to both these characteristics the applicant was ranked in the upper 20 percent of a professional service organization.

ESTIMATING PROCEDURES

The procedures used in the following example are defined and discussed in Chapter 10. These procedures, which make use of 17 separate sources of information (see Figure C.1), provide techniques for use in estimating values for the brain capacity factors, environmental factors, and com-

SELECTED INFORMATION SOURCES	BRAIN CAPACITY FACTORS			ENVIRONMENTAL FACTORS				COMPOSITE FACTORS			
						Ebx				BSQ × Ebx	
	IQ	PSQ	BSQ	Emi or Emi-e	Emps	Ebmo	Ebip	IQ × Emi	PSQ × Emps	BSQ × Ebmo	BSQ × Ebip
Early Family-Life Experiences							e				
Stability				a		c					
Social and economic status							f				
Religion						d					
Discipline and work											
Extracurricular Activities										p	
Organization and group activities									m	p	
Individual activities and hobbies					i				m		
Written communications					i						
Education Programs	j										
Psychological tests	k			g,h				k		p	
High school	k			g,h				k		q	
College	k			g,h	i			k	m		
Advanced study											
Work Experiences				o				l		p	
Analyst					b				l	p	
Synthesist										p	l
Supervisor											
Observed Personal Qualities								l			
Knowledge									l		
Problem-solving capability										l	l
Behavioral characteristics											
						a				a	
"Best-estimate" of factor values											

Effective mental capability

$$= \sqrt[3]{(IQ \times Emi)(PSQ \times Emps)(BSQ \times Ebx)} \;=\; \sqrt[3]{(\quad)(\quad)(\quad)} \;=\; (\quad)^n$$

a See text, Chapter 10, under heading of applicable factor
b Estimate from Table 10.3
c Estimate from Table 10.4
d Estimate from Table 10.5
e Estimate from Table 10.6
f Estimate from Table 10.7
g Estimate from Figure 10.4
h Estimate from Figure 10.5
i Estimate from Figure 10.7
j Estimate from Figure 10.8
k Estimate from Figure 10.9
l Estimate from Figure 10.10
m Estimate from Figure 10.11
n Estimate from Equation 8.3
o Estimate from Equation 10.2
p Estimate from Equation 10.3
q Estimate from Equation 10.4

Figure C.1 Capability evaluation form

posite factors employed in the capability evaluation process. Each of these factors serves a useful purpose.

Intelligence quotient or IQ, the only brain capacity factor for which estimating procedures have been defined, is useful because it indicates in quantitative terms a person's potential to acquire knowledge.

Environmental factors are useful because they indicate, also in quantitative terms, the quality of environment to which a person has been exposed. That is, they define the relative opportunity for a person to acquire information from the environment.

Composite factors, since they represent the combined influence of both brain capacity factors and environmental factors, are by far the most important qualities in the evaluation process. They define, within estimating accuracy, a person's knowledge, problem-solving capability, and behavioral characteristics—the factors that determine effective mental capability.

Even though some of the many factors are clearly more useful in the evaluation process than others, each is important. And for best results all must be carefully considered. To aid in these considerations, Figure C.1 identifies (with rectangular boxes) all the factors to be estimated and the applicable information source. It also identifies the tables, figures, and equations that provide the means for estimating each factor value.

The example that follows illustrates how the various procedures are used in the evaluation process. Using the previously established information about the job applicant, a step-by-step procedure is presented for determining each of the various brain capacity factors, environmental factors, and composite factors. The procedures for arriving at the "best-estimate" of each factor value are then illustrated, and the job applicant's effective mental capability is estimated.

BRAIN CAPACITY FACTORS

IQ (Intelligence Quotient)

EDUCATION PROGRAMS

Psychological Tests

Applicable Relationships: Figures 10.8, Chart A.

Pertinent Information: Applicant's combined SAT score — 1100.

Procedure: Enter Figure 10.8, Chart A, at an SAT score of 1100 and read

Measured IQ = 126

High School

Applicable Relationships: Figures 10.6 and 10.9, Chart A.

Pertinent Information: Applicant's class standing — upper 20 percent. Average SAT score of college-bound high school seniors — 1150.

Procedure:

Step 1 — Enter Figure 10.6 at an SAT score of 1150 for college-bound high school seniors and read class average SAT score of 1000.

Step 2 — Enter Figure 10.9, Chart A, at the upper 20 percent standing and for a class average SAT score of 1000 read

Apparent IQ = 134

College

Applicable Relationships: Figure 10.9, Chart A.

Pertinent Information: Applicant's class standing — upper 30 percent. College class average SAT score — 1200.

Procedure: Enter Figure 10.9, Chart A, at the upper 30 percent standing and for a class average SAT score of 1200 read

Apparent IQ = 142

Advanced Study

Applicable Relationships: Figure 10.9, Chart A.

Pertinent Information: Applicant's class standing — upper 50 percent. College (advanced study) class average SAT score — 1200.

Procedure: Enter Figure 10.9, Chart A, at the upper 50 percent standing for a class average SAT score of 1200 and read

Apparent IQ = 133

ENVIRONMENTAL FACTORS

Emi (Influence of the Environment on Knowledge)

EARLY FAMILY-LIFE EXPERIENCES

Social and Economic Status

The estimated influence of the applicant's early-life social and economic status is combined with the influence of education programs, as illustrated below.

EDUCATION PROGRAMS

High School Programs

Applicable Relationships: Figures 10.4 and 10.5

Pertinent Information: Family income during childhood—twice (200 percent) national average. High school class average SAT score—1000.

Procedure:

Step 1—Enter Figure 10.4a at student age corresponding to high school completion and read Emi-sd as 0.54.

Step 2—Enter Figure 10.4b at a class average SAT score of 1000 and read Emi-sq as 0.89.

Step 3—Enter Figure 10.5 at 200 percent of the national average income and proceed through Charts A and B as indicated by arrows and read △Emi-sq as +0.03.

Step 4—Add △Emi-sq (0.03) to Emi-sq (0.89) and estimate Emi-sq as 0.92.

Step 5—Multiply Emi-sd (0.54) by Emi-sq (0.92) and estimate that

$$\text{Emi-e} = 0.50$$

College (Bachelor's Degree)

Applicable Relationships: Figures 10.4 and 10.5.

Pertinent Information: Family income during childhood—twice (200 percent) national average. College class average SAT score—1200.

Procedure:

Step 1—Enter Figure 10.4a at student age corresponding to a bachelor's degree and read Emi-sd as 0.72.

Step 2—Enter Figure 10.4b at a class average SAT score of 1200 and read Emi-sq as 0.98.

Step 3—Enter Figure 10.5 at 200 percent of the national average income and proceed through Charts A and B as indicated by

arrows and read △Emi-sq as +0.01.

Step 4—Add △Emi-sq (0.01) to Emi-sq (0.98) and estimate Emi-sq as 0.99.

Step 5—Multiply Emi-sd (0.72) by Emi-sq (0.99) and estimate that

$$\text{Emi-e} = 0.71$$

Advanced Study (Master's Degree)

Applicable Relationships: Figures 10.4 and 10.5.

Pertinent Information: Family income during childhood—twice national average. College class average SAT score—1200.

Procedure: Use pertinent information listed, proceed as above, and estimate that

$$\text{Emi-e} = 0.75$$

WORK EXPERIENCES

Analyst

Applicable Relationships: Equation 10.2.

Pertinent Information: Applicable environmental factor from college work—Emi-e = 0.75. Work experience as an analyst—7 years in an applied research and development organization.

Procedure: Use Equation 10.2 and estimate that

$$\text{Emi} = 0.85$$

Emps (Influence of the Environment on Problem-solving Capability)

EXTRACURRICULAR ACTIVITIES

Individual Activities and Hobbies

Applicable Relationships: Figure 10.7.

Pertinent Information: Activity—high school science fair competition. Accomplishments of group members—frequently won statewide recognition. Student population represented in statewide competition—70,000.

Procedure: Enter Figure 10.7 at a population of 70,000 and read

$$\text{Emps} = 0.74$$

Written Communications

Applicable Relationships: Figure 10.7.

Pertinent Information: Activity—writing for college newspaper. Accomplishments of group members—articles frequently won statewide recognition. State population—1 million.

Procedure: Enter Figure 10.7 and, for a recognizing body representing a state with a population of 1 million, read

$$Emps = 0.80$$

EDUCATION PROGRAMS

Advanced Study

Applicable Relationships: Figure 10.7.

Pertinent Information: Activity—college graduate research programs. Accomplishments of other students—past participants frequently won national recognition for research accomplishments.

Procedure: Enter Figure 10.7 and, for a recognizing body representing the United States (240 million population), read

$$Emps = 0.93$$

WORK EXPERIENCES

Synthesist

Applicable Relationships: Table 10.3.

Pertinent Information: Work group—applied research and development organization (effective mental capability = 125).

Procedure: Use Table 10.3 and for an effective mental capability of 125, read

$$Emps = 0.95$$

Ebx (Influence of the Environment on Behavioral Characteristics)

Ebmo (INFLUENCE OF THE ENVIRONMENT ON MOTIVATION)

Early Family-Life Experiences

Social and Economic Status

Applicable Relationships: Table 10.4.

Pertinent Information: Income of family during childhood—twice the national average.

Procedure: Use Table 10.4 and estimate for this family that

$$Ebmo = 0.40$$

Discipline and Work

Applicable Relationships: Table 10.5.

Pertinent Information: Level of work and discipline imposed by parents—relatively high.

Procedure: Use Table 10.5 and estimate that

$$Ebmo = 0.90$$

Ebip (INFLUENCE OF THE ENVIRONMENT ON INTERPERSONAL RELATIONSHIPS)

Early Family-Life Experiences

Stability

Applicable Relationships: Table 10.6.

Pertinent Information: Level of cordiality, tolerance, and respect among family members—relatively high.

Procedure: Use Table 10.6 and estimate that

$$Ebip = 0.90$$

Religion

Applicable Relationships: Table 10.7.

Pertinent Information: Level of family participation in religious activities—reasonably high.

Procedure: Use Table 10.7 and estimate that

$$Ebip = 0.80$$

COMPOSITE FACTORS

IQ × Emi (Knowledge)

EDUCATION PROGRAMS

High School

Applicable Relationships: Figure 10.9.

Pertinent Information: Education completed—high school. Standing in graduation class—upper 20 percent. Average SAT score of class—1000.

Procedure: Enter Chart A at the upper 20 percent standing, proceed through the charts as indicated by arrows, and read

$$IQ \times Emi\text{-}e = 65$$

College

Applicable Relationships: Figure 10.9.

Pertinent Information: Education completed—college (bachelor's degree). Standing in class—upper 30 percent. Average SAT score of class—1200.

Procedure: Enter Chart A at the upper 30 percent standing, proceed through the charts indicated by arrows, and read

$$IQ \times \text{Emi-e} = 95$$

Advanced Study

Applicable Relationships: Figure 10.9.

Pertinent Information: Education completed —advanced study (master's degree). Standing in class—upper 50 percent. Average SAT score of class—1200.

Procedure: Enter Chart A at the upper 50 percent standing, proceed through the charts as indicated by the arrows, and read

$$IQ \times \text{Emi-e} = 100$$

WORK EXPERIENCES

Analyst

Applicable Relationships: Figure 10.10.

Pertinent Information: Work group—applied research and development organization. Rank in organization while working as an analyst—upper 40 percent.

Procedure: Enter Chart A at the upper 40 percent standing, proceed through the charts as indicated by arrows, and read

$$IQ \times \text{Emi} = 122$$

OBSERVED PERSONAL QUALITIES

Knowledge

Applicable Relationships: Figure 10.10.

Pertinent Information: Work group used by interviewer as basis for ranking—professional service organization. Ranking by interviewer relative to knowledge possessed— upper 20 percent of the organization.

Procedure: Enter Chart A at the upper 20 percent standing in the organization, proceed through charts as indicated by arrows, and read

$$IQ \times \text{Emi} = 120$$

PSQ × Emps (Problem-solving Capability)

EXTRACURRICULAR ACTIVITIES

Individual Activities and Hobbies

Applicable Relationships: Figure 10.11.

Pertinent Information: Activity—high school science fair competition. Accomplishments —won first place with a creative project. Stu-

dent population represented by competitors—70,000.

Procedure: Enter Figure 10.11 at a population of 70,000 and read

$$PSQ \times \text{Emps} = 125$$

Written Communications

Applicable Relationships: Figure 10.11.

Pertinent Information: Activity—writing for a college newspaper. Accomplishments— wrote several articles that received statewide recognition. State population—1 million.

Procedure: Enter Figure 10.11 and for a recognizing body representing a state with a population of 1 million, read

$$PSQ \times \text{Emps} = 142$$

EDUCATION PROGRAMS

Advanced Study

Applicable Relationships: Figure 10.11.

Pertinent Information: Activity—college graduate research program. Accomplishments—completed research and published results in a nationally recognized publication.

Procedure: Enter Figure 10.11 and, for a recognizing body representing the United States (240 million population) read

$$PSQ \times \text{Emps} = 168$$

WORK EXPERIENCES

Synthesist

Applicable Relationships: Figure 10.10.

Pertinent Information: Work group—applied research and development organization. Ranking in organization as a synthesist—upper 10 percent.

Procedure: Enter Chart A at the upper 10 percent standing, proceed through the charts as indicated by arrows, and read

$$PSQ \times \text{Emps} = 135$$

OBSERVED PERSONAL QUALITIES

Problem-solving Capability

Applicable Relationships: Figure 10.10.

Pertinent Information: Work group used by interviewer as basis for ranking—professional service organization. Ranking of interviewer relative to logic and judgment expressed—upper 10 percent.

Procedure: Enter Chart *A* at the upper 10 percent standing, proceed through the charts as indicated by arrows, and read

$$PSQ \times Emps = 125$$

BSQ × Ebx (Behavioral Characteristics)

BSQ × Ebmo (MOTIVATION)

Extracurricular Activities

Organization and Group Activities

Applicable Relationships: Equation 10.3.

Pertinent Information: Activity—high school football. Level of participation—during football season student spent 16 hours in supervised and unsupervised practice and workout.

Procedure: Use Equation 10.3 and estimate that

$$BSQ \times Ebmo = 117$$

Individual Activities and Hobbies

Applicable Relationships: Equation 10.3.

Pertinent Information: Activity—high school science fair competition. Level of participation—during the period of exhibit preparation the student spent 16 hours per week in his project.

Procedure: Use Equation 10.3 and estimate that

$$BSQ \times Ebmo = 117$$

Education Programs

High School

Applicable Relationships: Equation 10.3.

Pertinent Information: Level of study homework effort—approximately 10 hours per week.

Procedure: Use Equation 10.3 and estimate that

$$BSQ \times Ebmo = 90$$

College

Applicable Relationships: Equation 10.4.

Pertinent Information: Level of study homework effort—approximately 35 hours per week.

Procedure: Use Equation 10.4 and estimate that

$$BSQ \times Ebmo = 124$$

Work Experiences

Analyst, Synthesist, and Supervisor

Applicable Relationships: Equation 10.3.

Pertinent Information: Average amount of overtime spent on job-related matters—16 hours per week.

Procedure: Use Equation 10.3 and estimate that

$$BSQ \times Ebmo = 117$$

Observed Personal Qualities

Behavioral Characteristics

Applicable Relationships: Figure 10.10.

Pertinent Information: Motivation rating by interviewer—upper 20 percent of a professional service organization.

Procedure: Enter Chart *A* at the upper 20 percent standing, proceed through the charts as indicated by arrows, and read

$$BSQ \times Ebmo = 120$$

BSQ × Ebip (INTERPERSONAL RELATIONSHIPS)

Work Experiences

Supervisor

Applicable Relationships: Figure 10.10.

Pertinent Information: Work experiences as a supervisor—4 years in an applied research and development organization. Rank in the organization as a supervisor—upper 30 percent.

Procedure: Enter Chart *A* at the upper 30 percent standing, proceed through the charts, and read

$$BSQ \times Ebip = 123$$

Observed Personal Qualities

Behavioral Characteristics

Applicable Relationships: Figure 10.10.

Pertinent Information: Rating of interpersonal relationships by interviewer—upper 20 percent of a professional service organization.

Procedure: Enter Chart *A* at the upper 20 percent standing, proceed through the charts as indicated by arrows, and read

$$BSQ \times Ebip = 120$$

ANALYSIS AND INTERPRETATION

From the factor values estimated above, one important observation is clear: the different techniques used in estimating a particular factor value do not always produce the same result. In fact, as shown in Figure C.2, some of the differences are quite significant.

Two major reasons for the disparity of these results have already been stated. First, certain techniques are inherently less precise than others. Second, the information available is not always adequate. Also, it should be noted that the factor values estimated by some of the techniques are not independent of other factors under certain circumstances.

Thus, the "best-estimate" value for each of the factors can be established only after analyzing and interpreting the results produced by each of the procedures employed. For the individual included in the above illustration, the best-estimate values, shown on the bottom line in Figure C.2, are summarized as follows:

Brain Capacity Factors
    IQ = 126
    PSQ not estimated
    BSQ not estimated
Environmental Factors
    Emi = 0.85
    Emps = 0.95
    Ebx = 0.83
Composite Factors
    IQ × Emi = 122
    PSQ × Emps = 135
    BSQ × Ebx = 120

How these values were established can be best explained by individually examining each of the factors and the related estimating techniques.

Brain Capacity Factors

IQ

IQ by definition is a measured quantity. Thus, the *measured* IQ value of 126, determined from the applicant's SAT score, represents a reasonable estimate of this factor.

The *apparent* IQ values are influenced by factors not measured by IQ tests. They are only indicative of *measured* IQ. Their significance in the evaluation process is discussed later.

Environmental Factors

Emi

The knowledge a person acquires from the environment is, of course, always increasing. Thus, in this example, the lower Emi values tabulated in Figure C.2 are important only in that they show how the factor can be estimated during different periods of life. But for the job applicant, at the time being considered, the Emi value of *0.85* represents the best estimate.

Emps

In this example the environmental factor Emps, estimated by the different techniques, varies betweeen 0.74 and 0.95. However, the dominating exposure was to an applied research and development organization, for which an Emps value of 0.95 was estimated. Accordingly, the best estimate for Emps is *0.95*.

Ebx

The factor Ebx is by definition the average of the two factor values Ebmo and Ebip, and a best estimate must therefore be made for both the latter factors.

In estimating the factor Ebmo, information about two early-life environmental conditions were used. The affluent environment experienced by the applicant under study is, by its nature, known to have an adverse influence on motivation; thus, the assigned value of 0.40. The discipline and work imposed by the individual's parents, on the other hand, presented an environment very favorable to motivation, for which Ebmo was established at 0.90. More emphasis was placed on latter experiences under these circumstances, and the corresponding Ebmo was estimated at a value of *0.80*.

In estimating values for the factor Ebip, the only relevant information sources are the individual's family stability and religious life. For the conditions experienced by the applicant, the Ebip values were estimated at 0.90 and 0.80,

SELECTED INFORMATION SOURCES	BRAIN CAPACITY FACTORS			ENVIRONMENTAL FACTORS				COMPOSITE FACTORS			
						Ebx				BSQ × Ebx	
	IQ	PSQ	BSQ	Emi or Emi-e	Emps	Ebmo	Ebip	IQ × Emi	PSQ × Emps	BSQ × Ebmo	BSQ × Ebip
Early Family-Life Experiences											
Stability							e .90				
Social and economic status				a ⊠		c .40					
Religion							f .80				
Discipline and work						d .90					
Extracurricular Activities											
Organization and group activities										p 117	
Individual activities and hobbies					i .74				m 125	p 117	
Written communications					i .80				m 142		
Education Programs											
Psychological tests	j 126										
High school	k 134			g,h .50				k 65		p 90	
College	k 142			g,h .71				k 95		q 124	
Advanced study	k 133			g,h .75	i .93			k 100	m 168		
Work Experiences											
Analyst				o .85				l 122		p 117	
Synthesist					b .95				l 135	p 117	
Supervisor										p 117	l 123
Observed Personal Qualities											
Knowledge								l 120			
Problem-solving capability									l 125		
Behavioral characteristics										l 120	l 120
						a (.80 + .85)/2				a (117 + 123)/2	
"Best-estimate" of factor values	126			.85	.95	.83		122	135	120	

Effective mental capability

$$= \sqrt[3]{(IQ \times Emi)(PSQ \times Emps)(BSQ \times Ebx)} = \sqrt[3]{(122)(135)(120)} = (125) \text{ n}$$

a See text, Chapter 10, under heading of applicable factor
b Estimate from Table 10.3
c Estimate from Table 10.4
d Estimate from Table 10.5
e Estimate from Table 10.6

f Estimate from Table 10.7
g Estimate from Figure 10.4
h Estimate from Figure 10.5
i Estimate from Figure 10.7
j Estimate from Figure 10.8
k Estimate from Figure 10.9

l Estimate from Figure 10.10
m Estimate from Figure 10.11
n Estimate from Equation 8.3
o Estimate from Equation 10.2
p Estimate from Equation 10.3
q Estimate from Equation 10.4

Figure C.2 Capability evaluation form (illustration)

respectively, and the best-estimate value was established as *0.85*.

Thus, Ebx, the average of Ebmo and Ebip, is equal to *0.83*.

Composite Factors

IQ × Emi (KNOWLEDGE)

The applicant's work experience as an analyst provides the most accurate and complete source of information for estimating his knowledge (IQ × Emi). On this basis, the best-estimate of the IQ × Emi factor is established as *122*. Although the factors estimated from other sources are different in magnitude, they are in general agreement with this value (122).

The estimates made with information from the various education programs are, of course, lower than the above value. But they show an increase with school duration that is consistent with the estimated value. Also, the factor value estimated with information gathered from observed personal qualities is 125, essentially the same as the best estimate.

All the above notwithstanding, note that the product of IQ and Emi (when the factors are estimated separately) is appreciably different from the estimated value of IQ × Emi. Indeed, the product of the individual's *measured* IQ (126) and the environmental factor Emi (0.85), estimated from work experiences, yields a value of 107—far below the established IQ × Emi value of 122. This result, however, does not invalidate the best-estimate value, because the difference can be explained. The individual is an obvious "overachiever," a situation that is indicated when (as is the case here) *measured* IQ is lower than *apparent* IQ. As explained in the previous chapter, these differences may stem from higher than average levels of problem-solving capability, motivation, and early-life family affluence. These observations are used in later explanations; however, it is interesting to note that the product of Emi (0.85) and the apparent IQ (142) factor associated with college class standing yields a value of 121—almost the same as the best-estimate value.

PSQ × Emps (Problem-solving Capability)

The problem-solving capability of the individual in this illustration can be estimated with information from five different sources, but the best information is clearly that available from work experiences. From this source, the best estimate of the individual's problem-solving capability, in terms of PSQ × Emps, was established at *135*. Estimates based on information from other sources yield PSQ × Emps values that vary between 125 and 168.

The lowest value, determined from participation in an extracurricular activity, can be regarded as a lower limit—not a maximum. For example, the applicant's science exhibit may have won a national competition had it been entered. Thus, it is possible that his contribution may have justified a higher level of recognition.

The achievement in written communications, as indicated by an estimated PSQ × Emps factor value of 142, is reasonably close to and supports the best-estimate value of 135.

The extremely high problem-solving capability factor, which resulted from the applicant's success in research work, cannot be explained with the information available. However, it serves to indicate that the value of 135, established as the best estimate, may be conservative (on the low side).

The PSQ × Emps of 125, estimated from observed personal qualities, does not add great support to the value of 135 as the best estimate. Yet, in view of the results produced by the other estimations, a PSQ × Emps below 135 cannot be justified.

In addition to the above, information from the individual's high school and advanced study (college) programs provide further insight into his problem-solving capability. In both these programs the applicant's level of study was nominal. Yet his achievements, as indicated by class standings, were considerably above average. These standings, which correspond to *apparent* IQ values of 134 and 133, are appreciably above the *measured* IQ value. Since the level of study effort was only nominal, the difference cannot be attributed to motivation. Moreover, the influence of early-life family affluence, as shown earlier, is essentially nil. The difference, therefore, can be explained only by the presence of the superior problem-solving capability, indicated by the estimated PSQ × Emps value of 135.

BSQ × Ebx (BEHAVIORAL CHARACTERISTICS)

By definition, BSQ × Ebx represents the combined human characteristics referred to as motivation (BSQ × Ebmo) and interpersonal relationships (BSQ × Ebip). Accordingly, the value of this factor can be established only by developing the best estimates for both BSQ × Ebmo and BSQ × Ebip.

BSQ × Ebmo

In this example, the best source of information for use in estimating the individual's motivation is, again, work experiences. With this information, the evaluation procedures yield a best-estimate value of *117* for BSQ × Ebmo.

The estimated value that differs most from 117 is the one based on his high school study level, for which the estimate is 90. But in this latter case, the estimated value depends only on his motivation toward study. During the same period, the individual was engaged in two extracurricular activities that consumed much of his discretionary time. His participation level in these activities resulted in estimated motivation factor (BSQ × Ebmo) values of 117. Thus, in the interpretation process, it appears reasonable to disregard the lower value based on his level of study in high school.

Another observation that suggests an above-average level of motivation (117 versus 100) can be made from the applicant's achievements in his education programs. Based on class standings in high school and college, his *apparent* IQ was estimated as 134 and 142, respectively. Earlier, the difference between the *apparent* IQ (134), determined from high school class standing, and *measured* IQ (126) was attributed to superior problem-solving capability. The influence of other factors that affect *apparent* IQ—motivation and early-life family affluence—were assessed as nil. In the college study program, the influence of early-life family affluence may also be regarded as nil.

Thus, the higher value of *apparent* IQ associated with college can be explained only by higher motivation. That this is, indeed, the case is indicated by the relatively high estimated motivation factor.

BSQ × Ebip

Those human qualities identified as interpersonal relationships (BSQ × Ebip) are most clearly revealed from the individual's work experiences as a supervisor. With information from this source, the best estimate of BSQ × Ebip was established as *123*. This value is essentially the same as that estimated from observed behavioral characteristics.

Human Mental Qualities

For the individual considered in the preceding example, the estimated human mental qualities are as shown below:

Knowledge
(IQ × Emi)   = 122
Problem-solving Capability
(PSQ × Emps)   = 135
Behavioral Characteristics
(BSQ × Emps)   = 120
Effective Mental Capability

$$= \sqrt[3]{122 \times 135 \times 120} \quad = 125$$

Accordingly, the individual's human mental qualities (as established by the composite factor values) and the resulting effective mental capability equip him to perform successfully as a synthesist in aerodynamics for an applied research and development organization.

INDEX